Developing Web Information Systems

BUTTERWORTH-HEINEMANN INFORMATION SYSTEMS SERIES

Series Editors

Professor David Avison, BA, MSc, PhD, FBCS
Departement SID
ESSEC Business School
Avenue Bernard Hirsch
BP 105
95021 Cergy-Pontoise
FRANCE

Email. avison@essec.fr

Professor Guy Fitzgerald, BA, MSc, MBCS
Department of Information Systems and Computing
Brunel University
Uxbridge
Middlesex UB8 3PH
UK

Email. Guy.Fitzqerald@brunel.ac.uk

This is a new series under the Butterworth-Heinemann imprint which will provide a medium for quality publications in the information systems field. It will also provide continuity with the McGraw-Hill IS series, which has been discontinued. The new series of texts is aimed at first degree and postgraduate students, and the global research community in information systems, computer science and business management. IS is multi-disciplinary. Where formerly emphasis was placed on the technological aspects which remain significant, it now stresses the importance of, and the links to, the business environment particularly, in regard to the social and organisational aspects.

If you have a book proposal for this series, please contact either of the Series Editors.

BUTTERWORTH-HEINEMANN INFORMATION SYSTEMS SERIES

Developing Web Information Systems

From Strategy to Implementation

Richard Vidgen
School of Management, University of Bath

David Avison
ESSEC Business School, Paris

Bob Wood
Information Systems Institute, University of Salford

Trevor Wood-Harper
Information Systems Institute, University of Salford

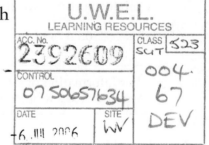

BUTTERWORTH
HEINEMANN

OXFORD AMSTERDAM BOSTON LONDON NEW YORK PARIS
SAN DIEGO SAN FRANCISCO SINGAPORE SYDNEY TOKYO

Butterworth-Heinemann
An imprint of Elsevier Science
Linacre House, Jordan Hill, Oxford OX2 8DP
200 Wheeler Road, Burlington, MA 01803

First published 2002

British Library Cataloguing in Publication Data
A catalogue record for this book is available from the British Library

ISBN 0 7506 57634

For information on all Butterworth-Heinemann publications visit our
website at www.bh.com

Printed in Great Britain by MPG Books Ltd, Bodmin, Cornwall

Contents

Preface

Wisdom [wis-dm] – capacity of judging rightly in matters
relating to life and conduct; soundness of judgement in the
choice of means and ends. (Oxford English Dictionary).

The Internet has undoubtedly changed the way that information systems are developed, particularly in the area of user interface design and increased openness and interoperability through the adoption of XML (eXtensible Markup Language) based data standards and .NET web services. As the Internet matures from a cyberbrochure into a space for inter-organizational information systems many of the old values of information system development, such as systems analysis methods and database design, have been rediscovered and their usefulness reinforced. The challenge for the information system developer of the 21st century is to respond to the opportunities afforded by the Internet while at the same time retaining traditional skills in information system development and software engineering.

This book introduces a web-based IS development methodology – WISDM – that provides a framework for bringing together traditional systems development methods with web-based techniques to provide a rounded framework that runs from e-business strategic analysis through to implementation in software. The WISDM framework draws on established methods and techniques, thus building on existing best practice rather than adding yet another methodology to an already crowded market.

A running case study of a theatre – the fictional Barchester Playhouse – is used to illustrate the ideas and methods introduced in each chapter of the book. A web-based theatre ticket booking system, TicketManager, is implemented using web software development tools. The accompanying web site for the book, www.wisdm.net, is the home of a working TicketManager prototype. The source code and database can be downloaded from the

WISDM web site and modified and extended by the reader. A second case study, of a research student admissions and tracking system, is provided to support teaching and self-paced learning.

The content of the WISDM framework was developed through action research, most notably during a two year Teaching Company Scheme (TCS) project run by the University of Bath and a local small to medium sized enterprise, Zenith International. We would like to thank Gary Roethenbaugh and Richard Hall of Zenith and the Teaching Company Associate, Tom Scotney, for their support and encouragement of the development of WISDM. The Barchester Playhouse case study draws on a range of resources, but thanks are due to Linda Macaulay of UMIST for providing an early draft of a theatre case study and to the Everyman Theatre in Cheltenham, England for giving us access to the workings of a real-life provincial theatre. The material in the book has benefited from several years experience of teaching a Masters level course in information system development at the University of Bath. Thanks are therefore due to the MSc students who have helped refine WISDM as a vehicle for teaching information systems development, and to Dominic Leaver in particular, who supplied the rich picture in chapter 6.

Richard Vidgen
July 2002

1

Information System Development

1.1 Information systems and IT

In the 21st century, the idea of an information system that does not rely on sophisticated information technologies is almost unimaginable. Information systems have always been essential to an organization's survival and effective computer-based information systems have come to be recognized as essential business assets. Laudon & Laudon (2002) suggest four factors that have altered the business landscape and made information systems strategically important:

- *The global economy*: Foreign trade in the United States represents more than 25% of economic activity, and successful organizations must be able to operate globally, compete in world marketplaces, and manage distributors, suppliers, and customers 24 hours a day in many countries. To be successful in the global market, organizations need powerful information systems to support this activity

- *Industrial transformation*: Industrial economies are becoming knowledge-based service-oriented economies. Services are information and knowledge intensive, and many jobs rely on creating and distributing information. Obvious examples include education and healthcare. Even the most tangible of products, such as motorcars, are becoming more and more knowledge intensive both with regard to the processes for designing and building them and in terms of the products themselves. For example, the *General Motors'* OnStar programme allows remote operators to detect when an accident occurs (the air bag is triggered) and to call the emergency services (the car can even set in motion processes that arrange for its own servicing, such as brake pad replacement). Consequently, manufacturers need less 'metal-bashers' and more designers, engineers, and IT specialists

- *Business transformation*: Traditional businesses are organized hierarchically and rely on standard operating procedures to deliver mass-produced product and services. New business organizations have flattened organizational structures and flexible combinations of resources that are organized around customer requirements to deliver mass-customized products and services. Organizations need considerable investments in information technology to meet these coordination and communication needs

- *Digital firms*: E-businesses conduct relationships with customers, suppliers, and employees and are able to sense and respond to changes in their environment rapidly. An example of a digital firm is *Egg*, a provider of financial services online, including mortgages, savings, insurance, and investments. We consider new forms of digital business in chapter 4.

An information system is a set of interacting components – people, procedures, and technologies – that together collect, process, store, and distribute information to support control, decision-making and management in organizations. The information system contains information about the organization itself, for example, the state of its internal operations, and about its environment, for example, information about customers, suppliers, and competitors. Without an information system an organization would not survive. This does not mean that the information system must use information technologies in the form of computers and communication networks. There are other forms of information system. Organizations have always needed information systems, although the formal aspects of these information systems would have been implemented using paper-based filing systems in the pre-IT era.

Our concern in this book is with *computer-based* information systems. By and large we will address the formal aspects of information systems, but must remember that many information systems in organizations are informal – the office grapevine and conversations at the water-cooler are typical examples of these. Although the informal aspects of information systems are difficult to manage and are not amenable to an engineering approach, their influence should not be under-estimated.

The definition of 'technology' is not without difficulty. Technology can and does often apply to devices such as computers and communications networks, but can also be applied to practices (for example, the software development process), and techniques (for example, database design). Information systems can be expected to make use of information technologies, but are not synonymous with technology. An information system is in essence a human activity system situated in an organizational context – technology is important to information systems but must be considered jointly with human and organizational dimensions. The WISDM framework for information systems development is in large part intended to help the development team keep organizational, human, and technological perspectives in balance.

1.2 Information systems development methodologies

Fitzgerald (1998) has summarized the evidence for a software crisis and reports that: average completion time for information systems development (ISD) projects ranges from 18 months to 5 years; 68% of projects overrun schedules; 65% exceed budget; 75% face major redesign following initial implementation; and 35% of companies have at least one runaway project. ISD is clearly a difficult task and some would argue that the answer lies in better and more professional approaches to development. One area that organizations have invested in is ISD methodologies. A methodology has been defined by Avison & Fitzgerald (2002) as:

> A collection of procedures, techniques, tools, and documentation aids which will help the system developers in their efforts to implement a new information system. A methodology will consist of phases, themselves consisting of sub-phases, which will guide the system developers in their choice of the techniques that might be appropriate at each stage of the project and also help them plan, manage, control and evaluate information systems projects.

There are many justifications for adopting a methodology to guide IS development. According to Fitzgerald (1996), these reasons include:

- The subdivision of a complex process into manageable tasks
- Facilitation of project management and control. One role of management is to manage risk and uncertainty
- Purposeful framework for applying techniques
- Economics – skill specialization and division of labour
- Epistemological – a framework for the acquisition and systemization of knowledge. A methodology should promote organizational learning
- Standardization – interchangeability of developers, increased productivity and quality.

However, Fitzgerald also identifies problems with methodologies. There is a basic issue about what is a methodology (definitional anomalies) and a tendency for methodology authors to engage in 'method wars'. Many methodologies have no or weak conceptual and empirical foundations, and where there are conceptual underpinnings these tend to be rooted firmly in a scientific and engineering paradigm. Engineering was possibly a suitable reference discipline when development was concerned with hardware and software support for repetitive processes, but it is a crude approach when dealing with social systems.

It is also possible that the methodology becomes an end in its own right. Wastell (1996) noted that:

> Methodology becomes a fetish, a procedure used with pathological rigidity for its own sake, not as a means to an end. Used in this way, methodology provides a relief against anxiety; it insulates the practitioner from the risks and uncertainties of real engagement with people and problems.

It is tempting to assume that a single methodology can be applied universally – to all types of project in all types of organization. Coupled with an inadequate recognition of developer-specific factors, IS development methodologies can become the 'one size fits all' solution. We do not suggest that the response to this should be to declare a free-for-all where IS development is tackled in an ad hoc manner, but it is important to be aware of the dangers of methodologically-induced blindness; a methodology helps organize and frame problems more clearly, but it can also be a way of not seeing.

1.3 Information systems development life-cycles

1.3.1 Waterfall life-cycle

The waterfall life-cycle of systems development subdivides the process into formal stages where the output of one stage forms the input to the next. The deliverables cascade down the waterfall with a completed software system at the bottom. The first stage, the feasibility study, is concerned with defining the scope and purpose of the new system, considering a range of alternative solutions and investigating the impact of the new system on the organization. The decision point following the feasibility study is for management to sign off on a preferred solution.

In the requirements stage, the requirements are specified in logical form, that is, in terms of 'what' is required rather than 'how' it will be achieved technically. The requirements specification should be signed off by the business user – an agreement that the system, if built as specified, will meet the needs of the business.

Design is concerned with translating the requirements into a software system specification that can then be turned into a working system by systems developers (coding). Thorough testing is vital and is often done at three levels. The first level of testing is for the programmers to unit test the program modules. Once the programmers are satisfied with the individual modules, then the system can be put together for a systems test. The systems development staff develop a comprehensive test plan and devise test data and subject the system to exhaustive testing. This might include peak capacity testing to see how many transactions the system can manage simultaneously before performance degrades to an unacceptable level or the system fails entirely. The third level of testing is the user acceptance test. Once the development team is happy with the systems testing, then the system is handed over to the users who then conduct their own (and independent) test of the system. Once the system successfully passes user acceptance it can be transferred to live operations, where it will then be monitored and maintained as software errors ('bugs') and enhancements are identified.

1.3.2 Problems with the waterfall life-cycle

Taken at face value, the waterfall life-cycle shown in figure 1.1 is appealing for its orderly and systematic stepwise refinement of a complex problem into smaller and smaller problems.

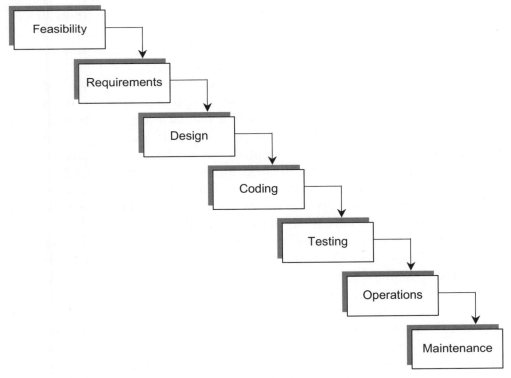

Figure 1.1: The waterfall life-cycle for systems development

The waterfall life-cycle has roots in hardware and software engineering and although suitable for designed artefacts such as computer chips and bridges, it is less appropriate to human activity systems where the human and organizational factors are less easy to identify. (We would also argue that bridges and chips are human activity systems that can also suffer from a strict engineering-only approach.) For information systems with well-structured requirements, such as an airline reservations system, or applications with a safety critical aspect (for example, a nuclear reactor control system), then the formality of the life-cycle model, possibly combined with formal methods, may well be appropriate.

However, for many information systems development projects, the life-cycle approach has limitations: it is expensive, time-consuming, and inflexible. Perhaps the most significant limitation is that the life-cycle approach assumes that the requirements can be specified with reasonable completeness before design begins. Often, users do not know (or cannot articulate explicitly) the requirements until the finished system is in use. Further, requirements are not fixed – they change over time as the project unfolds and the environment changes. This makes the formulation of a complete and permanently correct specification of requirements an unrealistic goal. It is also difficult to separate out the specification of an information system from its implementation, that is, the 'what' and 'how' of IS development are closely related and difficult to separate. Knowledge of how to implement and what is technically feasible affects perceptions of what can be done in the user world.

The waterfall life-cycle prescribes clear communication points between users and developers (for example, sign off of specification, sign off of user acceptance test) but it does not promote a mutual process of learning and coordination. Furthermore, the formal products of IS development, such as the specification of requirements, are often meaningless to users (even if they had the time and the inclination to read them). Any change to requirements after the sign-off point will be expensive – it is estimated that requirements errors cost 200 times more to fix if not discovered prior to implementation. All of these problems result in an inflation of the maintenance activity as developers attempt to fit the information system to actual working practices based on real experience. As maintenance often comes from a different budget than the original development, many organizations significantly underestimate the true cost of IS development.

So, why is the waterfall life-cycle still used? A cynical view would be that it is used to provide milestones and frozen deliverables to keep managers happy and to give them the illusion that they are in control of the IS development process. A more balanced view suggests that the life-cycle approach may work well in certain circumstances. Where the requirements can be articulated clearly, as might be the case where an existing IS is being replaced and the developers have in-depth experience of the application domain, such as a payroll or inventory application, the waterfall life-cycle approach may well be appropriate.

1.3.3 Alternative life-cycles

The shortcomings of the waterfall life-cycle have led to more flexible approaches being explored. Alternatives to the waterfall approach include evolutionary development (figure 1.2b) and incremental development (figure 1.2c).

Evolutionary development

In evolutionary development, shown as figure 1.2b, the system is developed using a prototype and refined through user feedback of the system in use and changes in the application itself. The operational system is improved all the time through responses to this user feedback. Change is therefore seen as the norm and catered for – a sharp comparison to the waterfall life-cycle discussed earlier, where change could be very expensive to implement.

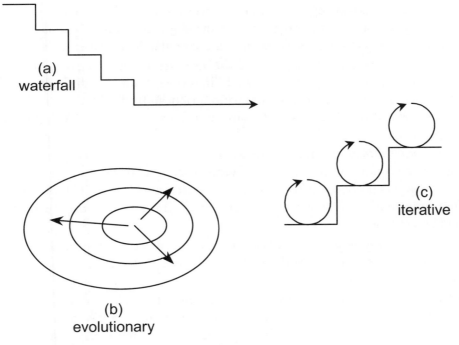

Figure 1.2: Life-cycles for systems development

Iterative (rapid) application development

The key objective of rapid application development (RAD) (figure 1.2c) is the delivery of working business applications in shorter timescales for less investment. With RAD the system is developed in chunks of functionality in accelerated and time-boxed cycles of development. RAD normally involves users and developers to jointly agree requirements in workshops. In particular, critical requirements (as against those 'nice to have') are identified. Different aspects of the system may be developed at different times, the most important usually being in the first time-box, and the overall system is therefore implemented incrementally in these chunks by small teams of users and developers. The assumptions underlying RAD include (adapted from Beynon-Davies et al., 2000):

- *Iterative incremental* development: an information system can be complete but it is never finished and must be allowed to evolve and adapt over time. Users cannot specify with absolute certainty what they want from an information system in advance and therefore an incremental and iterative approach is needed to explore the requirements as they unfold. RAD is a process of organizational learning through iteration of design, construction, testing, and evaluation of development artefacts

- *Top down refinement*: it is difficult for users to specify requirements accurately and in detail in advance; it is better to specify the requirements at a level that is appropriate to the stage of the development and to develop the detail as the project progresses through incremental development

- *Active user involvement*: the schism of the user/developer divide, which is structurally imposed in the waterfall life-cycle, leads to difficulties in requirements elicitation, ownership, and politics. In RAD the divide is broken down through co-located teams and joint application development workshops

- *Small empowered teams*: teams of four to eight are typical in RAD, promoting effective communications and empowered users. Small teams help reduce bureaucracy and enable quick and effective decision-making. The team is often supported by a facilitator and can benefit from extra-curricular team-building activities

- *Frequent delivery of products*: in RAD the delivery of working applications is constrained to shorter periods, such as 90 days – the aim is to deliver working product, not process

- *Software development toolset*: toolsets are available which allow developers to generate program code with graphical user interfaces from requirements specifications automatically, allowing them to provide the user with prototype applications quickly for evaluation. In RAD the application becomes its own self-documenting model, avoiding the tendency in the waterfall life-cycle to overwhelm the user with large amounts of paper-based documentation.

End-user development

A rather more radical approach to IS development is to hand over the development work to the users. The advantages are obvious, in particular, the users will know the requirements and once involved to the extent of developing the application, will have control over this aspect of their work, thus increasing job satisfaction. The approach has the potential of leading to more successful applications. Many of the limiting factors to end-user development are disappearing. Users use computer systems normally in their job, frequently on personal computers and use applications software, such as the Microsoft Office suite of word processor, spreadsheet and database, and other applications. Such software, particularly MS Excel and MS Access, can be used to develop quite sophisticated applications. Present-day users do not usually have the attitude that computers are nothing to do with them, which used to be commonplace. Further, there are software tools available which are designed to help less-experienced users carry out rudimentary system development for themselves.

1.3.4 Prototyping

Prototyping can be used in all three life-cycle models of figure 1.2. With the traditional waterfall life-cycle, prototypes can be generated in the requirements phase to test out the understanding of the user requirements. This gives the users an executable specification and gets round the problem of poor communications using formal paper-based specifications. It would seem far better to use a form of requirements specification that is similar to the final system. The prototype is typically to be thrown away – it is dispensed with prior to design. As a working system it might be inefficient, incomplete or inadequate in some other way.

In evolutionary development, the prototype evolves through a series of improvements until the users find a version acceptable. Even so, it might be operational fairly early on, but the prototype operational system develops further through incremental improvements and it may never reach a stage where it can be seen as the final version.

In RAD, the prototype typically becomes the final system or at least part of the final system as the time-box modules are implemented in turn. Nevertheless, it might also be thrown away in favour of a more robust design that follows the applicability of the prototype. Thus, to speak of prototyping as a life-cycle for IS development can be misleading.

1.3.5 Agile Development

Agile software development (ASD) encompasses approaches such as Extreme Programming (XP), Lean Development, and Scrum (Highsmith & Cockburn, 2001). As with rapid application development, the premise of ASD is that change is inevitable. Rather than treat the changes to requirements that arise as a project unfolds as an exception it is better to assume that requirements will change and to focus instead on reducing the cost of the associated rework. Extreme Programming encourages development teams to:

- Produce the first delivery in weeks – get feedback quickly and create credibility through an early win
- Go for simple solutions that can be changed easily and quickly
- Improve design quality so that subsequent versions cost less to build and implement
- Make testing an on-going activity so that errors are caught early.

ASD focuses on the 'keeping it real' through the creation of program code – code is less forgiving (it generally works or it doesn't) than requirement specifications and abstract designs. The Agile Software Manifesto (Highsmith & Cockburn, 2001) values:

- Individuals and interactions over processes and tools
- *Working software* over comprehensive documentation
- *Customer collaboration* over contract negotiation
- *Responding to change* over following a plan.

The manifesto recognizes there is value in the terms on the right, but values the left (italicized terms) more highly. Typical cycles are of two to six weeks duration with Scrum working on 30-day cycles. The agile approach is feature led, rather than project plan driven, with features being prioritized dynamically as circumstances change. The focus on program code and speed has opened ASD up to the criticism of being a hackers' charter. A more balanced view is to see agile methods in a spectrum that ranges from hacking to development based around micro-milestone ironbound contracts (figure 1.3). The choice of where to position a project on the spectrum must take account of a broad range of factors such as the organization culture, the external environment, type of application, and the level of risk.

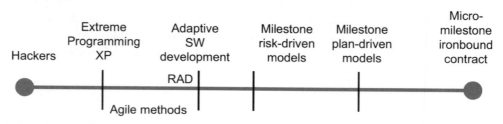

Figure 1.3: IS Development planning spectrum (adapted from Boehm, 2002)

1.4 Alternative strategies for information systems acquisition

In this book we will focus on custom systems development, that is, where the construction of the IS is part of the life-cycle. It is also possible to outsource IS development to a third party, to buy a package solution, or to rent an IS solution. We will look at these in turn.

1.4.1 Packaged solutions

Some organizations have decided not to embark automatically on major in-house system development activities but to first ascertain whether their requirements can be purchased in the form of application packages or 'turn-key' systems. This is regarded as a quick and relatively cheap way of implementing systems for organizations that have fairly standard requirements. A degree of package modification and integration may be required which may still be undertaken in-house. If there is a deep divide between requirements and provision, then the modifications may be very expensive to implement and a packaged solution a poor investment. On the other hand, many applications are similar between organizations, and these are likely to include all the accounting applications. In such cases, an application package is likely to be cheaper and quicker to implement.

1.4.2 Outsourcing

Outsourcing is the provision of services by an external company. In the IS context, it may be as small as the provision of a few contract programmers, to the external development of an application, hardware provision, and finally to the development and running of all applications. It is argued that an outsourcing company is more likely to have the human resources available for a new system and be quicker to develop the application. The vendor may agree to manage and be responsible for the provision and development of the information system for the organization who will be less concerned about how the system is developed and more interested in the end results. There is a trend toward outsourcing as it rids the organization of IT and IS responsibilities, which may be seen as being not of strategic importance – it is not their core business. Nevertheless, it is usually regarded as important that the organization maintains some residual IS specialists to ensure that the vendor is fulfilling both the contract and the organization's needs.

1.4.3 Application service providers

A combination of Internet and mobile technologies, IS skills shortage and growing application size and complexity has encouraged the development of a new kind of outsourcing, provided by application service providers (ASP). ASPs are sometimes formed from an alliance between a hardware vendor and a software provider such as Hewlett-Packard and SAP or IBM and Oracle, or may be third party providers such as the large consultancy groups. An ASP will build the data pool, develop applications, ensure the appropriate level of security, run the applications, allow access, monitor usage, tune, upgrade and enhance the application. Typically, these applications might relate to customer relationship management, enterprise resource planning or e-business. The relationship between an ASP and its client organization is critical, since an ASP places a further layer between the organization and its information resource.

Summary

- Information systems are central to organizational survival.
- A methodology for developing information systems is needed to bring order and structure to a complex technical and organizational process.
- Many traditional methodologies are inflexible, and end up being ignored or followed for their own sake rather than for organizational benefit.
- There are alternative approaches to the stepwise refinement approach of the waterfall life-cycle model that may be more appropriate to organizations.
- Although it is commonplace for organizations to develop their own applications, there are alternatives, such as packaged solutions, outsourcing and application service providers.

Exercises

1. Suggest different types of information system used at your university or another organization: formal, informal, clerical and computerized.
2. For any information system, argue for and against using an information systems development methodology.
3. What are the crucial differences between the waterfall life-cycle model and alternative models for information systems development?
4. What risks might an organization be exposed to in adopting extreme programming and agile development?
5. Argue for and against developing in-house applications and alternatives, such as packaged solutions, outsourcing and application service providers.

Further reading

Avison, D. and Fitzgerald, G., (2002). *Information Systems Development: Methodologies, Techniques and Tools*, 3rd edition, McGraw-Hill, Maidenhead.

Beynon-Davies, P., Mackay, H. and Tudhope, D., (2000). 'It's lots of bits of paper and ticks and post-it notes and things …': a case study of a rapid application development project. *Information Systems Journal,* 10: 195–216.

Boehm, B., (2002). Get Ready for Agile Methods with Care. *Computer,* January: 64–69.

Fitzgerald, B., (1996). Formalized Systems Development Methodologies: a Critical Perspective. *Information Systems Journal,* 6: 3–23.

Fitzgerald, B., (1998). A Preliminary Investigation of Rapid Application Development in Practice. In: Wood-Harper, A. T., Jayaratna, N., and Wood, J. R. G. (editors), *Proceedings of the Sixth International Conference on Information Systems Methodologies*: 77–87.

Highsmith, J. and Cockburn, A., (2001). Agile Software Development: the Business of Innovation. *Computer,* September: 120–122.

Laudon, K. C. and Laudon, (2002). *Management Information Systems: Managing the Digital Firm.* Prentice Hall, New Jersey.

2

Internet-based Information Systems

2.1 The Internet

Most IS development methodologies do not address the Internet in specific terms. This might be because the Internet is still relatively new for mainstream IS development, or that the methodology authors are only just beginning to catch up. In this chapter we provide a brief history of the Internet and how it works and then discuss information systems development in the context of the Internet. There are many histories of the Internet, but a few words here will provide some background and context. In a technological sense the Internet is relatively simple and obvious extension to computer networking. From a social and organizational perspective, however, it is a remarkable phenomenon, recent 'dotcom' failures and technology stock disaffection notwithstanding.

2.1.1 A brief history

In the Cold War of the 1950s and 60s, the US poured money into research in radar, communications, and computers (Hobbes, 2002). The US was concerned by the signs of Russian superiority in technology, as illustrated by the Sputnik space missions. New agencies were created to promote advances in science and technology. One of these was the Advanced Research Projects Agency (ARPA), which was formed in 1958 as part of the US Department of Defense (DoD). ARPA distributed funds to research institutes with one of the significant beneficiaries being MIT (Massachusetts Institute of Technology). MIT graduates worked for new technology companies, which were being set up close to the MIT campus and one of the companies, Bolt, Barenek &

Newman (BBN), helped develop ARPAnet in the late 60s. ARPAnet was deigned using packet-switching technology with the aim of being able to survive the loss of network nodes in a nuclear war. In 1969 four computers were networked using ARPAnet. By 1972 there were 40 network points and the need for common standards and protocols was recognized, leading to a file transfer protocol (FTP) in 1973 and transmission control protocol (TCP) in 1974. In 1976 Queen Elizabeth II sent out an email, but by the end of the 1970s the ARPAnet was still used mainly by academic institutions around the world.

From ARPAnet to the Internet

In 1982 the transmission control protocol (TCP) and the Internet protocol (IP), collectively known as TCP/IP, were adopted by ARPAnet – the Internet had arrived. The first name server was developed at the University of Wisconsin in 1983, which allowed messages to be sent without having to know the exact address of the recipient machine. In 1985 the domain name system (DNS) was introduced; the first domain name was symbolics.com with universities (for example, purdue.edu) and not-for-profit organizations (for example, mitre.org) following quickly on. In 1986, the NSF (National Science Foundation) made Internet support available to the research community via the NSFNET backbone. In 1989 there were 100,000 hosts connected to NFSNET and in 1990 the ageing ARPAnet was switched off. The growth in network connections was fuelled by the widespread adoption of developments in personal computers (Apple and IBM), networkable Sun servers and workstations, and networking infrastructure from Cisco and the Ethernet local area network pioneered by Bob Metcalfe.

Internet browser wars

Tim Berners-Lee was working at CERN (the European Laboratory for Particle Physics) in Switzerland in 1991 and wanted to be able to share documents and information easily over the Internet. Berners-Lee named the project the worldwide web (WWW). CERN released a line-driven browser for the WWW and distributed hypermedia had arrived. Use of a line-by-line browser was not user-friendly, but in 1992 Marc Andreessen, an undergraduate at the University of Illinois, saw the potential of the worldwide web and, together with colleagues, developed the first graphical browser, Mosaic. Jim Clark saw the value of the Mosaic browser and lured the original Mosaic developers away from Illinois to California, to work for a start-up that would later become Netscape. Clark's new browser was named Mozilla.

It was not until 1995 that Microsoft supplied Internet Explorer. Before 1995, the Internet was not licenced for commercial organizations seeking to make profits. Once the rules were changed, Microsoft entered the market and businesses started thinking about getting a web site. By 1996 the browser wars were in full swing as Netscape and Microsoft battled it out for dominance. Microsoft bundled Internet Explorer in with the Windows operating systems and made quick and large inroads into Netscape's dominance of the browser market. As most users had Microsoft Windows on their PCs and Internet Explorer was delivered free, Netscape's revenue earning opportunities from its browser disappeared. However, differences in implementation have led to browser incompatibilities and the need for developers to create two versions of web pages to cater for Internet Explorer and Netscape – so much for common standards! In 1998 Microsoft was taken to court after allegations of anti-trust violations, but it was too late for Netscape, whose original 90% share of the market had been shredded by Microsoft. In early 2000 Microsoft had 80% of the browser market share. By late 2001 Netscape had given up the browser battle, with Jim Bankoff (President, Netscape) announcing that Netscape would focus on being a content hub for Time Warner and that by 2002 Netscape would not be primarily known as a browser company. Netscape also saw inroads into its market share by the Norwegian developer of the Opera browser.

By the end of the 20th century, exponential growth of the worldwide web (by far the most heavily used service on the Internet) had led to Computer Sciences Corporation (CSC) no longer asking in its annual survey of 2000 if a company had a web site – more than 95% already did.

2.1.2 Internet statistics

As of 1 Jan 2000 there were 56.2 million computers connected, with 97 million users in the US (38% penetration) and 14 million users in the UK (25% penetration) (Forrester, 2001). The forecast for 2006 is that there will be 208 million users in the US (78% penetration) and 39 million users in the UK (68% penetration). In the early 1990s the typical Internet user was a young male with high technical knowledge; in 2000 there were various socio-economic groups with differing levels of technical knowledge, including business people, families, teenagers, and 'Golden Agers' (mature and retired people with time on their hands and disposable income to play the stock market).

Internet users are accessing the net anytime/anywhere, from home, office, and on the move. The devices they use to access the net include desktop computers, laptops, televisions, mobile telephones, and personal digital assistants. By 2006 there will be 0.92 billion Internet users using 549 million Internet PCs, 134 million Internet-enabled TVs, 705 million micro-browser devices, 161 million 'other' devices (for example, games consoles such as Sony's PlayStation). In terms of commerce conducted on the Internet, the $10 billion in 1997 grew to $250 billion in 2000 and is predicted to reach $2.7 trillion by 2005. Even if these forecasts do not prove 100% accurate, the signs are that the Internet will continue to be big business, and particularly so in a mobile context.

2.2 How the Internet works

2.2.1 Internet protocols

A protocol refers to the formalities and conventions observed by computers during communication. The more that protocols are shared then the greater the interconnectivity. The success of the Internet is due in large part to the agreement and adoption of a common standard for inter-computer communication. At the heart of the Internet is the TCP/IP protocol. The Internet can be thought of by analogy to postcards. Imagine that a message for one person is written out on a series of numbered postcards, for example, 1 of 10, 2 of 10, and so on, and the postcards then put into a post box. The cards will be collected and sorted at the post centre, but could end up separated, perhaps even going via different routes to the recipient, and even arriving on different days. The recipient of the postcards can put the message back together because each card is numbered and the total number of cards to be received is known – it is just a matter of waiting for them all to arrive. The TCP/IP protocol works in a similar way; messages are chopped up into fixed-size packets of data and the packets sent over the network. The route they take and the order they arrive in does not matter since the receiving computer can reassemble the original message. If parts of the network are congested or out of service then packets are automatically routed around the obstacles.

4	Application layer: programs and services that use the network	For example, the worldwide web, hypertext transfer protocol (HTTP)
3	Transport layer: end to end data delivery services	Transport control protocol (TCP)
2	Internet layer: handles routing of data and defines datagram types	Internet protocol (IP)
1	Network access layer: interface to physical networks	Underlying Local Area Network (LAN), for example Ethernet, and Wide Area Network (WAN)

Figure 2.1: Internet protocols and layers

The Internet uses multiple protocols, organized like the layers of a cake (figure 2.1) into layers. Working from the bottom up, the network access layer is concerned with shifting bytes across the network, for example, across a local area network running Ethernet. The Internet layer runs IP and is a connectionless protocol – it does not wait for an answer from the receiving computer, but sends packets of data (known as datagrams) regardless. The

TCP layer is a connection-based protocol that ensures reliable delivery by using 'handshaking' before sending data. The application layer is the one that the user sees and is the layer where services are implemented. One of these services is the worldwide web (WWW), which usually uses port 80. A port is a fixed length number – 16 bits – that serves to identify the sending and receiving users of TCP. There are a number of common users of TCP that have been assigned fixed numbers (as we have noted, the WWW uses 80); for example, SMTP (email – simple mail transfer protocol) uses port 25, and FTP (file transfer protocol) uses ports 20 and 21 for data and control information. It is therefore incorrect to see the WWW and the Internet as synonymous – the WWW is just one service implemented on the Internet (although the WWW is probably the most well-known).

The WWW service uses a further protocol, hypertext transfer protocol (HTTP). This is the agreed way for web page requests and web page contents to be communicated between computers.

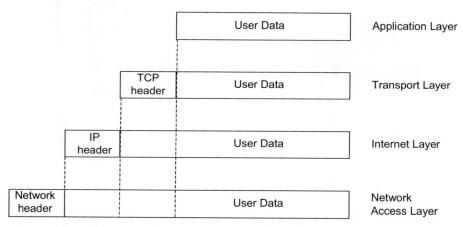

Figure 2.2: Internet layers and header data (adapted from Stallings, 2001, p. 79)

Working from the top down, when a service is invoked at the application layer, it passes the data to be communicated to the next level down (TCP). This layer adds header data associated with transmission control. The data and header are then passed to the IP layer, which adds further header data related to IP datagrams before finally passing it on to the network access layer. The receiving computer starts with the network access layer and strips off the headers as the user data is passed back up to the application layer.

2.2.2 The worldwide web

The worldwide web (WWW) is a distributed multimedia hypertext system. Multimedia files are distributed across *servers* and accessible by *clients* (figure 3.3). The Uniform Resource Locator (URL) makes access to WWW resources and the files delivered by the servers are displayed to the client using a browser, such as Internet Explorer, Netscape or Opera. The layout of the contents of the file and the hyperlinks to other files are specified using Hypertext Markup Language (HTML). The clients fetch files from servers using the Hypertext Transfer Protocol (HTTP). A URL indicates the method of access, the domain name, and the file location, for example,

http://www.wisdm.net/theatre/home.cfm.

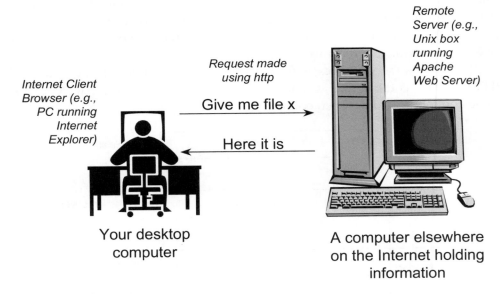

Figure 2.3: Client–server Internet model

Looking at this example URL in more detail, http:// specifies the protocol to be used for this request, the domain name is www.wisdm.net, and within this domain the specific file requested is located at theatre/home.cfm. The file extension ".cfm" indicates that the file is a ColdFusion template (ColdFusion is described in chapter 10); the most common file extension is ".htm" (sometimes ".html") which indicates the file is a standard web page. A domain refers to a specific group of networks under the control of a single entity, such as a university or a company. Domains are hierarchical: for example, in the University of Bath domain www.bath.ac.uk, the .uk specifies the geographical location (United Kingdom), ac.uk that it is a UK-based educational establishment, and bath.ac.uk that it is the domain for the University of Bath. Every domain name is unique – the IP address associated with the bath.ac.uk address is actually 128.119.40.195. Domain name servers (DNS) attached to the Internet translate the textual domain name into an IP address.

2.2.3   HyperText Markup Language (HTML)

HTML is the 'native language' of the WWW. HTML documents use markup tags, such as the heading tag:

```
<H1>Introduction</H1>
```

These markup tags are case insensitive, so <H1> has the same result as <h1>, although for aesthetics and ease of human readability it is better to be consistent with use of upper and lower case than to mix them. Although markup tags are not case sensitive, other attributes, such as filenames, can be (for example, on the UNIX operating system file names are case sensitive, but not so on Microsoft operating systems – another argument for being consistent with use of lower and upper case!). Markup tags are usually paired to denote the start and end of an element, for example, <H1> is closed by the tag </H1>.

Fortunately, browsers are pretty forgiving when rendering HTML content. Assume that the file, hello.htm, contains only the following text content:

```
Hello
```

The browser will display a window with the word 'Hello'. This file clearly does not comply with HTML standards, but the client browser will do its best to display it. A better version would be as follows:

```
<html>
<head>
<title>Hello WWW</title>
<meta http-equiv="Content-Type" content="text/html; charset=iso-8859-1">
</head>

<body bgcolor="#FFFFFF" text="#000000">
Welcome to the <i>worldwide web</i>. Find out more at the <a href="http://www.w3c.org">W3C</a>.
</body>
</html>
```

Only the content between the <body> tags is displayed in the browser. The rest of the tags give the browser information about the HTML standard used, the title of the document, and the colour of the background. The content contains plain text, some of which has italics <i>, and a hyperlink <a href>. When this file is displayed in a browser it looks like figure 2.4. This is a simple web page, but even the most complicated looking web sites are built up of similar tags.

2.2.4 Web site authoring tools

It is possible to build a web site by handcrafting the HTML tags using a text editor, such as Notepad – and some web developers still do this. For most developers, a wysiwyg (what you see is what you get) interface together with automatic generation of tags and syntax checking makes for faster and more accurate development. The simplest tools are often bundled in with word processors, such as Microsoft Word. These tools enable quick and easy building of a web site, particularly if the user is familiar with tables and image handling in the word processing software. Internet browsers often contain a basic web edit package, such as FrontPage Express (unfortunately, this software was removed from Internet Explorer version 5) or Netscape Composer. More sophisticated sites require a standalone authoring tool, such as Microsoft's FrontPage or Macromedia's DreamWeaver. However, these tools can hide the underlying HTML language and most developers find the need to work in native HTML at some point. Regardless of how good the authoring package is, there is no substitute for a sound working knowledge of HTML if one is to build sophisticated business web sites.

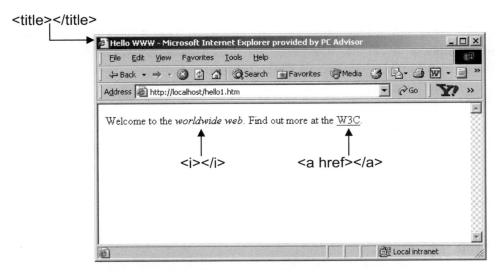

Figure 2.4: Browser rendering of HTML for hello1.htm

2.2.5 Beyond the basics

The vast majority of web pages are still written in HTML. However, HTML has been extended with Dynamic HTML (DHTML) and Cascading style sheets (CSS). But there is a need to beware of browser compatibility problems. In the longer term, the future surely rests with XML and related technologies (see chapter 11).

2.2.6   Mobile Internet

The wireless access protocol (WAP) allows Internet content to be delivered to a mobile phone. Unfortunately, mobile phones are limited in terms of display (they are small compared with the size of a PC monitor and not usually in colour), have limited processing power, have low bandwidth (9.6k in the United Kingdom – 6 times slower than the typical modem on a PC and much slower than a PC with a broadband connection), and are awkward to use (small numeric keypad with fiddly buttons). Further developments will address these limitations, such as the personal digital assistants/mobile phone combinations that are beginning to emerge. Although WAP enabled phones have failed to achieve the big success that was expected when they were launched in 1999, they have provided useful pointers to the future.

The key to mobile Internet is access on the move. Applications that have proven most successful include information services, such as railway and flight timetables, leisure resources, e.g., local restaurants and attractions, and time-fillers such as gambling and games. In the future, the killer application for mobility will be location-based services. For example, if a child has a mobile telephone then a parent can use an Internet browser to locate his or her precise position based on the cell phone number – and if it works for children then it will also work for other entities, such as pets and motorcars. Location-based services will also lead to a growth in 'push' advertising. For example, as I walk past a bookstore a message might arrive that they have a special offer for me today. The special offer will be based on my past purchases and preferences as a customer and might be valid for 15 minutes.

The key to the future of mobile applications is bandwidth and always-on services. These will come with the third generation of mobile technology – 3G. However, there are concerns about 3G that have led to it being dubbed 3D: doubt (will it work?), debt (did the telecommunications companies pay too much for their licences?) and delay (when will it be available?). Despite this, we believe the Mobile Internet is going to be big and that all organizations should spend some time considering how they might be affected by this emerging technology.

2.3 Open source software development

One way in which the Internet has affected IS development is through open source software. This is a radically different approach to the more traditional organization of IS development teams.

A software product can be categorized as Open Source Software (OSS) (see http://www.opensource.org) when: the source code is available to the user, the software can be redistributed, the software can be modified, and the licence is not restrictive and must apply to all users and groups. This does not mean that OSS products are necessarily 'free' or that products that appear to be free are in fact OSS. Because it costs no money to download, some software is called 'free', even though the source code is not available (the following is paraphrased from www.opensource.org/advocacy/free-notfree.html). The licence that covers Microsoft's Internet Explorer is a good example of this. Other software is 'free' because it (and the source code for it) has been placed in the public domain, free from copyright restrictions. Some software is called 'free' even though the source code for it is covered by copyright and a licence agreement. The licence usually includes a disclaimer of reliability, and may contain additional restrictions. The restrictions on non-public-domain 'free' software can range form mild to severe. Some licences may prohibit (or require a fee for) commercial use or redistribution. Some licences may prohibit distributing modified versions. Some licences may contain 'copyleft' restrictions requiring that the source code must always be made available, and that derived products must be released under the exact same licence. Some licences may discriminate against individuals or groups and therefore not fall under the requirements of OSS. Thus, the term 'free' software can mean different things to different people and the terms OSS and 'free software' should not be used synonymously.

The best-known example of OSS is probably the Linux operating system. The Linux development was started in 1991 by Linus Torvalds, a 22 year-old Finnish university student. Linux has achieved 25% of the server operating system market, while the Apache web server (another OSS product) has gained 65% of the web server marketplace. Netscape's move to make the Mozilla browser OSS was a less successful initiative, an act of desperation in the face of overwhelming competition from Microsoft.

2.3.1 The Linux phenomenon

Linux is a direct competitor to the UNIX operating system, which has seen marketshare fall over the last few years. Linux is not a direct competitor for desktop PCs running Windows ME/Windows 98, but it is a competitor for servers that run Microsoft Windows NT/Windows 2000/Windows XP. In 1998, internal Microsoft memos were leaked in which Linux was recognized as a serious competitor and the OSS process a potential threat to Microsoft products. The memos were sent to Eric Raymond, who published them with annotations the day after Halloween – hence the 'Halloween Papers'. From an IS development perspective, we may well ask: "how can a loose confederation of developers create a product that rivals Microsoft?".

Torvalds built a UNIX clone for the PC, based around a simple operating system core – the 'kernel'. Torvalds made the source code for Linux free to everyone and asked fellow developers to try it out, test it, suggest enhancements. The traditional view of system development for complex and mission-critical applications such as operating systems would be that it could only be done by the likes of IBM or Microsoft and that it would need large teams of software engineers working closely together under strict project and quality management. It would also take years rather than months to complete.

By contrast, Linux is developed by many part-time programmers, working in universities, for commercial organizations, and as free-lancers. Furthermore, the programmers are based all around the world. Linux developers are not paid for their contributions (although in many cases their employers are subsidising the cost through paying for their time). Although the Linux software is free to use and the developers typically do not receive financial compensation for their efforts, there are still opportunities for revenue generation. For example, Red Hat makes money from packaging Linux on CD media and providing support services, such as training and consulting.

2.3.2 How OSS works

OSS development is firmly grounded in the practical reality of programming, rather than the management-oriented (and arguably fantasy) world of the traditional waterfall life-cycle. Eric Raymond identified some of the lessons of OSS in the landmark essay 'The Cathedral and the Bazaar' (Raymond, 2001). Good programmers work on projects that they have an interest in – they need to 'scratch a personal itch'. They also know when to reuse code rather than develop from a clean slate. Torvalds did not write Linux but studied the code in Mimix; Clark did not reuse Mosaic code from Illinois, but he hired the programmers who built the original Mosaic browser. There is no substitute for enthusiastic, committed, and capable people.

Raymond also reiterates Fred Brook's (1975) lesson: 'plan to throw one away; you will, anyhow'. Once you have built a software system you begin to understand the problem – usually well enough to know that it needs to be re-written. A requirements specification by itself does not give this depth of understanding.

The organization of programmers in OSS networks means that co-developers will rapidly improve code and be effective in debugging. Together with frequent and early releases, this means that software can be tested and debugged quickly: 'Given enough eyeballs, all bugs are shallow' (Raymond, 2001, p. 30). By contrast, user acceptance tests in the traditional life-cycle are, very often, one-off software releases with a small user subset testing the software under severe time constraints.

One way in which software complexity is managed is to have smart data structures and dumb code rather than the other way around. Brooks says 'Show me your flowchart and conceal your tables, and I shall continue to be mystified. Show me your tables, and I won't need your flowchart; it'll be obvious'. We will be adopting a strongly data-driven approach to IS design in this book, based around class diagrams and database design.

Finally, Raymond recognizes the need to listen to and learn from users: 'The next best thing to having good ideas is recognizing good ideas from your users. Sometimes the latter is better' (p. 40). Development should not stop at implementation and then hand over into a separate phase of maintenance. It is possible that the developer's conceptualization of the problem was just wrong – it is also possible that the software will be used in ways unforeseen when it was developed: 'Any tool should be useful in the expected way, but a truly great tool lends itself to uses you never expected'.

Why OSS works

The fact that OSS works at all is surprising. Superficially, it appears that traditional management has been done away with and near-anarchy reigns. On closer inspection, OSS is a triumph of organization, although much of this is *self*-organization rather than hierarchical regulation. The core software that comprises Linux, the kernel, is guarded by a small number of gate-keepers who control what is included in a given release of Linux.

2.3.3 Implications of OSS for IS development

Whether OSS techniques will transfer to application development, such as a commercial banking system, remain to be seen. So far, Open Source development has tended to concentrate on software, such as operating systems, email servers, web servers, and content authoring systems. These are applications that relate to systems management and administration and used by IT professionals such as system administrators. There is less evidence that OSS is being used to develop business applications. An industry-specific information system such as a theatre booking system has a lower potential audience and will struggle to find the critical mass to support OSS. However, we expect to see further collaboration along the lines of the OSS model as commercial organizations, for example financial institutions, participate in joint systems development exercises. However, there are likely to be significant cultural barriers as traditional developers and commercial organizations try to adjust to the fluidity of OSS development. There may also be commercial barriers to the transfer of the gift economy into mainstream business.

Summary

- The Internet and Internet-based information systems have changed the form and content of information systems, the context in which they are developed, and the way in which they are developed.

- Although traditional software engineering skills are needed, for example, database design, program design, network design and security, these need to be reconsidered in the light of the Internet environment.
- The Internet has enabled a new form of software development organization – Open Source (OSS). Although this is more suitable for systems software we expect the lessons to be adopted and transformed by application developers in commercial environments.

Exercises

1. Discuss the future of the Internet – do you think the Internet will develop as rapidly as many forecast?
2. Discuss the potential differences between developing software by conventional means and using open source software.

Further reading

Brooks, F., (1975). *The Mythical Man-Month*. Addison Wesley.

Hobbes, (2002). *Hobbes' Internet Timeline* and *Internet 101,* PBS online.

Forrester Research, (2001). *Forrester Internet Research Survey 2000.*

Raymond, E. S., (2001). *The Cathedral and the Bazaar: Musings on Linux and Open Source by an Accidental Revolutionary.* O'Reilly and Associates, CA.

Stallings, W., (2001). *Business Data Communications.* Prentice Hall, Upper Saddle River, NJ.

3

Web IS Development
Methodology (WISDM)

3.1 Introduction

Many of the approaches to web development have focused on the user interface and in particular the look and feel of a web site, but have failed to address the wider aspects of web-based information systems. At the same time, traditional information system development methodologies – from the waterfall life-cycle to rapid application development (RAD) – have struggled to accommodate web-specific aspects into their methods and work practices. Although web sites are characterized historically as graphically intense hypermedia systems, they have now evolved from cyber-brochures into database-driven information systems that must integrate with existing systems, such as back office applications. web-based information systems (IS) therefore require a mix of web site development techniques together with traditional IS development competencies in database and program design. In this chapter we introduce the Multiview framework for information system development and illustrate how it can be used as a basis for a web IS development methodology (WISDM).

3.2 WISDM in context: the Multiview approach to IS development

Multiview originated as a response to approaches to IS development that had strong roots in engineering discipline and technical rationality. The extension of 1970s structured programming into 1980s structured analysis and design was, perhaps, a logical progression that resulted in IS development methods such as the UK's Structured Systems Analysis and Design Method (SSADM), James Martin's Information Engineering, and Ed Yourdon's Systems Modeling. The process of taking successful programming strategies and broadening them out into design and analysis methods continued unabated with the object-oriented (OO) paradigm, where OO programming was extended into 1990s OO analysis (by many of the same people who had earlier promoted structured methods) culminating in the Unified Modeling Language (UML). Although there are certainly differences between the structured and OO paradigms, the philosophical foundations are shared: a functionalist paradigm of objectivism and social order.

However, engineering-based approaches to IS development can lead to an over-emphasis on the design and construction of computer-based artefacts with insufficient attention given to the social and contextual aspects of IS development. Hirschheim et al. (1996) take the view that the changes associated with system development are emergent, historically contingent, socially situated and politically loaded. As a consequence of this position they argue that sophisticated social theories are needed to understand and make sense of IS development activity.

The fundamental assumption of Multiview (Avison & Wood-Harper, 1990; Avison, et al., 1998) is that an IS methodology that relies overmuch on an engineering approach and technical rationality is, by itself, an insufficient foundation for IS development. This is not to say that there is no place for technical rationality in IS development, but the search for an over-arching prescriptive methodology that claims to address and dissolve all the 'problems' inherent in IS development remains as elusive as the Philosopher's Stone. What then might be the role of methodology in IS development? In our view, IS methodologies are useful epistemological frameworks that can be drawn on during the process of information system definition and development.

The foundations of Multiview as an enquiring framework for IS development rest on a recognition that the needs of computer artefacts, organizations, and individuals must be considered jointly. An IS development exercise should generate robust technical artefacts that support purposeful organizational activity as well as taking into account the needs and freedom of the individual. Multiview is therefore a framework for making the tensions in IS development explicit, to avoid clear-cut distinctions between technical expediency and social justice. This concern with negotiating between the technological, organizational, and human aspects of IS development has constituted a central theme in the Multiview framework and differentiates it from other IS development approaches.

3.2.1 Using the Multiview framework to guide methodology generation

Multiview offers a systematic guide to any IS intervention, together with a reflexive learning process, which brings together the analyst, the situation and the methodology. Multiview is structured in three tiers:

- General framework
- Local, emergent methodology
- Methods/techniques.

Multiview is a framework that provides a basis for constructing a situation-specific methodology (figure 3.1). This contingent methodology is, at its best, the result of a genuine engagement of the IS developers (and other change agents) with the problem situation. This engagement, which is historically contingent and locally situated, informs the choice of methods and techniques, such as soft systems modeling and object-oriented design, that will be used to get things done and to improve the problem situation. The methods used also affect how the situation is perceived and the form of the intervention. Multiview is, therefore, more usefully seen as a metaphor that is interpreted and developed in a particular situation, rather than as a prescriptive description of some real-world activity.

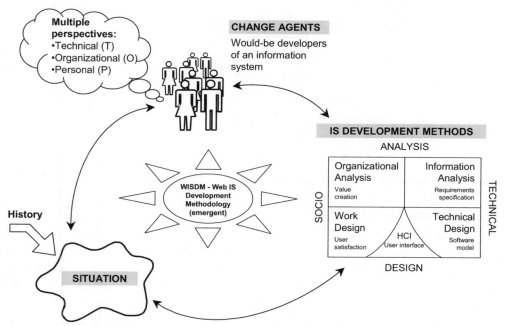

Figure 3.1: The Multiview framework for generating a web IS development methodology – WISDM (adapted from Avison et al., 1998)

Within the framework are methods that the developer (change agent) can draw on to make sense of and interact with the problem situation. The IS development methods are shown in the matrix. The matrix is deliberately presented as *methods* and techniques; they are general tools that can be drawn upon in a specific situation by particular people to create a local *methodology* (WISDM) in practice.

3.3 The WISDM matrix

The IS development methods matrix in figure 3.2 categorizes methods in two dimensions: socio (organizations and people) and technical (the things), on the one hand analysis ('what' is required) and on the other design ('how' it will be achieved). Hard, engineering-based approaches to IS development concentrate on the right hand side of the matrix: the generation of a requirements specification and its stepwise refinement into a software model. The Multiview approach is more even-handed, to seek a sociotechnical solution giving balance to the left and right hand sides of the methods matrix.

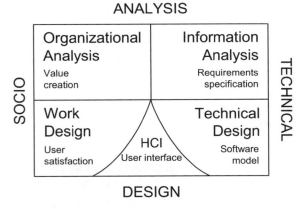

Figure 3.2: Information systems development methods matrix

3.3.1 Organizational analysis

Organizational analysis represents *value creation*. Vickers (1984) uses the word 'appreciation' to stress strategy as relationship building and maintaining, with a broad range of stakeholders that includes customers, employees, government, suppliers, labour organizations, and so on. The systems approach to organizational analysis is covered in chapter 5, where basic systems principles are introduced, and chapter 6, where systems theory is operationalized using the Soft Systems Methodology. A systems approach does not rule out goal-driven business strategies, but these are seen as a subset of a broader aim of relationship maintaining. Traditional business strategy frameworks, such as Porter's five forces and the many e-business models that have emerged, are pre-packaged models that provide specific content. Traditional approaches to e-strategy planning are covered in chapter 4.

3.3.2 Work design

Work design represents *user satisfaction*. The traditional concern of the sociotechnical approach to IS development has been with job satisfaction and genuine user participation in the development process, as reflected in the ETHICS method (Mumford, 1995). WISDM extends this view to incorporate the interests of external users, such as customers, who may be using the information system as part of their social activities. Customer satisfaction with a web-based IS is assessed using the WebQual method. Both of these topics are covered in chapter 7.

3.3.3 Information analysis

Information analysis represents the *requirements specification*. This is a formalized specification of the information and process requirements of the organization. The specification might be in the form of a document with graphical notations, but it might also be in the form of a software prototype (an executable specification). The indicative approach in WISDM is to use UML, which is described in chapter 8.

3.3.4 Technical design

Technical design represents the *software model*. A formalized model of the software in terms of data structures and program design is needed to support software construction.

3.3.5 Human computer interface design

HCI design represents the *user interface* and is located as an overlapping space in technical design and work design. The shape of this space reflects its role in pointing toward analysis but also that its foundations are solidly in design. The interface design draws on web site design principles for page layout, navigation schemes, and usability in the context of work design. Technical design and interface design guidelines are described in chapter 9.

3.3.6 Moving around the methods matrix

There is no a priori ordering of the five aspects of the methods matrix. For example, an organization might acquire an enterprise resource planning (ERP) software package and implement it without modification – this is one way of bringing in the best practice that has been incorporated in software through development and use in a large number of organizations. In such a situation there is less emphasis on information system modeling and software development and more on adapting organizational working practices to the software and learning from the experience of using the software in live operations.

We have found it useful to think of the methods matrix using the metaphor of a film camera. The focus of attention changes as the camera zooms in and then out of an aspect; moves from one aspect to another; revisits an aspect and finds the situation has changed. One particular aspect might be the focus of attention at a particular time, but the other aspects are in peripheral vision and can still make their presence felt even though they might be out of shot. It is possible to see all five aspects at the same time, but only by sacrificing the level of resolution. By contrast, it is possible to focus in and examine one particular aspect in great detail, but at the expense of losing some of the context. We can take the metaphor further and think of IS projects needing the services of a director to interpret the script and a producer to ensure that resources are available. Indeed, it might need all the other people that make up the 'film credits'. Perhaps IS projects are characterized better by multiple directors with multiple cameras endlessly re-making films for distribution straight to video or to sit on the shelf. Of course, this is only a metaphor, and can be stretched too far!

3.4 The role of the analyst: multiple perspectives

Avison & Wood-Harper (1990) suggested that methodologies often contained unstated and unquestioning assumptions about the unitary nature of both the problem situation and the analysts involved in investigating it. The focus is on methods with an underlying assumption that different people in different situations can use these methods in much the same way. As a result of this the methods and the methodology tended to be seen as one and the same thing. In Multiview we are concerned with how any given instantiation of the triad (analyst–methodology–situation) might come about in actual practice. When we talk of analysts, we refer to the role of change agents involved in IS development. This role can be assumed by IS professionals, user personnel, or consultants.

The multiple perspective approach described by Mitroff & Linstone (1993) can be used to inform the particular occurrence of Multiview under any given set of circumstances. In unbounded systems thinking, Mitroff and Linstone argue that complex problem solving requires the application of as many disciplines, professions, and branches of knowledge as possible, with each one employing different paradigms of thought. The idea of 'Multiple Perspectives' is used to describe the various ways of thinking which comprise unbounded systems thinking. The three perspectives identified are:

- Technical perspective (T)
- Organizational (or societal) perspective (O)
- Personal (or individual) perspective (P).

Mitroff and Linstone argue that each perspective yields insights not obtainable from the others, and that O and P perspectives are essential to bridge the gap between analysis and action. Thus, O and P perspectives are used to complement the T perspective, not to replace it. Using the O and P perspectives allows us to bring in the human and social factors that are replete in complex problems and thus focus on human beings both as individuals and groups, including ethical analysis (Wood-Harper et al., 1996). Making use of different perspectives in this way allows us to concentrate more on how we look at a problem rather than on what we are looking at.

A multiple perspective approach provides us with a richer base from which to investigate complex problem situations. Any problem may be viewed from any perspective; the different perspectives may reinforce each other, cancel each other out, or operate in the dialectic mode. Choosing a particular perspective to adopt is in itself problematic and involves the investigator's ethical values and moral judgments. All complex problem situations, however, will inevitably require the adoption of all three perspectives. It is therefore an essential aspect of IS development that the analyst develop reflection and self-awareness and become capable of thinking and acting on the joint basis of the three perspectives.

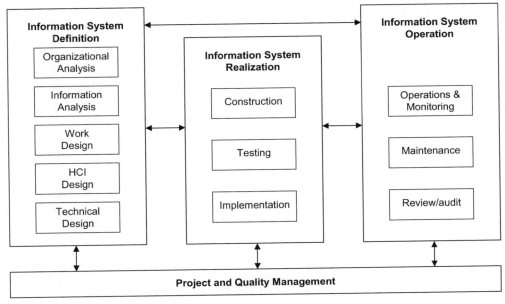

Figure 3.3: The dynamics of WISDM

3.5 WISDM and the IS development life-cycle

WISDM covers the analysis and design activities of system development. An IS development project also encompasses the construction of software and its operation and maintenance (figure 3.3). Software construction is discussed in chapter 10. There must also be testing and implementation, followed by operations and monitoring. These are largely outside the scope of this book, but they are essential aspects of the IS development life-cycle. There is no unidirectional flow seen in figure 3.3. The different life-cycles discussed in chapter 2 – waterfall, iterative, and evolutionary – are catered for in WISDM dynamics since all approaches must address the basic issues of analysis and design, software construction and implementation, and operation and maintenance. Thus, the traditional waterfall life-cycle is a special case: a requirements specification is produced and frozen and then passed on for refinement into a design and implementation in subsequent stages of the life-cycle. The specification might also be produced iteratively through RAD or evolve through successive prototypes.

Running throughout any IS development project is a concern for project management and quality management. This might be formalized as, for example, in PRINCE, the UK Government sponsored project management methodology, and the ISO9000 series of quality standards, or it might be less formal, for example, being driven by customer expectations and self-organizing teams.

3.6 Is web IS development different?

In a review of three companies working in Internet time, Baskerville & Pries-Heje (2001) identified ten concepts relevant to IS development for the Internet. We will explore these concepts to gain an insight into the real-world characteristics of web development projects.

Time pressure: Competitive pressures may mean that any advantage is short-lived and will be copied quickly – time is of the essence.

Vague requirements: Requirements are often imprecise or not known at all and have to be created through imagine and innovation.

Prototyping: The software prototype is the specification of requirements rather than the models in a paper-based specification. Fred Brooks' adage noted in chapter 2 that developers should aim to throw one away ("because you will anyway") is particularly pertinent to web-based applications where the requirements are vague and fast changing.

Release orientation: Release early and often – the adage of rapid application development is also highly relevant to Internet projects.

Parallel development: Database development can take place at the same time as the graphical design; requirements analysis and design become hard to separate.

Fixed architecture: Complexity needs to be tamed. A three-tier architecture where the business data, business logic, and the user interface are separated out and this allows team members to work in parallel with a degree of independence.

Coding your way out: When the going gets tough the developers need to code their way out of problems. Hacking was not originally a pejorative term, but was used to identify programmers who could write elegant and effective code quickly (see the 'Hacker Ethos').

Quality is negotiable: Do you want it: good, quick, or cheap. Pick any two. In a sense, quality has always been negotiable. In web-based projects the over-riding view of quality tends to be the customer perspective and experience, rather than by a defined and repeatable development process or a software product that survives an internal audit.

Dependence on good people: Internet projects are completed under time pressure and typically in small teams where all members need to pull their weight. Key staff can make or break a project.

Need for structure: The old structures of systems development, e.g., business analysts separate from software engineers may be inappropriate to building applications in Internet time.

Although the ten concepts capture the emergent aspects of web IS development well, if the term 'business urgency' is substituted for the concept 'Internet time' then it is clear that the ten concepts have a more general relevance to understanding the IS development process. In situations characterized by time pressure and definitional uncertainty the response of IS developers has long been to adopt a flexible strategy to IS development using techniques such as rapid application development and prototyping. However, there are some concrete differences between Internet projects and traditional IS development:

- *Internet time*. The development time is reduced greatly – two years is unthinkable, 6 months is often unacceptable and many significant e-commerce projects are implemented in weeks. This means that the 10 concepts above tend to be the norm rather than the exception.
- *Strategic implications*. The strategic implications are directly related to business goals, particularly in e-commerce projects where a revenue stream is generated.
- *Emphasis on graphical user interface*. There is a need for talented graphic designers to work with software engineers.
- *Customer-orientation*. The user is a customer rather than an employee. E-

commerce applications need customer focus and marketing input. Again, these are not traditional areas of software engineering.

On the other hand, there are also similarities:

- *Databases.* Sophisticated Internet applications rely on databases and require traditional software engineering skills to implement them.
- *Integration.* Internet applications need to be integrated with enterprise applications. For example, a front office car ordering system that gives consumers a delivery date will need to communicate with the back office manufacturing requirements planning (MRP) module of an enterprise resource planning (ERP) software suite. Tying together the front office and back office business systems – enterprise application integration (EAI) – will continue to be a major challenge to organizations.

As Internet projects become broader in scope requiring greater integration with front office, back office, and legacy IT systems of all sorts, then Internet projects will become yet more difficult to distinguish from traditional IT projects. Traditional IS projects would also benefit from being given more attention to strategy, customers, and design aesthetics and therefore the distinctions should, over time, become less pronounced and even disappear altogether as web-based IS development becomes 'business as usual'.

Summary

- WISDM builds on Multiview and is a contingent approach to IS development that provides a general framework for understanding the triad of analyst, problem situation, and methods.
- The web IS Development Methodology (WISDM) is an emergent property of an instantiation of the triad in practice.
- The IS Development Methods matrix is multi-perspective, being a balance of organizational analysis, information analysis, work design and technical design.
- WISDM requires the developer to construct a particular methodology from these ingredients that is suitable to the situation at hand.

Exercises

1. What are the different situations that might lead to different emphases on organizational analysis, information analysis, work design and technical design in IS development projects.
2. Consider various case studies in IS development. What was the balance struck in terms of organizational analysis, information analysis, work design

and technical/HCI design? In the light of the project successes and failures, was the correct balance struck?
3. What are the particular features of web development applications that might lead to different aspects being emphasised in a real-world instantiation of WISDM?

Further reading

Avison, D.E. and Wood-Harper, A.T., (1990). *Multiview: An Exploration in Information Systems Development.* Blackwell Scientific Publications, Oxford.

Avison, D.E., Wood-Harper, A.T., Vidgen, R.T. and Wood, J.R.G., (1998). A Further Exploration into Information Systems Development: the Evolution of Multiview2. *Information Technology & People*, 11(2): 124–139.

Baskerville, R. and Pries-Heje, J., (2001). Racing the e-bomb: How the Internet is Redefining Information System Development Methodology. In: Russo, L., Fitzgerald, B. and DeGross, J., editors, *Realigning Research and Practice in Information System Development*, Proceedings of the IFIP TC8/WG8.2 Working Conference, July 27–29, Boise, Idaho, USA.

Himanen, P., (2001). *The Hacker Ethic and the Spirit of the Information Age.* Secker & Warburg, London.

Hirschheim, R., Klein, H.K. and Lyytinen, K., (1996). Exploring the Intellectual Structures of Information Systems Development: a Social Action Theoretical Analysis. *Accounting, Management & Information Technology*, 6(1/2): 1–64.

Mitroff, I. and Linstone, H., (1993). *The Unbounded Mind: Breaking the Chains of Traditional Business Thinking.* Oxford University Press, New York.

Mumford, E., (1995). *Effective Systems Design and Requirements Analysis – the ETHICS approach.* Macmillan Press, Basingstoke, UK.

Vickers, G., (1984). *The Vickers Papers.* Edited by the Open Systems Group. Harper and Row.

Wood-Harper, A.T., Corder, S., Wood, J. and Watson, H., (1996). How We Profess: the Ethical Systems Analyst. *Communications of the ACM*, 39(3): 69–77.

4

e-Business Strategy

4.1 Introduction

The information system (IS) development team should be prepared to answer the question: how does this IS development project fit with the organization's business strategy? In pre-Internet IS developments, the question of strategic fit is often implicit and taken as given. The project is part of a portfolio of IS developments that in some way, at some higher and more abstract level, align with the organization's business strategy.

ANALYSIS

	Organizational Analysis Value creation (business strategy)	Information Analysis Requirements specification	
SOCIO	Work Design User satisfaction	HCI User interface	Technical Design Software model	TECHNICAL

DESIGN

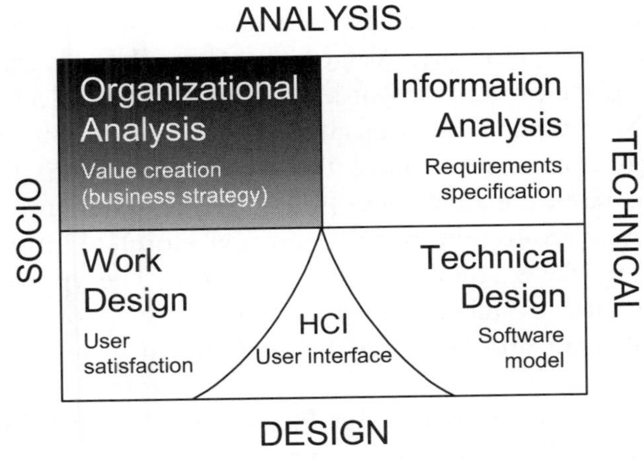

Figure 4.1: Organizational analysis – the strategic context

With Internet based development projects there is often a direct and tangible relationship between information systems and strategy – the IS development may have implications for the way the organization deals with customers and other partners as well as a direct impact on revenue flows. In some organizations, particularly the dot-com, the information systems *are* the very embodiment of the organization's business strategy.

There are many definitions of strategy, but Porter's (1980) definition is succinct and to the point:

> Strategy is a broad based formula for how business is going to compete, what its goals should be, and what policies will be needed to carry out those goals. The essence of formulating competitive strategy is relating a company to its environment.

At the close of the 20th century, dot-com mania set in as Internet companies achieved valuations of startling proportions. In the last quarter of 1999 Lastminute.com, a specialist in late bookings for holidays and theatre tickets, had revenues of £0.6 million, a loss of £6 million and a market capitalization of £770 million. The high street bricks and mortar travel agent Thomson Travel had a turnover of £3 billion in 1999, a profit of £77 million, and a market capitalization of £980 million. In January 1999 Amazon.com had a market capitalization of $29 billion (despite never having made a profit at that point) while the retail giant Sears had a value of a 'mere' $16.5 billion. Clearly, many of the business models that underpinned these staggering dot-com valuations were not going to be sustainable.

Porter (2001) argues that the age of the 'new economy' is over and that the terms e-business and e-strategy have been dangerous and misleading. To view Internet operations as separate from the rest of the business can lead to simplistic ways of competing and a more general failure to integrate the Internet into traditional value-creating business activities. Some companies have struck a good balance. For example, Walgreens, a large US pharmacy chain, allows customers to place prescription orders online and to collect the order at their local store. Ninety per cent of customers prefer to collect their prescription from the local store than to have the order delivered to their home. Walgreens have integrated the *marketspace* (the convenience of Internet ordering) with the *marketplace* (collection from a physical store) to provide customers with a bricks and clicks solution – the *marketface*. The approach adopted by Walgreens does not cannibalize the sales of physical stores, but uses the Internet to complement and build on their traditional value-adding activities.

Similarly, for our case study of the Barchester Playhouse (see appendix A for details), the aim must be to use the Internet to support its business strategy – how it will create value and how it will compete and sustain itself in its environment. Although we might have reservations about dot-coms and the dangers of separating out the 'e' aspect of business and strategy, there are indeed innovative ways in which the Playhouse might use the Internet to create business models that go beyond the obvious: using e-commerce to add sell theatre tickets online.

4.2 Business models

Rappa (2001) defines a business model as:

> In the most basic sense, a business model is the method of doing business by which a company can sustain itself – that is, generate revenue. The business model spells out how a company makes money by specifying where it is positioned in the value chain.

This generic definition is consistent with a view of strategy as survival in a competitive environment. Timmers' (1999) definition of a business model is yet more specific:

> An architecture for product, service and information flows, including a description of the various business actors and their roles; and

> – a description of the potential benefits for the various business actors;

> and

> – a description of the sources of revenue.

Timmers argues that a business model in itself is necessary, but not sufficient. To assess the commercial viability of the business model we also need to know the marketing strategy of the organization. A marketing model comprises a business model together with the marketing strategy (how we are to compete) of the business actor under consideration. Timmers identifies a range of business models, the most basic of which is the e-shop.

The Barchester Playhouse could, with relative ease, implement an e-shop for ticket and merchandise sales. The e-shop would constitute an additional sales and marketing channel for the Playhouse, allowing customers to buy tickets online rather than in person or by telephone at the box office. Although this basic approach to the Internet may well result in operational benefits for the Playhouse, such as reduced transaction costs through automated ticket sales, and convenience for the customer, including 24-hour ticket bookings and electronic ticket delivery, it can hardly be classified as a significant change in business strategy and the way in which the Playhouse competes. Timmers identifies a range of further business model archetypes, such as the auction, the value chain integrator, and the community, which would have greater strategic implications for the Playhouse.

Using Timmers' definition of a business model, we can produce a generic template that acts as a useful checklist to think about both the broad business strategy and the specifics of how the strategy will be implemented in terms of how to compete (table 4.1).

The apparent simplicity of a question such as 'What business are we in?' can surface a wealth of taken for granted assumptions and highlight a lack of shared understanding about an organization's core business. For example, should the Playhouse provide popular entertainment using actors seen on television? Should it create a cultural experience through the staging of the classics? Should it aim to educate young people on the intricacies of stagecraft? Many organizations do not have a clear view of what business they are in and even where the view is clear at the top it is not necessarily communicated and shared throughout the organization. In chapters 5 and 6 we introduce systems thinking as a way of surfacing assumptions and discussing what might constitute purposeful activity for an organization such as a theatre.

- **Business (strategy)**
  - What business is the Organization in?
  - What are the products and services?
- **Products and services**
  - What are the sources of revenue?
  - What are the benefits to the business actors?
- **Who are the Customers?**
- **Who are the Competitors?**
- **Marketing strategy (how to compete)**
  - What is the Organization's marketing strategy?

Table 4.1: Business planning template (adapted from Timmers, 1999)

Using the template in table 4.1 we might state that the core business of the Playhouse is the staging of productions in order to provide live entertainment to the theatre-going public. Additional and complementary services include bar and restaurant facilities, and conferences. The source of revenue is therefore primarily from ticket sales, with ancillary streams from catering and the hire of conference facilities. The customers are the people of Barchester, tourists visiting the town, and corporate clients. The Playhouse stages productions for the entertainment of the public, but it also has a mission to educate, particularly local school children, through its outreach programme. Competitors include other theatres in the town and other forms of entertainment, such as cinemas and television. In order to compete the Playhouse needs to have a clear marketing strategy that will inform the choice of productions and a communications strategy to promote the Playhouse and its productions.

4.3 Business webs for the theatre industry

A straightforward approach would be for the Playhouse to adopt the e-shop business model to provide an additional ticket sales and marketing channel, i.e., e-commerce. Although it is important that the operational benefits of the e-shop are not overly downplayed (the success of the business model of a budget airline, such as EasyJet, derives in part from the reduction in transaction costs of Internet-only ticket booking), the e-shop often represents the line of least resistance. It is the 'obvious' option, but is easy to copy, and in isolation is unlikely to confer any significant or enduring competitive advantage.

Tapscott et al. (2000) identify generic business webs that enable organizations to create value in ways that could only be achieved through leveraging the power of the Internet (figure 4.2).

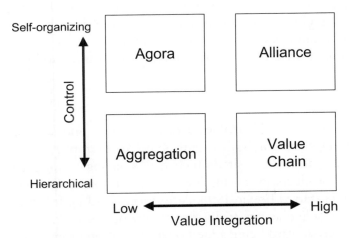

Figure 4.2: Business webs (adapted from Tapscott et al., 2000, p. 28)

The two dimensions of figure 4.2 relate to economic control and value integration. Hierarchical business webs have leaders who control the pricing and the flow of transactions. Amazon.com selects the products it will offer and sets a price for the books and CDs it sells. By contrast, the online auction house e-Bay accepts any item for sale (within reason – nuclear warheads are not allowed) and facilitates the discovery of the price for that item. So, eBay does not set prices: it provides a mechanism for buyers and sellers to discover a price. Where a business web integrates the activities of multiple members of the value chain then the value integration is high.

For example, at the University of Bath there is project investigating the feasibility of producing a motor-car in three days from the time the customer places their order at the dealer to the customer taking delivery of their new car (Howard et al., 2001). Typical best practice in the industry in 2001 is around 40 days. Weeding out inefficiencies in the supply chain will not be sufficient to reduce the current 40 day lead time to 3 days. In order to achieve a three-day car it is necessary to integrate the activities of dealers, manufacturers, first tier suppliers, second tier suppliers, and logistics companies through a business web. The value integration will be high and the benefits for the customer substantial in terms of product customization and convenience. For some business webs value integration is low, as is the case where a business web focuses on giving customers a broad product selection through providing accessing to a wide range of third party suppliers.

Using these two dimensions, four stereotypical business webs are defined: the agora, the aggregation, the alliance, and the value chain (figure 4.2). In practice, organizations will display characteristics of more than one type of business web. For example, Amazon.com works with fixed prices but it also has auction facilities and community aspects through reader reviews of books. However, the four business webs provide a useful framework for thinking about how the Playhouse might exploit the Internet to move beyond the e-shop. It is also a useful framework for thinking about the threats to any individual business that might arise from the emergence of business webs in that business's industry.

4.3.1 Aggregation

The Aggregation business web (b-web) enables a flow of goods and services between producers, creating value for both (figure 4.3). An exemplar of the aggregator is the Egg financial services site, which offers savings, mortgage, credit card, and insurance products (Seybold, 2001). The UK based financial services company Prudential started Egg in 1998. At its inception Egg followed the e-shop model, offering online access to Prudential savings products, with further products such as a credit card being added over time. When Egg began to offer third party products it moved from the e-shop model into an aggregation b-web. Egg now offers motor insurance, drawing from a panel of insurance underwriters. Customers enter their details online (personal details, driving history, vehicle particulars) and are matched with a suitable insurance product. Egg do not provide access to motor insurance products and by acting as an intermediary they add value for both the end customer and for the third party suppliers of insurance products. The third party producers gain by having access to the Egg customer base, while customers benefit from a comprehensive service that includes selection, organization, matching, price, convenience, and fulfilment.

Selection entails providing the consumer with a wide range of products. Egg clearly does this through access to its mortgage supermarket where many mortgage providers' products can be accessed. It is not enough to provide a wide range of products, since this can be overwhelming. To help users find the right product for them the offerings should be *organized* in a way that is appropriate to the consumer. For example, with a mortgage product there might be categories such as 'first time buyer' and 'empty nester'. A *matching* process will help the user find suitable products that fit their individual profile. For a mortgage this could include age, number of dependants, income, mortgage term, and degree of risk aversion (e.g., a mortgage denominated in the Japanese Yen might not be for everyone).

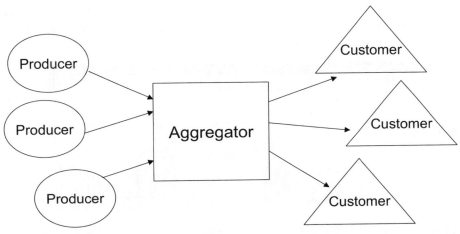

Figure 4.3: Aggregator b-web. Source: Digital Capital, p. 32, © Don Tapscott, David Ticoll, and Alex Lowry, 2000. This material is reproduced by permission of Nicholas Brealey Publishing.

The aggregator should assist the consumer in finding the best *price*, but can go beyond this into customization, for example they might reward loyal customers by giving them a discount on buildings insurance if they already hold a mortgage account. A key requirement for aggregations is *convenience*; Egg credit card holders can print off their statements from the web and make payments online at any time of the day or night, avoiding trips to the bank or writing out and posting cheques. The ultimate in convenience is doing nothing – if your fridge knows that you are running low on milk then it can email the local supermarket to order some more. The final stage is *fulfilment*, which is where many Internet businesses fall down. For intangible goods, such as insurance, it is relatively easy to process the transaction and to post out a certificate (improved security and digital certificates will eventually mean that postage is not needed). For tangible items, particularly where the ratio of value to weight is low, such as groceries, fulfilment can make Internet sales uneconomic. Webvan was set up to provide a US-wide infrastructure for the online ordering and distribution of groceries. Unfortunately, Webvan underestimated the cost and difficulty of their enterprise and from a valuation of $9bn in 1999 were reduced to filing for bankruptcy protection in July 2001.

What role might an aggregator play in the theatre industry? An aggregator could aggregate multiple theatres, offering consumers access to many productions, thereby providing a wide selection, with appropriate organization (e.g., families, corporate entertainment, art-house), matching to individual tastes, and a loyalty scheme to reward regular theatre-goers. More interestingly, the Playhouse might aggregate local restaurants and hotels to provide the theatre-goer with the convenience of a self-selected package that includes a theatre performance, supper, and accommodation. Third parties, such as tourist information offices and hotels, could be enrolled as affiliates and paid a commission for selling tickets and services.

Figure 4.4: Egg web site

A useful and visually powerful way of representing and imagining a b-web is to create a value map (figure 4.5). The value map shows the flows between the involved parties of:

- goods and services, revenues
- information and knowledge
- intangible benefits.

The value map shows the reach of the aggregator and how and where it can create value for a range of parties. Value maps can be created for all types of business web.

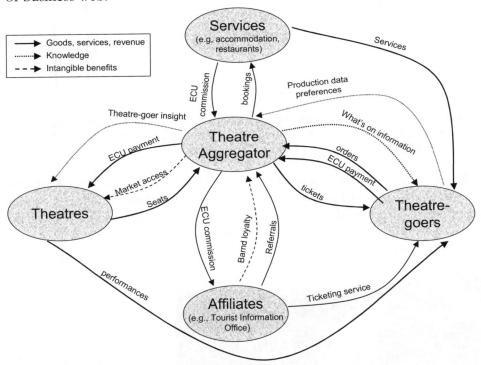

Figure 4.5: Barchester Playhouse aggregator value map

4.3.2 Agora

In Ancient Greece an agora was a public meeting where commercial activity was conducted. Tapscott et al. (2000) use the term to refer to a business web where buyers and sellers come together to negotiate and assign value to goods (figure 4.6). The fundamental point of the agora model is that it provides liquidity: assets can be converted into cash. The agora achieves this by providing a price-discovery mechanism that allows buyers and sellers to be matched and to carry out mutually beneficial exchanges. One of the best-known examples of the agora is eBay, which is primarily a consumer to consumer auction site (although there are also full-time traders operating on eBay who are better classified as small businesses).

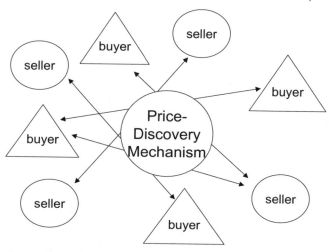

Figure 4.6: Agora b-web. Source: Digital Capital, p. 31, © Don Tapscott, David Ticoll, and Alex Lowry, 2000. This material is reproduced by permission of Nicholas Brealey Publishing.

eBay is an example of a sell-side auction. There are also buy-side auctions, such as FreeMarkets, who work with businesses to meet their procurement needs (figure 4.7). FreeMarkets spend months setting up an auction, vetting suppliers to ensure they can meet quality requirements and checking that they are financially stable.

Figure 4.7: FreeMarkets – a buy-side agora

Once the suppliers have been short-listed the auction can take place. In less than an hour millions of dollars worth of contracts for the supply of components can be awarded, with suppliers from around the world bidding to offer the lowest price. Following the auction there is still work to be done by FreeMarkets, who will tie up the detail of the contracts. Through buy-side auctions FreeMarkets claim to be able to reduce procurement costs by around 12%.

The agora model is particularly appropriate for perishable goods, such as flight seats and theatre seats. In the theatre industry a business web could transform the pricing mechanism, moving from fixed prices to price discovery where ticket prices are allowed to vary directly with market demand. One affect of such an agora in the theatre industry would be to disintermediate the 'ticket tout' by offering and buying back tickets at prices based on demand – i.e., the creation of a market for theatre seats. Although a provincial theatre such as the Barchester Playhouse would probably not be in a position to become a market maker for theatre seats it could adopt dynamic pricing mechanisms to improve the yield of its performances. Airlines already do this, recognizing that it is better to sell flight seats and make a small margin than to run the flight with empty seats.

4.3.3 Value chain

A more complex and innovative business model is the value chain integrator (figure 4.8). In this business model the organization integrates multiple steps of the value chain and exploits the information flows between the stages.

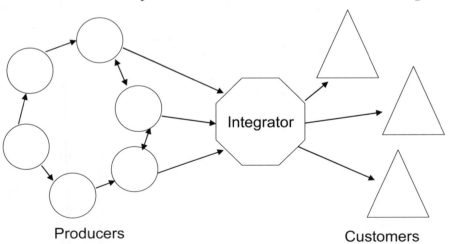

Figure 4.8: Value chain integration. Source: Digital Capital, p. 33, © Don Tapscott, David Ticoll, and Alex Lowry, 2000. This material is reproduced by permission of Nicholas Brealey Publishing.

We have already mentioned the Three Day Car initiative as an instance of how a business web would be needed to support the transformation of the motor industry. The Three Day Car requires a shift from suppliers building for stock and pushing cars through a supply chain to a situation where customer demand pulls cars through a supply network, i.e., build to order. There is much to be done in the motor industry – in the CSC (Computer Sciences Corporation) 2001 survey of critical issues in IS they estimated that savings of $100bn to $200bn could be made annually through an e-business driven reconfiguration of the industry.

Figure 4.9: Cisco web site

Business webs are emerging in other industries, for example in the computer industry where companies such as Dell are building computers to order. Another computer industry example is Cisco (figure 4.9). Cisco builds the networking infrastructure that powers the web. Cisco designs the core technologies, such as routers and switches, coordinates business processes, manages relationships between partners, and does the marketing. But Cisco does not need to manufacture all of the products (Cisco owns two out of the 38 plants that manufacture its products), does not need to sell and distribute the products itself, or even perform all of the customer support (customers can do this for themselves in large part via online communities). In value chain integration all of the partners – chip manufacturers, component manufacturers, distributors, and system integrators – act like one firm to create value for the customer. Cisco provides the context in which information sharing and collaboration take place to achieve this value creation.

In the theatre industry value chain integration could bring together participants such as production companies, artistes, playwrights, promoters, agents, and theatres to create value for the ultimate customer, the theatre-goer. A theatre business web could provide a forum for matching artists with productions and the creation of performance schedules with theatres. Such integration might threaten the role of traditional intermediaries such as theatrical agents, who would need to reconsider how they add value to the theatrical production process in a business web context. However, the transformation of an industry is going to be a technologically, socially, and politically complex undertaking and the power of the current incumbents in the industry to resist change should not be under-estimated.

4.3.4 Alliance

The fourth business web stereotype is the alliance. An excellent example of the power of the alliance is the Open Source Software (OSS) movement where industrial strength software, such as the Linux operating system (see chapter 2) is produced through a community of prosumers. A prosumer is both producer and consumer: the organizations and individuals that contribute code to Linux are also using the software to run the computers that run their businesses. Contributors are not paid for their contributions and the resulting software can be downloaded from the Internet and used free of charge.

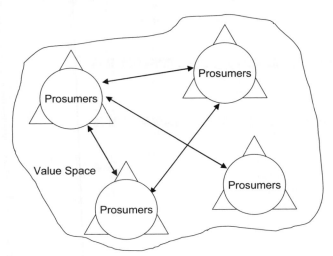

Figure 4.10: Alliance business web. Source: Digital Capital, p. 34, © Don Tapscott, David Ticoll, and Alex Lowry, 2000. This material is reproduced by permission of Nicholas Brealey Publishing.

Another example of the alliance that has proven to be successful in 2001 is FriendsReunited (figure 4.11). FriendsReunited was set up by Julie and Steve Pankhurst to put people in touch with old school friends. A vast community with a common interest and a strong incentive to return was created entirely by 'word of mouse' – FriendsReunited did not use traditional advertising and marketing channels. Despite this, by October 2001 FriendsReunited had 2 million unique users per month – up from 191 thousand in June 2001. With a subscription £5 and some advertising revenue FriendsReunited has a significant income stream, achieved with minimal overheads.

In the context of the theatre industry, prosumption could take many forms. For example, the Internet would enable authors to engage in collaborative writing of a piece of theatre and the resultant work could then be made available for download and performance by any theatre company free of charge. Of course, whether this would work for artistic endeavour as well as it does for the creation of software such as the Linux is debatable. By looking at different types of virtual community it is possible to get a deeper insight into how this type of business web could support the Playhouse.

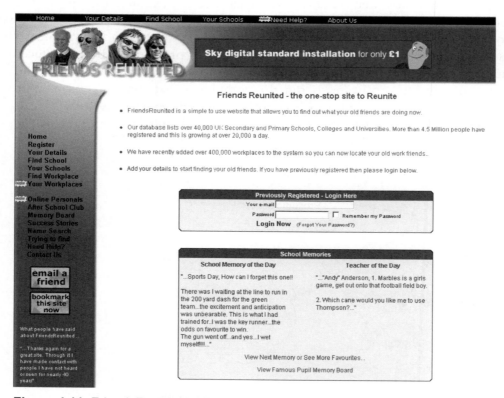

Figure 4.11: FriendsReunited.com web site

4.4 Virtual communities

According to Rheingold (2000) virtual communities are 'Social aggregations that emerge from the Net when enough people carry on those public discussions long enough, with sufficient human feeling, to form webs of personal relationships in cyberspace.' A virtual community has the capacity to integrate content and communication, gives access to competing publishers and vendors, and promotes member-generated content. In a business setting the focus is likely to be on developing business networks, conducting business transactions, and job-hunting; the personal and social interaction aspects of an online business community will likely be less well-developed than a non-commercial community. Hagel and Armstrong identify four types of community orientation: interest, relationship, fantasy, and transaction.

Interest-oriented communities typically have high levels of interaction between members on topics of shared interest and are supported by chat rooms, message boards, and discussion groups. The community has a shared interest, such as a sport, music, or hobby. The Motley Fool investment advice site is an example of an interest-oriented community. In the theatre context, an interest-oriented community could provide a forum for theatre-goers to discuss performances they have attended, or for stage managers to share their expertise and to advertise job opportunities.

Relationship-oriented communities are typified by shared life experiences, such as divorce or cancer and the focus is on sharing information and opinions and community support. FriendsReunited is a good example of the power of relationship-oriented community and in the theatre industry a copycat initiative would be ActorsReunited, providing a forum for actors to get together with fellow actors they worked with in the past.

Fantasy-oriented communities are associated with role-playing and imaginary environments. Role-playing games of the Dungeons and Dragons variety are typical examples of fantasy communities. In the theatre context, a fantasy-community could provide an online environment for those who want play out acting roles but don't want to appear live on a physical stage acting in 'real roles'.

Transaction-based communities aid buying and selling. For example, Virtual Vineyards is a commercial site for selling wine but it also has community aspects that deliver expert advice and a forum for wine drinkers to chat with each other. A transaction-based virtual community for the theatre industry could allow members to buy and sell theatre memorabilia supported by discussion forums.

Value can be created for the organizer of a virtual community by selling products and services, taking subscriptions, placing advertising, and selling market research data (figure 4.12). FriendsReunited generate revenue streams from an annual subscription and from advertising (see figure 4.11). A virtual community in the theatre industry would have potential revenues from subscriptions, commissions on ticket sales, and advertising. Selling demographic data is also a potential source of revenue but has to be approached with care if personal privacy legislation is not to be breached or the trust of the community lost.

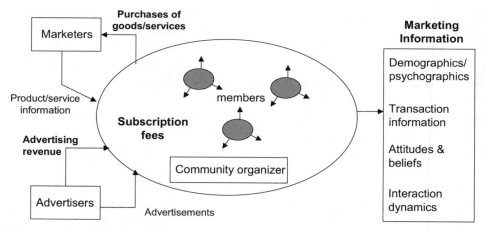

Figure 4.12: Value creation in virtual communities (after Kannan et al., 1998)

The benefits of a successful virtual community are appealing to businesses. According to Forrester Research the paybacks for creating a successful community (in order of greatest importance) are:

- Customer loyalty increases
- Sales increase
- Customer participation and feedback increases
- Repeat traffic to the site increases
- New traffic to the site increases.

However, creating a viable community is not a simple task. The community facilitator needs to monitor content quality, monitor the free-riders (people who take from the community but make no contribution), protect the privacy of members, and nurture the community in the early stages so that it attains critical mass.

4.5 Marketspace transformation and relationship capital

The business webs and virtual community stereotypes are useful broad-brush tools for thinking about how the Internet might transform business models in the theatre industry. At a more tangible level we can use the *marketspace* model (Dutta & Segev, 2001) to think in more detailed terms about how the traditional 'four P's' of marketing (product, price, place, promotion) might be transformed in cyberspace.

The marketspace model (figure 4.13) is built on two dimensions: a technological capability and a strategic perspective. The technological viewpoint comprises interactivity and connectivity. The real-time, online nature of the Internet enables more interactive and richer relationships between organizations and customers. The open and global nature of the Internet increases connectivity and fosters the creation of a shared global marketspace.

The strategic dimension of the model takes the traditional '4 Ps' of marketing and adds a customer perspective, which is particularly significant in an Internet context where personalization and one-to-one marketing are possible. Using the strategic dimension to analyse the Playhouse case we see that there is potential for a significant degree of transformation (table 4.2) that goes beyond simple online ticket sales.

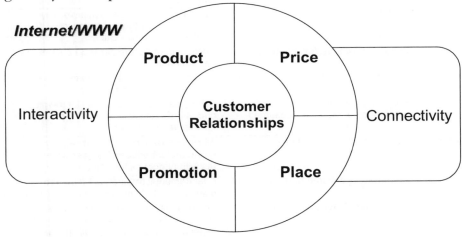

Figure 4.13: Marketspace model (Dutta & Segev, 2001)

The key aspect of Internet marketing is to manage the market*face* – the mix of the market*space* (e.g., buying tickets online, seeing video excerpts, engaging in online promotions) and the market*place* (e.g., buying tickets in person from the box office and other physical outlets, experiencing a live performance). However, above all else the Playhouse must not lose sight of its core business: the provision of a live theatre experience. An indiscriminate use of technology, such as the introduction of live 'theatre-cams', which would reduce theatre to an inferior form of cable television, would damage the Playhouse's product.

Dimension	Aspect	Possibilities
Product	Availability of product-related information online	Online access to reviews; video-clips of performances, online matching of user preferences to available productions
	Customization of products for individuals/groups of customers	Customization of merchandising, e.g., artwork for mugs and T-shirts
	Customer participation in product specification and design	Allow theatre-goers to vote for the actors they want to see in a production
Promotion	Use of online advertising	Advertise the Playhouse on search engines and listings sites
	Use of online promotions such as sales and discounts	Provide special offers, such as family tickets for the pantomime season
	Customization of online promotions	Target promotions to individual theatre-goers based on their personal profile
	Participation of customers in online promotions	Quizzes and online games to win theatre tickets and merchandise
	Links with other organizations in organizing online promotions	Provide theatre package deals in partnership with local restaurants and hotels
Pricing	Pricing information online	Full pricing information available, any special rates for the unemployed, disabled, and senior citizens
	Dynamic customization of prices	Auctioning of theatre seats 3 hours before performance
	Availability of online price negotiation	Reverse auction – allow theatre-goers to make offers for theatre seats
	Possibility to charge customers for proportions of products consumed	If the theatre-goer does not like the play offer a 75% refund on the ticket price if they leave at the interval
Placement	Availability of online ordering	Allow theatre-goers to buy theatre seats online and introduce paperless ticketing (as with budget airline EasyJet)
	Availability of secured online payment	A fundamental requirement if theatre-goers are to trust the web site
	Distribution of products online	Video feeds could be streamed in real time and 'theatre-cams' deployed, but the experience of being physically present at a live performance will be eroded
	Involvement of partner organizations in online distribution	Cable television companies could screen live performances
Customer relationships	Provision of online customer service	Online ticket returns, email response to queries
	Online identification and tracking of customers to provide customized services	Initiate a scheme, e.g., 'Friends of the Theatre', to reward loyalty with ticket price discounts and special offers
	Provision of online communications to customers	Email newsletters, discussion forums
	Creation of online communities for customers	Establish a virtual community for the 'Friends of the Theatre'
	Solicitation of online feedback from customers	Monitor discussion forums, encourage email communication, use online questionnaires to assess customer satisfaction

Table 4.2: Marketspace transformation of the Playhouse (adapted from Dutta & Segev, 2001)

Summary

- e-business goes beyond the simple e-commerce approach of offering theatre seats for sale on the Internet.
- Business webs are emerging that harness the power of the Internet to facilitate new business models that would not be possible without the reach and communication power of the Internet.
- Despite the opportunities offered by the Internet, e-business models are still just business models. A sound strategy for how to compete is still a fundamental requirement.
- Virtual community aspects can be blended into the operations of all types of business webs and traditional businesses.
- Organizations need to manage the marketface: the intersection of their traditional business (marketplace) and their online operations (marketspace).

Exercises

1. Use the template in table 4.1 to create a business model for a University MBA or undergraduate degree programme.
2. Create a value map using the notation in figure 4.5 for a theatre industry value chain integrator.
3. How might a University offering a weekend programme to senior executives create value from a virtual community?

Further reading

Dutta, S. and Segev, A., (2001). Business Transformation on the Internet. In: Barnes, S. and Hunt, B., *E-Commerce & V-Business*, Butterworth Heinemann.

Hagel and Armstrong, (1997). *Net Gain*. Harvard Business School Press, Boston, Mass.

Howard, M., Vidgen, R., Powell, P. and Graves, A., (2001). Planning for IS Related Industry Transformation: the Case of the 3DayCar. In: Smithson, S., Gricar, J., Podlogar, M. and Avgerinou, S., editors, *Proceedings of the 9th European Conference on Information Systems*, Bled, Slovenia, June, pp. 433–442.

Kannan, P., Chang, A. and Whinston, A., (1998). Marketing Information on the I-Way. *Communications of the ACM*. 41(3): 35–43.

Porter, M., (1980). *Competitive Strategy*. Free Press.

Porter, M., (2001). Strategy and the Internet. *Harvard Business Review*, March, 63–78.

Rappa, M., (2001). Business Models on the Web.
   http://digitalenterprise.org/models/models.html

Rheingold, H., (2000). *The Virtual Community*. MIT Press (original edition published in 1993).

Seybold, P., (2001). *The Customer Revolution*. Random House Business Books, London.

Tapscott, D., Ticoll, D. and Lowy, A., (2000). *Digital Capital: Harnessing the Power of Business Webs*. Nicholas Brealey, London.

Timmers, P., (1999). *Electronic Commerce: Strategies and Models for Business-to-Business Trading*. Wiley, Chichester.

5

Systems Thinking

5.1 Introduction

Reductionist approaches to problem solving take wholes apart and examine the parts to see how they work to gain an understanding of the whole. This approach can work with certain types of problem where it is possible to isolate them to a part of the whole and to then fix it. For example, I might well be able to identify a hard disk failure on my personal computer as the cause of it not working. Fixing the hard disk may well fix the problem and get me a fully functioning computer once again. Unfortunately, not all problems are amenable to this treatment and in many situations it is better to think of the situation as a 'mess' to be explored than a problem to be solved.

In this chapter we will consider the principal ideas behind systems thinking and contrast them with the reductionist approaches of traditional analysis. The aim of this chapter is to build an understanding of systems theory and systems thinking to provide a foundation for the soft systems methodology (SSM) introduced in chapter 6.

5.2 Difficulties and messes

Mental models affect how we see the world. How we view the world is an important factor in what action we take. If we view the situation non-problematically as a difficulty to be resolved then the situation is perceived as being bounded (figure 5.1).

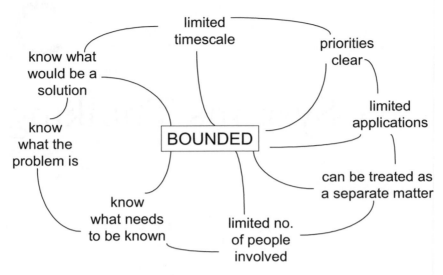

Figure 5.1: Bounded situation – a difficulty

With a 'difficulty', it is possible to identify the 'problem' and thus to recognize what would constitute a solution. We know what needs to be known and can isolate and treat the problem as a separate matter.

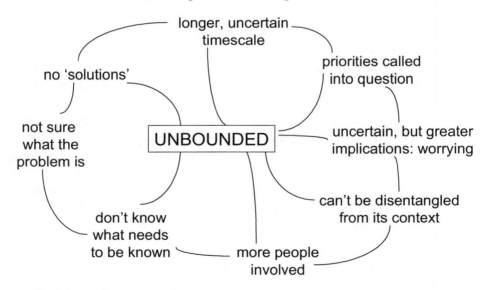

Figure 5.2: Unbounded situation – a mess

In contrast, with a 'mess' (figure 5.2) there are no 'solutions' since no one is sure what the problem is – or if they are, then different people have different opinions concerning what the problem is and agreement is difficult to reach.

With a mess, the 'problem' cannot be disentangled from its context and the priorities are unclear and need to be questioned. With a difficulty the situation is bounded and the boundaries are taken as given. With a mess the situation is unbounded and the boundaries of the problem need to be explored and defined jointly with the process of defining what the problem is.

Real-world situations are not in themselves either difficulties or messes. The degree of difficultness or messiness is an attribute of the relationship between the observer and the situation. What is a local difficulty for one can be a mess with wide implications for another. It is more appropriate to think of problem situations as being perceived by a would-be problem-solver as lying on a spectrum delimited by a difficulty at one end and a mess at the other. The tendency of the system thinker will be to see messes and interconnectedness as well as difficulties and localizable problems. The art of judgment is in knowing where to position a particular intervention on the spectrum of difficulties and messes.

5.3 Themes in systems thinking

Systems thinking is particularly powerful in situations that are perceived as messes, where exploration and discussion are needed to define what the problem *is* before rushing in and trying to solve it. We will now look at the underpinning themes of the systems approach in a general way before considering how systems ideas can be used in information system development in chapter 6. For an in-depth study of the history and traditions of systems theory, see Checkland (1981).

5.3.1 Systems and patterns of organization

A *system* is an entity that maintains its existence and functions as a whole through the interaction of its parts – change in one part changes all parts. In systems thinking it is necessary to understand the whole in order to understand the parts. The opposite of systems thinking is reductionism; the idea that a whole is simply the sum of the parts, that wholes can be broken down into their constituent parts and studied in order to gain an understanding of how they work.

The key to understanding systems is to think about organization not as a noun, but as a verb. It is the organization, or arrangement, of the parts that give a system its identity, that make it recognizably the system that it is. The parts can be interchanged but the system remains recognizable. If the arrangement of the parts changes then the behaviour changes and the system identity is transformed.

A *viable* system (Beer, 1979) is one that is capable of maintaining a separate existence. Viable systems are not completely autonomous – they must survive in some environment, which will be the source of a range of perturbations to the system. Survival is the maintenance of identity – i.e., the preservation of the system's pattern of organization.

Autopoietic systems are able to specify and maintain their organization, to produce and reproduce themselves over time. The word autopoiesis was coined by Maturana & Varela (1980) and is derived from the Greek 'self' + 'to produce'. An autopoietic system is a living system. Cultural objects and productions in general are not autopoietic; a car, a wristwatch and my computer (with its faulty hard drive) are organizations of processes but their identity arises from a source outside of themselves and they cannot be said to self-creating.

Cybernetics is 'the science of effective organization' (Beer, 1985). In cybernetics the term *organization* has a specific meaning, being concerned with the relationships between the processes that define a system as a unity. This notion of a pattern of organization is contrasted with *structure*, which is concerned with the components and relations that constitute a particular unity. Organizations come in all shapes and sizes and include commercial concerns, such as manufacturing and banking, as well as social 'enterprises', such as local government, charities, local communities and schools. Enterprises can even be non-human, such as a bee colony (Foss, 1989). The common factor is that all of these enterprises have an identity, that is, they can be perceived as having a separate existence, and, from a cybernetic perspective they all seek viability. Thus, an important theme in systems thinking is the notion of a *boundary* that helps give a system an identity by allowing it to be perceived as separate, although embedded within, its environment.

An enterprise can endure significant structural changes, but while it retains its *pattern* of organization then its identity will be preserved. For example, a bank might go through deep structural change – such as shutting down all of its high street branches and replacing them with telephone banking, Internet services, and cash dispensers located in retail areas – but, it might still be recognizable as a bank since the nature of its activities, the provision of financial services, has not changed. Of course, it is not always quite so easy to ascertain the purpose of an organization in practice. If supermarkets begin to offer banking services, such as cash dispensing and offering loans, then they might still be recognizable as supermarkets. However, if the supermarket's banking operations assume yet greater prominence it might be more appropriate to recognize the occurrence of organizational (rather than structural) change. The supermarket might be re-classified as a bank or indeed as a new type of organization, such as a 'retail-based bank'. A change in the pattern of organization is always associated (by definition) with a change of identity, since the enterprise becomes a unity of a different type. Conversely, an enterprise can retain its identity through significant and far-reaching *structural* changes if the pattern of organization is maintained.

5.3.2 Systems and emergent properties

A system is a whole and the whole has properties above and beyond the parts that comprise the system. These properties are *emergent*. An emergent property of an aircraft is flight, assuming that the parts – power unit, fuselage, wings etc. – are organized appropriately. Put the components down on the runway or put them together according to another pattern and the result will be a collection of parts – junk – that does not have the emergent property of flight. This means that you cannot take the whole apart and work out what the system does by analysing its parts, since the emergent property is not a characteristic of the parts but of their pattern of organization. A further implication of the systems approach is that you do not need to understand how all the parts work together to be able to use it; I can drive a car without knowing how to service it or how to rebuild the engine. In many situations, taking a system apart and analysing its components can indeed gain knowledge, but the only way to understand the properties of the whole is to make a synthesis and to see the system in action as an entity.

5.3.3 Recursion and system hierarchies

Systems are organized recursively and hierarchically – systems within systems and all sharing the same systems topography (as we will see clearly in chapter 6). Although systems are often shown as a hierarchy, it is better to view them as a series of embedments. These embedments can be laid out flat to show that they are a network of inter-related entities rather than a hierarchical decomposition. Capra (1996) captures the spirit of embedments and systems networks:

> Since living systems at all levels are networks, we must visualize the web of life as living systems (networks) interacting in network fashion with other systems (networks).... We tend to arrange these systems, all nesting within larger systems, in a hierarchical scheme by placing the larger systems above the smaller ones in pyramid fashion. But this is a human projection. In nature, there is no 'above' nor 'below', and there are no hierarchies. There are only networks nesting within other networks.

5.3.4 Communication and control

A fundamental concept in systems thinking is communication and control. Cybernetics is translated as 'steersmanship'. Taking this translation literally, we might think of setting off for an island from the shore in a motor-powered boat with a hand-held rudder. As the boat moves off course the steersman makes adjustments to the rudder position to put the boat back on course.

These adjustments typically over or under compensate and further adjustments are needed to keep the boat on course for the island. Through a continuous process of making adjustments the boat finally reaches its destination, but it can hardly be said to have travelled directly, rather it has wended its way through a series of more and less fine adjustments. It is not possible to set the rudder once at the point of departure and expect the boat to arrive at its destination since even the smallest error in setting the rudder is magnified into a large error over distance, in all likelihood causing the boat to not just miss the harbour on the island but to miss the island altogether. Even if the course can be set accurately it won't compensate for and adapt to water currents and changes in the wind direction and wind force.

The process of adjustment is triggered by a feedback loop (figure 5.3). The desired output is to keep the boat on a course such that it will reach the island; the process is the steering mechanism with its (human) controller. The comparator looks at the gap between the course we are on currently (the output) and the course we wish to be on (the desired output). The error triggers changes in the rudder position, and so on ad infinitum, until we reach the desired destination.

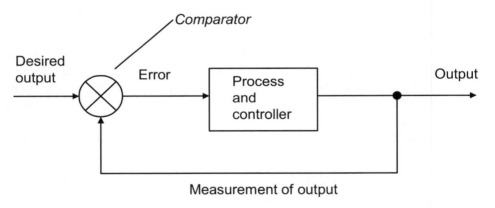

Figure 5.3: A classical feedback loop. Source: Systems: Concepts, Methodologies and Applications, p. 15, Brian Wilson, 1984, 1990. © John Wiley & Sons Limited. Reproduced with permission.

5.4 Thinking in loops

One of the more difficult aspects of systems thinking is to stop thinking in terms of cause and effect and to begin to think in terms of loops and circles of causality. We can see how loop-thinking works in the example of the steersman. The simple, cause and effect view says, 'I set the position of the rudder on a heading (cause); this makes the boat head toward my destination (effect)'. As we have already seen, this activity is rather more complex than it seems. As our boat makes progress through the water we monitor the gap between the current course and the desired course and make adjustments to bring the boat back on course. Larger changes to the position of the rudder will result in larger changes in the course of the boat. Such a navigational system has five variables:

- The desired course
- The current course
- The gap between the desired course and the current course
- The rudder position
- The magnitude of the change in direction.

These five variables are linked in a loop diagram in figure 5.4 (see Senge's (1990) *The Fifth Discipline* for further details). The arrows represent influences: the rudder position influences the direction of the boat, which affects the course. The change in the course of the boat affects my perception of the gap and as the gap changes then my hand changes the position of the rudder …

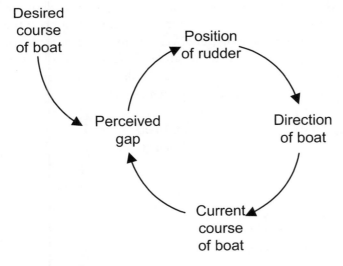

Figure 5.4: Steering system

Causality suggests that I am in control and that there is a one-way arrow of cause and effect through which I cause the course of the boat to change. But this is only half the story, that is, setting the rudder position determines the direction of the boat and the current course. It is also possible to see the other half of the story, which says that the current course of the boat affects the perception of the gap which influences the position of the rudder. In this version of the story the course of the boat is controlling the movement of my hand. The **whole** story is that there is intent to set a course in order to reach a specific destination (the purpose of the system) and that the system allows the direction of the boat to change course when a gap between the desired course and the current course is perceived. The pattern of organization of the system gives rise to the behaviour that can be observed, i.e., the emergent property of steering a boat on a course.

5.4.1 Feedback loops

All the elements of a system are connected, either directly or indirectly. Since feedback is a loop, any change in one element of the system will lead to changes in all the other elements; as these elements are changed so the effect of these changes will ripple out in turn to affect the original element. The influence, modified by its journey, returns to the originating element in a loop, making the discernment of cause and effect difficult – it depends on where one starts in the loop and from where one is observing.

Negative (or balancing) feedback

Figure 5.4 is an example of a feedback loop. In this instance it is an example of negative, or balancing, feedback. In balancing feedback, changes in one part of the system result in changes in the rest of the system that limit or oppose the initial change. We use the term balancing feedback to avoid the sense of something bad that can accompany the word 'negative'. Balancing feedback is neither good nor bad; it simply helps to maintain the stability of the system by reducing the gap between what is desired and what currently exists.

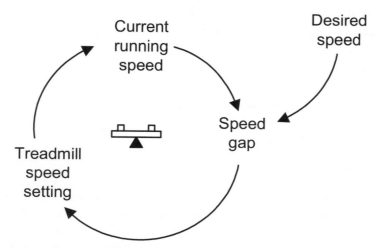

Figure 5.5: Treadmill balancing feedback loop

For example, the treadmill in a gym has a speed setting that is used to set the running speed in kilometres per hour (kph). This is a balancing loop, as indicated by the scales symbol (figure 5.5). Starting at the gap, the difference between what is desired and the current state of affairs, there is a difference between the speed I want to run at and the speed of the treadmill. The action taken is to increase or decrease the speed of the treadmill depending on whether the desired speed is less than the current speed or greater than the current speed. The balancing process will continue to work even if the desired speed is moving, as would be the case as the runner gets more and more tired.

The treadmill in a gym does not respond to requests to change the speed instantaneously. When the increase speed button is pressed the speed of the treadmill does not make an immediate and step change to the new setting; the speed increases slowly at first and then more rapidly the longer the increase speed button is held down. Because nothing seems to be happening at first, it is only natural to hold the button down, but that leads to the speed surging and increasing too rapidly and the target being overshot (figure 5.6). The more frantically one stabs at the speed control the longer it takes to get to the right speed – the actions produce instability and oscillation in the system.

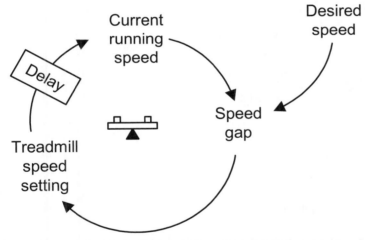

Figure 5.6: Delay and the treadmill balancing feedback loop

With the treadmill the delay is small – a couple of seconds. Some delays are very short and the feedback immediate (try putting your hand on a hot car exhaust pipe). But in other cases the delay can be substantial. For example, after a hard session on the treadmill and the weights muscle pain and stiffness set in 48 hours later rather than the next day. Other delays are even longer, as workers in asbestos producing factories found out when lung cancer appeared many years after they had stopped working with asbestos.

Delays can lead us into adjusting too late and by too much, destabilising the system as it swings from one extreme to another. To deal with delay we have to either get more immediate feedback (perhaps the way the speed mechanism on the treadmill works can be changed) or take the delay into account when making adjustments. Over time, one learns to compensate for the delay of the speed control, but possibly only after having had a nasty shock in trying to keep up with a runaway treadmill.

Positive (or reinforcing) feedback

Reinforcing, or positive feedback, occurs when changes in the system feedback amplify the original change, leading to the system, moving it away from its steady state. A small change can be amplified into large consequences. This 'snowball' effect is illustrated in figure 5.7. With a good web site more site visits mean more satisfied users, which means more positive word of mouth (an important factor in driving up web site accesses). Reinforcing feedback *can* lead to exponential growth, but does not always do so. However, reinforcing feedback *always* amplifies change in the same direction, such as increasing the number of site visitors.

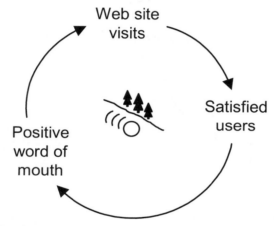

Figure 5.7: Reinforcing feedback loop

The web site visitor growth is a virtuous cycle, but it is also possible for it to be a vicious cycle. Imagine that those who visit the site hate the design and give poor word of mouth reports, leading over time to less site visits. The change is amplified in the same direction, but this time it is a downwards spiral.

5.4.2 Feedforward loops

In balancing and reinforcing feedback, cause and effect go in circles. Feedforward takes into account our ability to anticipate the future. This is the case in management when action is taken on the basis of forecasts or where disturbances are anticipated that cannot be controlled (figure 5.8). The process and the controller have been separated in figure 5.8 with a classical feedback loop whereby the controller monitors the outputs of the process and uses this information to set the values of the input variables.

An example of this is a sales manager responsible for the activities of a sales team. The manager makes adjustments to the current inputs based on the outputs from the sales processes. There will also be uncontrolled and possibly unexpected inputs to the process, such as a product failure at a customer site, which might require the department's activities to be rescheduled in the light of adverse publicity. The sales manager can also anticipate uncontrollable events, such as budget cuts to the sales department that arise from a drop in sales as result of a downturn in the economy. The anticipation of a downturn might lead the manager to take action in advance of the imagined budget cut, such as to reduce the number of sales staff. The cut in sales staff contributes to the sales target not being met and the likelihood of budget cuts – a self-fulfilling prophecy.

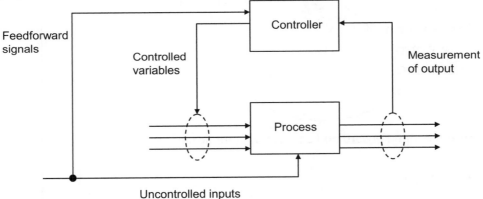

Figure 5.8: Feedback and feedforward (adapted from Wilson, 1990, p. 16)

In short, when you expect to succeed you often do – nothing succeeds like success. However, the converse is also true – nothing fails like failure. The easiest way to have an IS development failure is to convince yourself in advance that it will never work and that the users will resist it. An example of the self-fulfilling prophecy arose in the UK in September 2000 when lorry drivers protesting against what they considered to be the high price of fuel blockaded fuel depots. The outcome of this action was that it was difficult to get fuel to petrol stations and as a consequence there were long queues at the stations and empty pumps. However, the petrol pumps emptied much more quickly than they need have done as a result of panic buying and motorists queuing just to squeeze a few more drops of fuel into their cars. The expectation that petrol would run out ensured that it did so more quickly than it need have done. Our fears (or hopes) for the future can lead to the very situation we would wish to avoid. A couple of days after the fuel crisis had been resolved, a radio announcer in South Wales commented (mistakenly) that the blockades might start again. Other radio stations picked up the story and the next day the spectacle of queuing motorists was back again. Now, the rumour was wrong, but petrol stations do not hold enough fuel to meet the demands of panic buying and a very real shortage was manufactured from a false rumour (figure 5.9). What we and others believe and take action on does indeed shape our future.

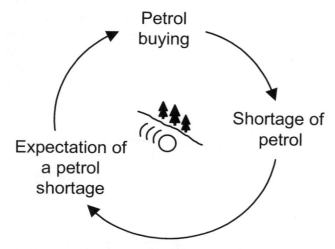

Figure 5.9: Feedforward and self-fulfilling prophecies

5.5 Patterns

Loop stereotypes are useful templates that help us in systems thinking. In 'The Fifth Discipline' Senge (1990) identifies a range of patterns that help us understand real-world problems. We will look at three patterns here: 'limits to success', 'fixes that fail', and 'success to the successful'.

5.5.1 Limits to success

Why don't reinforcing loops just go on increasing forever? It is because all loops will experience some limiting factor at some stage. For example, the virtuous circle in figure 5.9 may well lead to more satisfied users, but more users spending more time on the site (because they are satisfied) will also lead to more web site hits. An increase in web site hits will put more load on the server causing longer response times (especially at popular times) and the balancing loop kicks in as positive word of mouth reduces with the increase in response time. This situation arose with the UK Internet financial services provider, Egg (www.egg.com). Offers of zero-rate interest on credit card purchases for six months in January 2001 resulted in the servers being out of action as they failed to cope with the surge in demand. The capacity of the server is used as an illustration – it is just one of a number of potential limits to growth, some of which will be interdependent and therefore increase complexity. However, putting two simple loops together gives a pattern for limits to success (figure 5.10).

In figure 5.10 each of the connections is labelled with a plus or minus sign. A plus sign indicates that the two elements move in the same direction – for example, faster response times lead to increases in positive word of mouth and slower response times reduce the occurrences of positive word of mouth. The converse is the case with a minus sign – an increase in web site hits leads to slower (decreased) response times, while a reduction in web site hits leads to faster (increased) response times. The general rule is that if the number of negative connections is even (including zero) then the loop is reinforcing. If the number of negative connections is odd then the loop is balancing.

Leverage points

When the balancing loop begins to limit the growth of the reinforcing loop it is tempting to push harder, to do more of the same thing that led to the initial success: if the number of web site hits is down then spend even more money on advertising. But, the more strongly you push the levers in the reinforcing loop the more the balancing process resists. The way to gain leverage is to look for the limiting factors rather than continue to throw resources into the development of the reinforcing loop. Finding the leverage points is a key aspect of systems thinking.

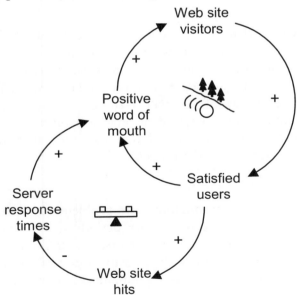

Figure 5.10: Limits of success

When looking for leverage points, first, look for limits early – nothing can grow forever, so look for limiting factors while everything is going well. Ask the question 'what limits am I likely to encounter?' and consider how to manage growth jointly with the limits that will arrive. It may be necessary to change strategies before growth has slowed, particularly if there are delays in the system that mean growth will continue for a time while the limits work their way through.

The second leverage point comes from asking 'what is limiting growth?' Examine the limiting factor (balancing loop) and remove or weaken the constraint. For example, upgrade the server before the system crashes under peak loading and avoid the 'victim of success' syndrome. Unfortunately, dealing with one limiting factor just means further limits emerge to take its place. The fundamental lesson is that growth *will* eventually stop.

The third leverage point is to consider the mental models behind the actions. Continuous growth may be unsustainable or undesirable. Ask these questions:

- Is growth always a good thing?
- What will this growth get for you?
- Is there a better way to get it?
- Do you want sustainable growth?
- How far ahead are you looking for the effects?

In our web site scenario we need to at least consider these points. Is it desirable to attract more and more web site visitors? If it is, then what will the growth in visitors get us? Word of mouth is one way to increase visitors, but what other ways might it be achieved (e.g., advertising on public transport)? Do we need this growth to be sustainable or will a surge in visitors be sufficient (e.g., to satisfy the venture capitalists)? What time horizon need we plan for? Perhaps new issues and problems will arise in 6 months' time that are different in kind from those faced in the next three weeks.

5.5.2 Fixes that fail

Another common problem is the short-term fix, long-term problem. Consider the theatre box office, where bottlenecks occur in busy periods such as the pantomime season. A short-term fix might be to hire in temporary staff in busy periods. This is a balancing loop – more bottlenecks lead to more staff being brought in, and as more clerks are brought in then the bottlenecks are reduced (figure 5.11). More staff result in less space in the box office, and less box office space leads to less ticket processing efficiency, which in turn leads to more bottlenecks. The outer loop is a reinforcing loop – more staff results in more bottlenecks as box office clerks hinder each other's work. In the box office situation, hiring more staff is not the answer, unless changes to the way the box office operates are made, such as more physical space, better layout, or possibly the introduction of an Internet ticket booking system.

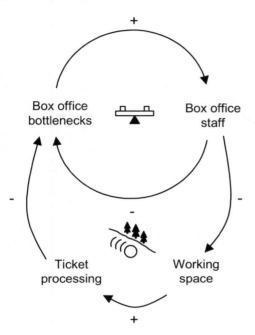

Figure 5.11: Short term fixes that fail

5.4.3 Success to the successful

In this scenario two activities are competing for a scarce resource, such as finance or moral support. The more successful one becomes then the more support it gets – a reinforcing loop. The other activity is also subject to a reinforcing loop, but in this case it is reinforcing failure as the activity is starved of resource by the more successful activity. In the case of the theatre this pattern is illustrated by the success of alternative comedy and stand-up comedians, a form of production whose popularity at a particular point in time leads to strong demand (figure 5.12).

Good ticket sales result in more resources being made available for comedy, allowing better-known acts to be booked, reinforcing the popularity of this type of act. Dramatic productions are starved of resources and fail to book productions with big name cast members and well known directors. The fall in ticket sales for drama results in less resources being allocated, which in turn reinforces the cycle of failure. However, the theatre needs a balanced portfolio of productions if it is to survive the vagaries of fashion in the longer term. From a systems perspective the theatre should look at the overarching goal (a portfolio of production types) and balance resource allocation and achievement between comedy and drama. This pattern is typical of situations where the coupling is unintended and leads to a climate of unhealthy competition for scarce resources.

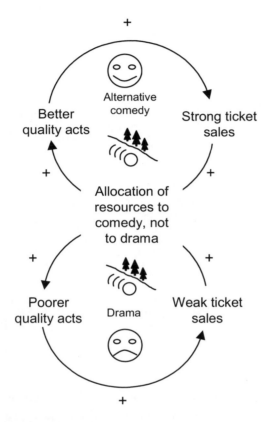

Figure 5.12: Success to the successful

5.6 Mental models

The 'limits to success' pattern and the feedforward loop demonstrate how beliefs can affect our future and how our actions are informed by our beliefs. The mental models we hold are going to affect the way we view the world and the way we act in the world. Mental models can help us achieve goals and solve problems, but they can also be limiting. Language is often an indicator of limiting mindsets. O'Connor and McDermott (1997) give examples of limiting mindsets:

'*Obviously*, we cannot expect to find experienced e-business developers'
'Web site hits will get worse before they get better'
'Online sales are bound to be affected by worries about Internet security'

'No pain, no gain'

'Changing our Internet service provider is the *only* answer to this problem'

These phrases demonstrate weasel words, such as 'obviously' and 'only', things outside of our control (Internet security) for which we can abrogate responsibility, and clichés concerning pain/gain and worse/better that allow us to continue on as before. The response to these statements is to ask 'why', 'so what?', and 'why not?'. Language also shows where rules are operating:

'We *must* cut spending on graphic design for the web site'

'You *should* upgrade the database server'

'You *have to* make these web pages compatible for all browser types'

'You *must* wear a jacket and tie when meeting with clients'

In the above phrases, the presence of 'must', 'should', and 'have to' indicate that a rule is working. Respond to these types of statement by asking 'What would happen if we did not?'. There may be a good reason for the rule, but by getting behind it and asking the question then the rule can be rephrased as a choice rather than a necessity.

The third type of language to be aware of are the 'universals':

'You should *never* use frames on a web site'

'*No one* has ever complained about our online ordering system'

'We have *always* used C++ to build server side objects'

'You should never transfer code to the live server without testing it'

The universal operators here are words such as 'all', 'never', and 'always'. The response to a universal is to ask whether there have ever been any exceptions.

Summary

- Systems theory is a way of dealing with situations perceived to be 'messes'.
- Systems thinking is about loops rather than cause and effect.
- Systemic patterns such as 'limits to success' and 'fixes that fail' help us recognize actual and potential problems in the real world.
- Making mental models explicit helps us to question our basic assumptions and beliefs in support of radical change.
- An understanding of systems theory and systems thinking provides a grounding for applying systems ideas to information system development in general and the soft systems methodology in particular.

Exercises

1. Using the research student admissions case (appendix B) identify and model situations that can be typified by 'fixes that fail' and 'success to the successful'.
2. For an IS development project that you are working on, been involved in, or know about, what are the 'limits to success' from a business perspective.
3. Review a project proposal or business case and highlight passages where the language indicates a limiting mindset.

Further reading

Beer, S., (1979). *The Heart of Enterprise*. Wiley, Chichester.

Beer, S., (1985). *Diagnosing the System for Organizations*. Wiley, Chichester.

Capra, F., (1996). *The Web of Life: a New Synthesis of Mind and Matter*. Harper Collins, London.

Checkland, P., (1981). *Systems Thinking, Systems Practice*. Wiley, Chichester.

Foss, R., (1989). The Organization of a Fortress Factory. In: Espejo, R. and Harnden, R., editors, *The Viable System Model: Interpretations and Applications of Stafford Beer's VSM*. Wiley, Chichester.

Maturana, H. and Varela, F., (1980). Autopoiesis: the organization of the living. In: Maturana, H. and Varela, F., editors. *Autopoiesis and Cognition*. D. Reidel, Dordrecht, Holland.

O'Connor, J. and McDermott, I., (1997). *The Art of Systems Thinking*. Thorsons, London.

Senge, P., (1990). *The Fifth Discipline*. Doubleday, USA.

Wilson, B., (1990). *Systems: Concepts, Methodologies and Applications (second edition)*. Wiley, Chichester.

6

Soft Systems Methodology

6.1 Introduction

In chapter 5 we looked at systems thinking and introduced the basic tenets of systems theory. In this chapter we show how systems thinking can be applied to complex organizational interventions, such as information systems development projects, using the 'soft' systems methodology (SSM).

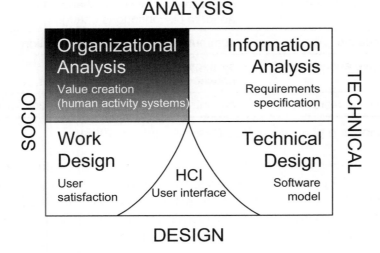

Figure 6.1: Organizational analysis – the systems perspective

Peter Checkland and others developed SSM at the University of Lancaster in the 1970s as an antidote to 'hard' systems thinking typified by the work of the Rand Corporation in the 1960s.

6.2 Hard and soft systems thinking

6.2.1 Organizations

The traditional view of organizations is of autonomous entities that seek to tame and control their environment while engaging in conflict and competition with other organizations. This view of organization is illustrated in the left hand column of table 6.1. Alternatively, we might take a systems perspective and view an organization as the entire set of relationships it has with itself and its stakeholders, as do Mitroff & Linstone (1993, p. 142). This view would also be consistent with the work of Geoffrey Vickers, whose notion of *appreciation* emphasizes relationship-maintaining and judgement rather than the 'poverty-stricken notion of goal-seeking' (Checkland & Casar, 1986). Looking at the right hand column of table 6.1 organizations act as verbs rather than nouns, and organization becomes an active process of maintaining identity and viability – two of the central themes in cybernetics and systems theory that were introduced in chapter 5.

Old organizational metaphor	Recast metaphor
organization as autonomous entity	organization as a web of relations among stakeholders
organizations enact and control their environment	organizations thrive on chaos and adapt to discontinuous change
conflict and competition	communication and collective action
strategy as objective analysis	strategy as solidarity in relations between agents and stakeholders
power and authority in hierarchies	decentralization and empowerment

Table 6.1: Metaphors for organizations (see Calton & Kurland, 1996)

In the age of the Internet and business to business industry portals, value chain integration, and virtual business communities, to view organizations as being constituted by networks of relationships (internal and external) with fluid and permeable boundaries – rather than as hierarchically-structured entities with fixed and clearly-defined boundaries – is highly appropriate.

6.2.2 Hard and soft traditions

In looking at systems principles we have yet to make any clear statement about the status of the systems models we might develop. Should they be models of the real world insomuch as the world behaves like a system and can therefore be 'engineered'? The 'hard' tradition sees organizations as goal-seeking entities operating in a world that is systemic, i.e., that entities with systemic properties exist in the world (table 6.2). As we did in table 6.1, we might posit organizations as relationship-maintaining entities that use information systems (and e-business applications) to understand, build, and maintain relationships. To survive, therefore, an organization needs to maintain relationships with various parties, including employees, customers, finance institutions, and competitors.

	The 'hard' tradition (Simon)	The 'soft' tradition (Vickers)
Concept of organization	Social entities which set up and seek to achieve goals	Social entities which seek to manage relationships
Concept of information system	An aid to decision-making in pursuit of goals	A part of interpreting the world, sense-making with respect to it, in relation to managing relationships
Underlying systems thinking	'Hard' systems thinking: the world assumed to be systemic	'Soft' systems thinking: the process of inquiry into the world assumed to be capable of being organized as a system
Process of research and inquiry	Predicated upon hypothesis testing; quantitative if possible	Predicated upon gaining insight and understanding; qualitative

Table 6.2: Hard and soft traditions (adapted from Checkland & Holwell, figure 2.4, 1998)

In adopting a soft approach we do not maintain that the world contains systems. When talking of the transport system or the health system (or even an information system) people tend to use the word system loosely; the transport 'system', for example, in the real-world is *not* organized systemically (i.e., it does not display the properties of a system). With hard systems thinking, a *systematic* approach is taken in the problem situation to make changes to real world systems. With soft systems thinking it is the intervention that is organized *systemically* and the best we can say about the problem situation is that it is problematic (and probably best perceived as being 'messy'). This is an important difference between hard and soft approaches and is the source of considerable debate and confusion between hard and soft thinkers. To show how soft systems thinking can be used to learn about a problem situation we will use the soft systems methodology (SSM) to conduct an analysis of the Barchester Playhouse case study (see appendix A for details).

6.3 Soft systems methodology

Soft systems methodology (SSM) was developed as a response to hard systems thinking and its failure to address messy situations in which no clear problem definition exists. We have an understanding of 'systemic' through the systems fundamentals introduced in chapter 5, i.e., thinking with wholes, or holism. In soft systems thinking we organize our thinking about the world systemically, while recognizing that the perceived world is problematic. The word 'problem' can have negative connotations in some organizational settings, where people talk along the lines of having 'opportunities' rather than problems. In SSM the phrase 'problem situation' is not used pejoratively, in the same way that 'negative' feedback does not in itself indicate good or bad. To avoid this mental trap the negative feedback loop in chapter 5 is often known as a reinforcing loop. Similarly with SSM, the phrase 'problem situation' does not indicate good or bad and therefore encompasses 'opportunity' situations as well. However, custom dictates that we will continue to use the term 'problem situation' in the context of SSM.

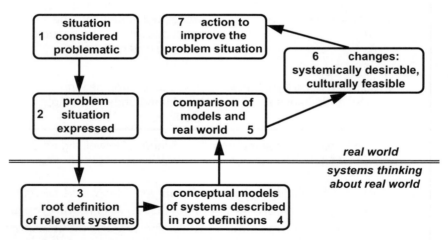

Figure 6.2: Seven-stage model of SSM (adapted from Checkland & Scholes, 1990, p. 27)

SSM supports an enquiring process and is most commonly presented as a seven-stage model (Checkland & Scholes, 1990) (figure 6.2). A key aspect of figure 6.2 is the division between the real world and systems thinking about the real world, which we can think of as 'above the line' thinking and 'below the line' thinking respectively. Above the line is concerned with our perceptions of the real world problem situation; below the line is the province of conceptual thinking, using systems models that help us gain insight into the problem situation by comparison with the perceived, above the line, world. Possibly the most difficult aspect of SSM to grasp, but an essential one if the potential of SSM is to be leveraged – is that the below the line systems models are not models of the real world problem situation. The models are devices that serve to inform our understanding of the problem situation above the line, to foster discussion and debate, and to surface deep-rooted assumptions held by those involved in the intervention. The below the line models are not models of the situation and it follows that neither are they statements of what should be, ought to be, might be, or could be (see Checkland, 1995 for a discussion of the role of conceptual models in SSM). This is an important aspect of SSM and the point will be reiterated as we work through the basic SSM activities.

A further word of caution is needed before we look at the content of the 7 stages of SSM. The 7-stage model is helpful insofar as it makes visible a process for 'doing' SSM. It is also unhelpful in that it reduces SSM to a set of stages that suggests a step-by-step method that can be picked up and applied. In practice, experienced SSM practitioners use SSM ideas and frameworks as a guide to organizing an intervention and not as a recipe book. The experienced SSM practitioner will take account of the interplay between the situation, the people involved (including the self-awareness of the SSM practitioner), and the problem situation. It might not, for example, be appropriate to begin an intervention by the SSM facilitator introducing the project team to the principles and terminology of SSM, as this might not be perceived as meaningful. Systems thinking can still be applied, but not in a directive or prescriptive way. For the purposes of understanding we will use the seven-stage model to structure our description of SSM using the Barchester Playhouse case study as an illustration, but these concerns about the application of a stage model should be borne in mind.

6.3.1 Exploring the problem situation

Situation considered problematic [1]

The starting point is for someone to perceive a situation as problematical. The issue does not pre-exist in the real world; it must be perceived and recognized as problematic by a would-be improver of the situation. For example, a new manager joins the company and is concerned that there is poor representation of women and minorities on the staff. This might be the motivation for an enquiry into why this situation prevails. In the Barchester Playhouse case study one motivation is the Chief Executive's concern with the inability of the box office to cope during the last pantomime season. A further motivation might be the web site manager pushing for box office operations to be Internet-enabled. In this situation there is a senior management top-down concern for a business issue and a bottom-up technology push from an Internet evangelist. Either or both of these concerns — one a 'problem' and the other an 'opportunity' — might be the catalyst for an intervention.

Problem situation expressed [2]

The second stage is to attempt to express the situation that is considered problematic. In traditional systems development this might take the form of the development of a process model and a list of problems associated with the current business process. In SSM the aim is to open out the situation, to avoid the temptation of closing the situation down into a neat box and line graphical representation. The rich picture diagram is one way of representing our mental models of a problem situation, helping us to surface and record our assumptions about the relationships and interconnections between the elements we perceive as being pertinent in the problem situation. The rich picture diagram is not a formal technique and each person will develop their own style (and work around their drawing skills as necessary!). Rich pictures can be created using graphics software, such as Microsoft Visio, but there is a danger that the result will be rather stiff and formal and the use of standard clip-art can make it clichéd.

Rich pictures develop over time as the intervention unfolds. This means that the original diagram will be elaborated or re-drawn entirely as the project develops. The rich picture is not an objective representation of an external reality; it says as much about the person(s) creating the diagram as it does about the problem situation. Rich pictures can be created collaboratively with the client or used as an internal thinking device by the SSM practitioner. What is appropriate depends, as usual, on the situation and on the characteristics of the would-be improvers of the situation. Our experience is that it is useful to develop rich pictures collaboratively in a workshop with members drawn from different areas of the organization. This would not work in all organizations in all interventions and the SSM practitioner must therefore be sensitive to the setting.

Although the technique is informal, a few conventions are seen as being useful and have therefore gained general acceptance. Crossed swords are used to represent conflict, an eyeball to represent a watching interest, and a hurdle to show a difficulty in communication between elements, such as departments in an organization. Human actors are often represented by stick figures and their opinions by speech bubbles; hidden or unarticulated views can be shown with thought bubbles. Practitioners are encouraged to create their own symbols that work for them and are relevant to the specific problem situation being explored.

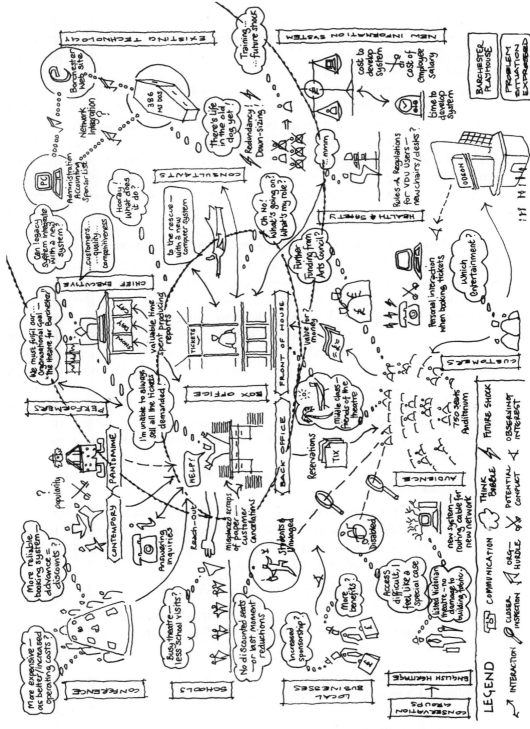

Figure 6.3: Barchester Playhouse rich picture (courtesy of Dominic Leaver)

The rich picture in figure 6.3 was developed by Dominic Leaver, an MSc student taking the IS Development course at the University of Bath. Dominic has used a magnifying glass to represent scrutiny, a lightning flash to represent 'future shock', and scales to show the trade-off between people issues and financial cost together with their impact on the project timescale. Dominic's background as an architect and his strong graphical skills have enabled him to produce a rich picture of complexity and aesthetic appeal. But, don't worry if your drawing and drafting skills are not up to this level of aspiration.

The rich picture is about the communication of perceptions of a problem situation and aesthetics are only part of the mix. If your abilities with a pen are limited try using a mixture of clip art and hand drawing to produce recognizable icons while retaining a sense of the situation as grounded, organic, and messy.

6.3.2 Below the line: root definitions and conceptual models

The dividing line between the real world and systems thinking about the real world is fundamental to SSM. Above the line activities are concerned with the real world; below the line thinking is concerned with developing systemic models that help us to think about and debate the real world. These models are not models of the real world. They are not models of how the real world ought to be. They are simply devices that are more or less relevant to the problem situation being investigated and offering more or less insight into the issues. A model can therefore be formally correct but offer very little insight into a problem situation. A successful model is one that promotes discussion and debate, surfaces hidden assumptions, and questions deep-rooted beliefs. There are two main components of below the line thinking: root definitions and conceptual modeling.

Root definition of relevant systems [3]

A root definition is a short textual definition of the purpose and means of the system to be modeled. The root definition should tell us what the system will do (X), how it will do it (Y), and why it is meaningful for it to be done (Z). This can be encapsulated in template form as:

A system to do **X**, by (means of) **Y**, in order to **Z**

Before we look at a root definition, we will consider the purpose of a system, i.e., the transformation that it might achieve. There are two key things to hold in mind here:

- The system is not a representation of the real world. Therefore there is an unlimited number of possible transformations that can be generated. These models will be more or less relevant and more or less useful in exploring the problem situation;

- A transformation is akin to a state transition; a system in one state is transformed into the system in another state (figure 6.4). For example, it is not a *systemic* transformation for a model to take in labour and materials and produce products.

Figure 6.4: Purpose as a systemic transformation

Part of the spirit of systems thinking is in an opening out of a problem situation, the perception of a mess rather than a difficulty. To understand the role of the box office in the Barchester Playhouse it is likely that we will need to consider the box office environment. An understanding of the theatre may be necessary to gain insight into making change in the box office. What might be the purpose of a theatre? Some relevant transformations are developed in figure 6.5, where 'T' stands for transformation.

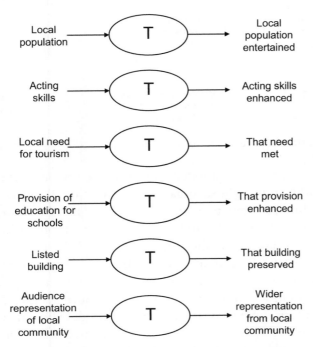

Figure 6.5: Primary task transformations relevant to a theatre

These are all possible systemic transformations that might be used to discuss the role of the theatre in Barchester. Some are obvious. Surely a theatre is there to entertain? Well, yes and no. Entertainment might be best served by taking off productions and turning it into a bingo hall. It might then be argued that the identity would change as the operation would no longer be recognizable as a theatre. What if entertainment is provided by putting on sexually explicit material? The organization might still be recognizable as a theatre but questions of who is entertained and what constitutes entertainment are raised, as are external constraints such as censorship. Although it is counter-intuitive perhaps to think of a theatre as a system to maintain the fabric of a building, the theatre happens to be a grade 1 listed building with a unique interior by a famous Victorian designer. Considerable insight into the theatre can be gained by creating a model that considers the theatre in this setting. For example, the historic nature of the building might constrain the ability to provide disabled access.

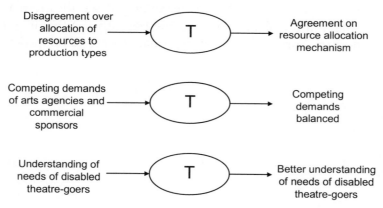

Figure 6.6: Issue-based transformations relevant to a theatre

In figure 6.5 we consider *primary* task models. Typically, a primary task model reflects some real-world entity whose organized activity does indeed coincide with the notional human activity system described by the root definition. As figure 6.5 shows, there is an unlimited number of potential models that might be relevant to discussion about the purpose of the theatre. Each of those models can be sub-divided into a number of systems that together cooperate to achieve the transformation of the higher level of recursion. For example, a system model to entertain the local population might have a subsystem to allocate theatre time to different types of production, such as drama and comedy. An issue arising from this primary task activity might be disagreements concerning how much resource should be allocated to each type of production. Such a model formulation is known as an *issue*-based system. Further examples relevant to a theatre could include how to balance the competing demands of arts funding agencies and commercial sponsors, and how to ensure that disabled people in the local population are represented in the audience (figure 6.6).

A Weltanschauung (W) – or worldview – is what makes the transformations (T) in figures 6.5 and 6.6 meaningful. Why is it meaningful to entertain the local population? One W might be that it would improve quality of life. Another W might be that it demonstrates the good judgment of the Barchester Council in funding the Playhouse. It is, therefore, quite possible to associate a single transformation, e.g., local population entertained, with different Ws. The pairing of a T and a W form the heart of the CATWOE mnemonic (table 6.3).

Customer	The victims or beneficiaries of the transformation
Actor	Those who would do the transformation
Transformation	The conversion of input to output
Weltanschauung	The worldview which makes the transformation meaningful
Owner	Those who could stop the transformation
Environmental constraints	Elements outside the system which it takes as given

Table 6.3: CATWOE mnemonic (after Checkland & Scholes, 1990, p. 35)

In the CATWOE the Customer is the beneficiary or victim and should not be confused with the more everyday sense of customer as the purchaser or consumer of a product. If we posit a model of the theatre as an entertainment system then it is indeed possible that the Customer would be the local population and in this case there is congruence between the Customer of SSM and the customer of everyday usage. However, if we model the T as promoting tourism with a W that 'local businesses, such as restaurants and hotels, will benefit from the trade that results from the increased numbers of tourists visiting the town to see plays' then the CATWOE Customer is more appropriately local businesses than tourists. Tourists do have a role to play but they are not the direct beneficiary – to ascertain the beneficiary of a Transformation it is necessary to look at the T and W jointly.

The actors are those who would carry out the T. In the case of the theatre as entertainment system the Actors could be box office staff, theatre management, and tourists – the Actors could even be the stage actors! The Owners are those who could stop T. In an entertainment system this could be the management of the theatre. The environmental constraints are things that will be accepted as given. For example, the local council might put restrictions on the theatre with regard to safety or the police with respect to the laws of censorship. If we construct an entertainment model that allows productions to contain sexually explicit content or dangerous acts, then environmental constraints could be censorship laws and health and safety legislation. This exposes further Owners who could stop the T taking place – the local council and the police. If we shift the boundaries then environmental constraints can be brought inside the model. This might involve a subsystem to campaign for changes in the censorship laws in order to allow more explicit material to be presented in the interests of entertainment – however we might define it.

These fragmented examples can now be brought together into an example model that has a consistent and coherent root definition and CATWOE (table 6.4). The root definition (primary task) is as follows:

A theatre-owned and operated system to entertain the local population (X) by promoting and staging live theatrical productions (Y), in keeping with health and safety legislation and the laws of censorship, in order to improve the quality of life of the people of Barchester (Z).

Customer	The people of Barchester
Actor	Production companies, marketing
Transformation	Local population → Local population entertained
Weltanschauung	The quality of life for the people of Barchester will be improved through the provision of live entertainment
Owner	Theatre Board, Local council, Police
Environmental constraints	Health and Safety legislation, censorship laws

Table 6.4: CATWOE mnemonic for a primary task model of a theatre

A further example of a root definition is now given, but this time it is relevant to the box office level rather than the theatre as a whole. The root definition is formulated as follows (with accompanying CATWOE in table 6.5):

A senior management-owned system to shorten the queues at the box office (X) by the introduction of an Internet-enabled box office ticketing system (Y), subject to theatre-goers having Internet access and being willing to pay online, in order to increase the number of ticket sales (Z).

Conceptual models [4]

Now that the CATWOE has been produced we will model the purposeful activity using the minimum number of necessary activities to meet the requirements specified in the CATWOE (figure 6.7). Each of the activities is itself a system (the principle of recursion from chapter 5) and can be modeled with its own root definition and CATWOE. Similarly, the whole model is itself just one activity in a wider system.

Customer	Barchester Playhouse management
Actor	Theatre-goers, software companies, box office staff, Internet
Transformation	Box office queues → Box office queues shortened
Weltanschauung	Theatre revenues will increase as frustration with box office queues is reduced
Owner	Barchester Playhouse management
Environmental constraints	Internet access by theatre-goers, willingness to pay online

Table 6.5: CATWOE mnemonic (box office level)

The arrows between subsystems in figure 6.7 represent logical dependencies. For example, it is not possible to 'schedule performances' until the productions to be staged have been decided. In this model it *is* allowable to promote a production in advance of the performance schedule being fixed.

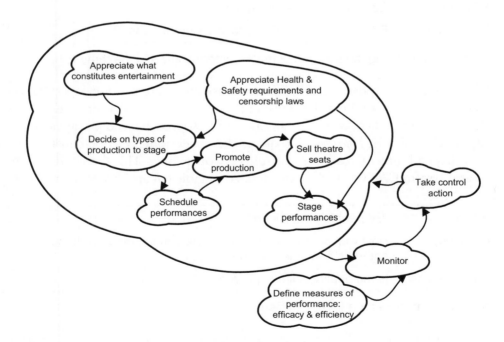

Figure 6.7: Conceptual model of a theatre

The logical activity 'sell theatre seats' is preferred to 'sell tickets', which would be a rather physical representation of the purposeful activity; indeed, we might go further and replace the notion of ticket by a more abstract notion such as 'entry token'. This would help us to think about novel ways of communicating entry tokens to customers, such as by mobile phone.

In this model an appreciation of Health and Safety requirements and censorship constraints is needed when deciding which productions to stage; this appreciation is also needed when the performances take place. Monitoring and control is needed to regulate the system – is the Transformation being achieved? How well? Monitoring and control in the conceptual model is one of the characteristics of the systems approach identified in chapter 5. At the level of recursion shown in figure 6.7, monitoring and control are concerned with two of the three measures of success for a Transformation (in this case, the entertainment of the local population): efficiency and effectiveness. In a wider context there is a concern about whether the system contributes to the wider purpose, i.e., effectiveness. These three success factors are known as the Three Es (table 6.6).

Efficacy	E1	Does it work?
Efficiency	E2	Does it use minimum resources?
Effectiveness	E3	Does it contribute to the wider purpose?

Table 6.6: Regulating the success of the Transformation with the three Es

The stated purpose of the system is to entertain the local population. Therefore, *Efficacy* answers the question: 'is the local population entertained?' *Efficiency* is concerned with the amount of resource needed to achieve the output. The third E, *Effectiveness*, requires the wider context to be considered – is the expenditure of resource and effort worthwhile? The three Es for the Theatre system CATWOE that was defined in table 6.4 are shown in table 6.7.

Efficacy	Are people entertained?
Efficiency	How well are they entertained? How much resource is needed to entertain each theatre-goer?
Effectiveness	Is the quality of life improved?

Table 6.7: Three Es for a theatre system

According to the Weltanschauung in the CATWOE, it is meaningful to entertain the local population since it will contribute to the quality of life of the people of Barchester. The assessment of effectiveness requires consideration of the wider system in which the Theatre is embedded and awareness that many other (possibly non-theatre) initiatives could contribute to the quality of life of the people of Barchester. In figure 6.8 there is an activity 'appreciate local population quality of life', which sits at a higher level of recursion from the entertainment system. Without a concern for the bigger picture it is possible for the Theatre system to be efficient in entertaining people, but to fail or only make a marginal contribution to the wider goal of improving the quality of life.

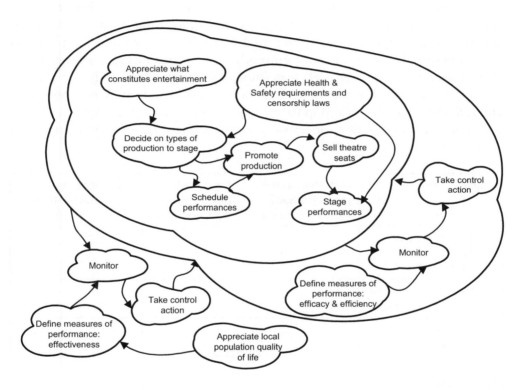

Figure 6.8: Conceptual model elaborated with effectiveness

6.3.3 Back above the line: taking action in the problem situation

The conceptual models developed are **not** models of a real world theatre. The models help us to organize our thoughts *about* the problem situation in a systemic manner. It is therefore important to develop more than one conceptual model, where each model has its own root definition and CATWOE. Figures 6.5 and 6.6 show multiple Transformations that might be relevant to both primary-task and issue-based conceptual modeling in the theatre domain. If there is only one model then it will be very difficult for the SSM practitioner and others involved in the intervention to stop themselves from slipping into viewing the single model as a representation of the real world problem situation. Once this happens, then much of the value of the

SSM approach is in danger of being lost. For example, think about how the conceptual model might be structured if the Transformation were to educate the local population. What might be some of the Weltanschauungs that would give such a Transformation meaning?

Comparison of models with real world [5]

The rigorous, coherent and defensible conceptual models developed below the line can now be compared with the messy, real world problem situation. To support such an analysis, a matrix can be prepared listing both the activities and the logical dependencies in the model as rows. The columns are used to show whether the activity is done currently in the problem situation and if it is, then how it is done, how well it is done, and the criteria used to judge the activity (table 6.8). For example, how does a theatre know what constitutes entertainment for the local population? Perhaps it is just an assumption based on 'expert' artistic opinion, or possibly some market research might have been conducted.

Activity	Is it done in the real situation? How is it done?	How well is it done? How is it judged?	Comments and recommendations
1. Appreciate what constitutes entertainment			
2. Decide on types of production to stage			
3. Schedule performances			
4. Promote productions			
Links 1 → 2			
2 → 3			

Table 6.8: Comparing conceptual model and real world situation (partial matrix)

Evaluating change [6] and taking action [7]

In hard systems thinking the rubric is that change must be systemically feasible and should be culturally feasible. This comes from a belief that the system model is a representation of a real world problem, that the situation can be addressed through problem solving. Cultural acceptance is nice to have but is of secondary concern to the systems engineering task at hand.

The soft systems view turns this on its head. The change should be systemically desirable, given the analysis conducted during the preceding stages of SSM. However, cultural feasibility is of paramount importance since if the change is not perceived to be meaningful by those involved in the problem situation then it will not succeed. The implication of this is that large scale change can be achieved if it is perceived as meaningful, while small-scale and seemingly insignificant changes will fail because they are not perceived as meaningful. Does this mean that there must be a consensus before the intervention can proceed? Not necessarily, but there needs to be an accommodation where people can agree on the ends, that is what can be said to constitute an improvement in the situation and then act in general accordance with the ends that have been agreed. In other words, there is give and take in which the parties are happy, to a greater or lesser extent, to go along with what has been agreed. Consensus is therefore best seen as a special case of accommodation, lying at the end of the spectrum where there are less demands on the affected parties to compromise as their ends and their understanding of what constitute reasonable means are congruent.

As a consequence of this there is much emphasis within SSM on the need to create shared understandings as the basis for change that will be perceived as meaningful in the problem situation. This is very much an exercise in the kind of organizational change that accompanies many information system development projects, but which tends to be overshadowed by the technical worldview.

6.4 Beyond the basic form of SSM

A successful SSM intervention is characterized by a genuine engagement with the problem situation, the participation by those affected, and cycles of learning. The seven-stage model of figure 6.2 may give the impression that all that needs to be known about the situation can be found out in stages 1 and 2. In practice, however, there needs to be regular revisiting of the problem situation as understanding grows, perceptions change, and the situation unfolds. The developed form of SSM (Checkland & Scholes, 1990) contains a cultural stream of enquiry that runs in parallel to the logic-based enquiry of stages 3, 4, and 5 of the seven-stage model in figure 6.2. The cultural stream supports stages 2, 6, and 7 in particular, and involves three analyses: the intervention, the social system, and power.

Analysis 1: the intervention. This is the analysis of the intervention itself, recognizing that intervening in a problem situation is itself a problem! With regard to the SSM intervention, this analysis clarifies the roles of the *client,* the *problem solvers(s)* and the *problem owner(s).* The client is the person who commissioned the study or caused it to take place and who can often be identified in the real world situation. The problem solvers are those who wish to do something to improve the problem situation. Depending on how the problem solvers formulate their models there can be different and multiple problem owners. Clarifying roles is a useful way of generating ideas about which of the infinite number of possible models that could be constructed below the line are likely to have greatest relevance for informing understanding of the real world situation.

Analysis 2: the social system. The social system analysis examines the situation using *roles*, *norms*, and *values*. Roles reflect the social position of people in the problem situation. A role may be defined by the institution, such as lecturer, programmer, or graphic designer, but can also be given less formally, such as 'Java guru', 'hacker', or 'good guy'. Norms relate to the expected behaviours of the people in the roles, and values reflect the local beliefs about the merit of the behaviours of the role holders.

Analysis 3: political system. The political analysis is concerned with power – the process by which the differing parties reach (or do not reach) an accommodation. In SSM, power is explored by finding out how power is expressed in the problem situation. One way to do this is to look at the commodities of power, such as formal authority, personal charisma, and external reputation.

It is fair to say that SSM is weaker in analyses 2 and 3 – social and political systems – than it is in the logic-based analysis. This has led to the criticism that SSM tends to support the status quo, that it is weak in addressing issues of power from a critical perspective. Furthermore, it can be argued that in pushing the systemic aspects of SSM below the line opportunities for applying cybernetic 'laws' in the real world (as would be the case with the Beer's Viable Systems Methodology) are missed out in SSM. There is much debate amongst academics and SSM practitioners about the underpinning philosophy of SSM, but it is outside the scope of this chapter (see Flood & Jackson, 1991 for a critique of SSM).

6.4.1 Using SSM to support IS Development

Two approaches to the incorporation of SSM into the development of information systems are grafting and embedding. On the face of it, the simplest way is to simply front-end, or graft, SSM on to an existing methodology, as has been done with SSADM (structured systems analysis and design methodology). With regard to Object-Oriented methods, such as UML (Universal Modeling Language), a similar approach could be adopted, i.e., conduct an SSM analysis before commencing with the analysis and design of an information system. This approach is rather mechanistic and reminiscent of the step-wise refinement of the waterfall life-cycle approach to IS development. A second approach is to embed traditional methods, such as

SSADM and UML, into SSM and to view the IS development process as just another SSM intervention, albeit with specialist activities embedded within it.

There are numerous examples of the application of SSM to IS development including Lewis (1994) who uses SSM as a basis for interpretive data modeling, Stowell and West (1994) who link SSM conceptual models to the data flow diagrams of structured systems analysis, and Savage and Mingers (1996) who have combined SSM with Jackson Structured Design.

Our view is that the strength of SSM is as an enquiring framework to support an exploration of a problem situation with the aim of defining and building support for an intervention to improve that situation. Although there may be value in linking SSM more explicitly with traditional system development techniques, such as data and process modeling, there is an ever-present danger that the value of systems thinking will be overwhelmed by the technical rationality of software engineering.

Summary

- In hard systems thinking the world is assumed to be systemic (having the properties of a system). In SSM the process of enquiry is organized according to systemic principles (as described in chapter 5) and the problem situation ('real world') is perceived as a mess.
- The messiness of the problem situation is represented using a rich picture diagram.
- SSM can be applied as a seven-stage model to gain insight into the differences between the real world and systems thinking about the real world.
- Experienced users of SSM tend to use systemic principles to guide the intervention rather than relying on a systematic application of the stage model.
- For IS developers SSM helps hidden and unarticulated assumptions about the problem situation to be expressed and can help developers think in terms of radical change and breakthrough.
- SSM has been criticized for weaknesses in addressing critical aspects of organizational change related to power and vested interest.

Exercises

1. Create a rich picture diagram of the research student admission problem situation (appendix B). Be sure to portray the context and the issues in the problem situation rather than just the process flow.
2. Study the research student admission case (appendix B) and specify ten or more primary task transformations that could inform discussion about the role and purpose of the admissions process.
3. Take one of the primary task transformations for the research student admissions process and develop a CATWOE and root definition.
4. Develop a conceptual model with two levels of hierarchy for your primary task root definition and CATWOE. Specify the success criteria E1–E3 at each level.
5. What ethical issues might arise as a result of the analysis and the intervention? How might these be addressed?

Further reading

Calton, J. and Kurland, N., (1996). A Theory of Stakeholder Enabling: giving voice to an emerging postmodern praxis of organizational discourse. In: Boje, D., Gephart, R. and Thatchenkery, T., editors. *Postmodern Management and Organization Theory*. Sage, California.

Checkland, P., (1995). Model Validation in Soft Systems Practice. *Systems Research*, 12(1): 47–54.

Checkland, P. and Casar, A., (1986). Vickers' Concept of an Appreciative System: A Systemic Account. *Journal of Applied Systems Analysis*, 13.

Checkland, P. and Scholes, J., (1990). *Soft Systems Methodology in Action*. Wiley, Chichester.

Checkland, P. and Holwell, S., (1998). *Information, Systems and Information Systems – making sense of the field*. Wiley, Chichester.

Flood, R. and Jackson, M., (1991). *Creative Problem Solving, Total Systems Intervention*. Wiley, Chichester.

Lewis, P., (1994). *Information Systems Development*. Pitman, London.

Mitroff, I. and Linstone, H., (1993). *The Unbounded Mind, breaking the chains of traditional business thinking*. Oxford University Press, New York.

Savage, A. and Mingers, J., (1996). A framework for linking Soft Systems Methodology (SSM) and Jackson System Development (JSD). *Information Systems Journal*, 6: 109–129.

Stowell, F. and West, D., (1994). *Client-led Design*. McGraw-Hill, Maidenhead, UK.

7

Designing for User Satisfaction

7.1 Introduction

In applying traditional systems analysis methods, whether structured or object-oriented, the developer tends to place an emphasis on functional requirements that can be specified explicitly using simple but technically powerful diagramming notations, such as UML class diagrams and interaction diagrams.

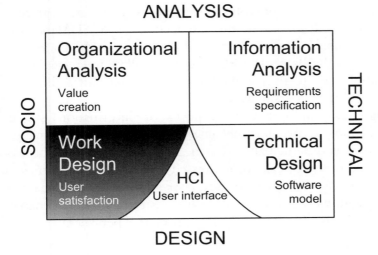

Figure 7.1: User satisfaction – the work and play perspective

Sociotechnical approaches seek to engage the user of the information in genuine participation and to achieve an acceptable fit between people and technology rather than attempting to force one to change and adapt to the other. In an invited talk on participatory design Ellen Bravo (1993) described the winner of the 'pettiest office procedure' competition, a law practice that installed a new carpet in their offices. They wanted to keep the carpet looking pristine, so to stop the secretaries rolling back and forth on the carpet on their chairs they nailed the chairs to the floor. The lawyers did not consult anyone in making this decision. When the secretaries came back to work they could not do their jobs since they needed to roll their chairs from typewriter to telephone to computer. These workers had been excluded from the design process. If we extrapolate this exclusion to different levels of user and a full range of business processes we begin to see the implications of leaving the user out of the IS and work design process. As Bravo (1993) went on to say:

> Leaving out the users isn't just undemocratic – it has serious consequences for worker health, human rights, job satisfaction, and also for the work process and the bottom line (p. 4)

Information systems should not conflict with the essential activities of the organization. If, for example, the response time of a sales recording system is long, the computer terminal awkwardly situated on the counter, or the printer too slow then the sales assistants will struggle to serve customers, queues will build, and sales and customers will be lost.

The province of sociotechnical design approaches has typically been the interest of the user in the role of employee, or worker. With the advent of the Internet it is likely that many of the users of the information system will be external to the organization, in the role of customers, suppliers, partners, collaborators, investors, and so on. In this explication of WISDM we will concentrate on two key user roles: employee and customer. In the context of an Internet box office for the Barchester Playhouse we will be interested in the job satisfaction of employees (work) and the level of customer satisfaction with the Internet service of theatre-goers (play/leisure).

In investigating the employee/work aspects of information system development we will look at two sociotechnical approaches to information system design: ETHICS and participative design. The interests of the theatre-goer as customer would more typically be addressed by market researchers and customer services personnel. To assess theatre-goer satisfaction with the box office information system we will use the WebQual instrument, which enables an organization to understand web site quality from the perspective of the customer.

7.2 Sociotechnical design with ETHICS

ETHICS (Effective Technical and Human Implementation of Computer-based Systems) is a sociotechnical approach to information system design and implementation developed by Enid Mumford. The aim of ETHICS is to foster genuine participation, going beyond users 'participating' by providing input to requirements specifications and after-the-event prototype evaluation. In ETHICS users work with technical designers to identify the issue the new information system is to tackle, to set objectives for the new information system, and to redesign work practices and organizational structure so that the sociotechnical system as a whole works efficiently and effectively. The ETHICS approach builds on Leavitt's framework (figure 7.2), which illustrates the need to align and integrate people and tasks with technology and organization.

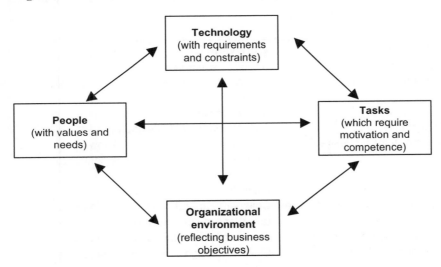

Figure 7.2: The Leavitt (1958) framework for sociotechnical design (from Mumford, 1995)

In the context of the Playhouse, this might lead to box office clerks and supervisors identifying problems with the current operations and systems, specifying their information needs to address the problems, setting performance targets for a new system, and reorganizing their work as appropriate to get the best out of a new booking system. Genuine participation is a multi-way process in which users, managers, developers, and others influence each other's plans, policies, and decisions, thus affecting future outcomes. IS technical staff, therefore, do indeed have an important role to play as advocates for technology, but their role is not to come in and nail the box office staff's chairs to the floor!

Perhaps one of the fundamental problems of relying on formal specifications of business processes is the assumption that it is possible to make a rational description of how work really gets done in practice. This problematical theme has been investigated by Sachs (1995) who describes a case study of a Trouble Ticketing System (a database for recording and scheduling jobs) in which new technology and new working practices are introduced. On the face of it, the new technology and redesigned work processes should have led to gains in efficiency. Unfortunately, in actuality, the opposite happened – work became less efficient. The systems analyst had failed to understand how the experienced maintenance engineers shared their knowledge through informal mentoring schemes, how knowledge was shared through social interaction (the 'coffee machine' effect), and how the new data entry requirements would slow productivity. In the extreme, we can imagine two different worldviews, one a mechanistic view of the organization and the other a social work view (table 7.1).

Organizational view	Work view
Analytic assumption	*Analytic assumption*
People produce human error	People discover problems and solve them
Design assumptions	*Design assumptions*
Deskilling is desirable	Skill development is desirable
Routine work, rote thinking desirable	Development of knowledge, understanding, deciphering is central to skill
Flexibility = interchangeable jobs	Flexibility = skilled people
Standard operating environments are necessary to the business	Collaboration and collaborative learning take place in communities
Social interaction is non-productive	Communities are funds of knowledge
Automation produces reliability	Skills through learning produces reliability
Consequence	*Consequence*
Learning is not encouraged	Learning is supported

Table 7.1: Organizational and work views (adapted from Sachs, 1995)

The dangers of assuming that the analyst knows best, coupled with the difficulty of workers being able to articulate clearly just exactly how they accomplish work, points to the need for users to participate fully in information system development.

7.2.1 Participation

Mumford suggests three motivations for organizations to adopt a participative approach:

- because it is morally right – those affected by an information system development project should have input and influence on their destinies;
- because participation can build an involved and committed work force;
- because participation is an educational experience that provides insight, understanding and knowledge that will help an organization better achieve its policies. The people actually doing a job usually know more about it than the people who direct and manage it.

Participation can be categorized as consultative, democratic, and responsible (Land, 1982). In *consultative* participation, the lowest level of participation, users input ideas and suggestions to the design process, but the system analysts make the majority of decisions. With *democratic* participation all user groups are involved and given an equal say on the development of the information system. However, although the users make the decisions, management are responsible for implementing them. In the highest level of participation, *responsible*, all participants are involved in making the decisions and in implementing them. With responsible participation there is the chance of building a genuine commitment to an information system development rather than merely involvement.

Achieving genuine participation is not a trivial undertaking and Mumford is realistic about the difficulties involved. There needs to be trust between workers and management; workers have to believe that management's intentions are good and management believe that workers will work in the interests of the organization. Members of the design group have to be identified – this could be by selection or, more democratically, by election. With genuine participation, the role of the IS designer is altered; rather than playing the role of 'expert' the IS professional has to work as a consultant to the design group. The role of the departmental manager, such as the box office manager or the sales and marketing manager, also changes. The manager might decide not to be a permanent member of the design group so that they do not stifle discussion or overly direct the outcome of the design process. On the other hand, the manager needs to be informed and kept uptodate of progress since the manager will still be responsible for approving the solution the design group suggests.

7.2.2 Job satisfaction

In addition to the idea of participation is a concern with job satisfaction (figure 7.3), which Mumford defines as the goodness of fit between what employees expect and need from work and what they are required to do by the organization. The ETHICS framework for job satisfaction draws on the work of Talcott Parsons, an American sociologist, to give five dimensions of fit (table 7.2). If an employee's needs are met in all five areas then a good fit is obtained and high job satisfaction should result.

Knowledge fit: some of the older box office clerks might be looking for routine work with limited responsibilities and challenges. Other clerks might need more opportunity to use skills already acquired and to develop new ones. The degree of knowledge fit is the extent to which employees believe their skills are being used and the extent to which they are being helped to develop those skills and to acquire new ones.

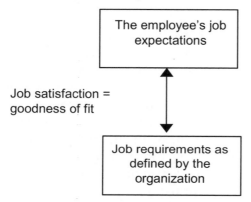

Figure 7.3: Job satisfaction (adapted from Mumford 1995, p. 31)

Psychological fit: according to Herzberg people have psychological needs for recognition, achievement, responsibility, and status. The workplace is one setting in which these needs can be fulfilled and the design of work should, wherever possible, help people satisfy these needs. Organizations need to be aware that a new information system and accompanying work practices might indeed worsen the efficiency fit. The introduction of new technology can lead to deskilling, the taking away of responsibility, and the creation of an environment where it is more difficult for workers to create a sense of achievement.

Efficiency fit: however good the psychological fit people still need to be compensated at a level that they consider to be fair. Controls over their working life should be acceptable and support services available to help them carry out their tasks. For the effort-reward bargain to work, both parties – the employer and the employee – must feel that a fair balance has been struck between what is required by the organization in terms of skills and competences and the employee's assessment of what they are worth to the organization. The new working practices and organizational structures associated with business process redesign need to be considered in the light of compensation plan factors such as salary levels and bonus plans.

Task structure fit: there should be sufficient variety in the tasks employees are required to carry out. A task should have a clear boundary so that employees know when they have completed a task, and targets to allow them to evaluate how well they have performed. In any given situation there will be many ways of designing work and using IT, but a good design will stimulate employees by providing variety and scope for discretion while not overwhelming employees with overly onerous tasks or unrealistic performance expectations.

Fit	Employees needs
KNOWLEDGE	Wants personal skills and knowledge to be used and developed
PSYCHOLOGICAL	Seeks to further personal interests, e.g., sense of achievement, recognition, advancement, status
EFFICIENCY	Seeks equitable effort–reward bargain and acceptable supervisory controls. Seeks efficient support services such as information and technology
TASK STRUCTURE	Seeks a set of tasks with variety, interest, targets, feedback, task identity, and autonomy
ETHICAL	Seeks to work for employer whose values do not contravene personal values

Table 7.2: ETHICS Fits for job satisfaction

Ethical fit: a company focused on sales to the exclusion of pretty much all else is likely to concentrate on hard measures of success, such as the number of leads converted into sales. A provincial theatre might lay emphasis on a range of values, such as a belief in community service and an empathy with the creative arts and performers. Employees in the theatre setting would expect to participate in the design of a new information system and the ethical fit would be poor if they were not consulted or not involved.

7.2.3 Sociotechnical systems design process

From an IS development process perspective the ETHICS method entails a matching of business/technical objectives with job satisfaction/social objectives (figure 7.4). By 'technical' we are not referring only to information technology but also to things that are now technically possible in the organization, such as theatre-goers making ticket bookings for themselves. Wherever possible, people should be allowed to see the alternatives through the use of prototypes and have the opportunity of acting them out. It is important to note that the same piece of information technology can be blended with different business processes and social objectives to produce very different results. For example, assume an insurance company builds a new customer information system allowing customer service representatives to see the details of each product a customer has purchased from the insurance company. Using this information system the insurance company could pursue a business efficiency objective of improving customer service while at the same time reducing the number of customer representatives. This business objective would require that personnel are trained to deal with customers quickly using the information in the customer system while human resources would need to ensure that the compensation plan rewards short 'customer moments' (as well as reallocating representatives and negotiating severance packages).

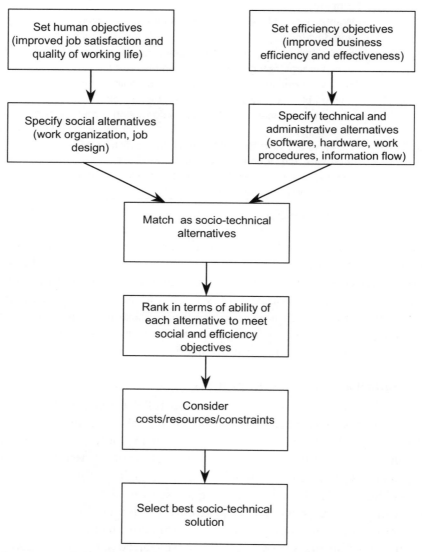

Figure 7.4: Socio-technical systems design (Mumford, 1995, p. 46)

Using the same customer information technology the insurance company could decide to use the information about the relationship the customer has with the company to cross-sell more insurance products. In this case employees would need to be trained to identify cross-selling opportunities and the compensation plan revised to reward sales. Although the two business objective scenarios use the same piece of IT (a customer information software system) they lead to very different outcomes: the first scenario (the efficient handling of customer enquiries) will lead to redundancies and the possibility of repetitive and dull work for the service representatives remaining; the second scenario (cross-selling) will require extensive retraining for existing staff and possibly the introduction of new staff with different skills.

One way of assessing the level of job satisfaction quality is to use a questionnaire (table 7.3). This instrument was developed by Mumford as a practical guide to assessing the five fits of table 7.2. Application of this instrument before and after the information system implementation should provide a guide to how well the social objectives of increasing the quality of work life have been met.

Some general questions that might be asked of any information systems development project are:

- Are the existing staff going to use the system?
- Will some staff be lost or redeployed?
- Will the good features of the existing system be kept? Such features could include an acceptable level of job variety, easy interaction between people, and a friendly working atmosphere
- What emphasis is to be placed on general objectives such as improving job satisfaction or acceptability to all employees?

Once the social and business objectives have been identified and matched they need to be ranked, costs and constraints considered, and then the 'best' sociotechnical solution selected. The task of assessing the costs and benefits is considerable and even then there is no guarantee that there will be enough information to ensure a successful outcome. There will be some people or groups who will not be happy about the proposed system – indeed there will be situations where the new system is seen as a direct assault on vested interests leading to a power struggle.

KNOWLEDGE FIT		
A.1	My skills and knowledge are fully used in my present job	1 2 3 4 5
A.2	I find my work extremely interesting	1 2 3 4 5
A.3	I do not like my present job	1 2 3 4 5
A.4	I would like a different job in this organization	1 2 3 4 5
A.5	I would like to be doing a more difficult job	1 2 3 4 5
A.6	My job does not provide enough opportunities for me to learn new things and develop my talents	1 2 3 4 5
A.7	I would like the opportunity of learning and doing a more challenging kind of job	1 2 3 4 5
PSYCHOLOGICAL FIT		
B.1	Status is important to me: I like to be respected	1 2 3 4 5
B.2	Working here gives me a feeling of status	1 2 3 4 5
B.3	I have considerable responsibility in my job	1 2 3 4 5
B.4	I would like to carry even more responsibility	1 2 3 4 5
B.5	If I do good work, I feel management recognizes this	1 2 3 4 5
B.6	I would like to receive more recognition	1 2 3 4 5
B.7	My job is a very secure one	1 2 3 4 5
B.8	I enjoy the opportunity of making friends which my job provides	1 2 3 4 5
B.9	There are sufficient opportunities for promotion in this department	1 2 3 4 5
B.10	I would like to get promoted soon	1 2 3 4 5
B.11	I want to achieve a great deal and get to the top	1 2 3 4 5
B.12	I get my feelings of achievement from doing a good job	1 2 3 4 5
EFFICIENCY FIT		
C.1	I could earn more if I did not work here	1 2 3 4 5
C.2	I am paid adequately for the work I do	1 2 3 4 5
C.3	I have to work too hard in my job	1 2 3 4 5
C.4	We are expected to be accurate in our work	1 2 3 4 5
C.5	Control mechanisms are too lax	1 2 3 4 5
C.6	Supervision here is strict	1 2 3 4 5
C.7	I like to be allowed to do my work without interference from supervision	1 2 3 4 5
C.8	My supervisors give me all the help I need	1 2 3 4 5
C.9	The performance rating system is fair to everyone	1 2 3 4 5
C.10	I get all the information and materials I require to do my job efficiently	1 2 3 4 5
ETHICAL FIT		
D.1	Top management here is to ruthless	1 2 3 4 5
D.2	Managers and staff here are very friendly	1 2 3 4 5
D.3	This department puts productivity above the interests of its employees	1 2 3 4 5
D.4	The organization looks after the welfare of its staff very well	1 2 3 4 5
D.5	A person's character and experience count far more here than formal qualifications	1 2 3 4 5
D.6	I believe that character and experience are more important than qualifications	1 2 3 4 5
D.7	Communication in this department is very poor	1 2 3 4 5
D.8	In my department, we are told as much as we want to know about day-to-day matters	1 2 3 4 5
D.9	Senior management is out of touch with the way people feel	1 2 3 4 5
D.10	We have sufficient say in the way this organization is run	1 2 3 4 5
D.11	Staff should be consulted more about major decisions	1 2 3 4 5
D.12	We cannot sufficiently influence decisions about changes made in the way we do our work	1 2 3 4 5

Table 7.3: Job satisfaction survey

TASK STRUCTURE		
E.1	There is not much variety in my work	1 2 3 4 5
E.2	I would like a job that is less routine	1 2 3 4 5
E.3	There is little opportunity for using initiative	1 2 3 4 5
E.4	I would like a job that expects more initiative	1 2 3 4 5
E.5	In my job I have to rely on my own judgement and decision	1 2 3 4 5
E.6	It would be better for me if I could make decisions without having to ask someone first	1 2 3 4 5
E.7	There is a lot of pressure in my job	1 2 3 4 5
E.8	I would like less pressure in my work	1 2 3 4 5
E.9	I have clear-cut work targets and know when I achieve these	1 2 3 4 5
E.10	I would like clearer targets to aim at	1 2 3 4 5
E.11	How well I can do my work depends on my co-workers	1 2 3 4 5
E.12	It would be better for me if I could do my work without depending on others	1 2 3 4 5
E.13	I can organize and carry out my work the way I want	1 2 3 4 5
E.14	I would prefer more freedom to plan my work myself	1 2 3 4 5
E.15	I believe my job to be important	1 2 3 4 5
E.16	I believe others recognize the importance of my job	1 2 3 4 5
E.17	I would prefer a job that made a larger and more important contribution to the work of the department	1 2 3 4 5

Table 7.3 (cont.): Job satisfaction survey. Source: New Partnerships for Managing Technological Change, pp. 158-160, © Nancy H. Bancroft, 1992. This material is reproduced by permission of John Wiley & Sons, Inc. Bancroft uses original material from Designing Human Systems, © Enid Mumford, 1983. This material is reprinted here with permission of the author.

7.3 The Scandinavian tradition of participative design

The provenance for the sociotechnical underpinnings of ETHICS is in the seminal work of the Tavistock Institute of Human Relations in London, which operated from the 1950s onwards. A criticism that can be levelled against a sociotechnical approach such as ETHICS is that it can be used to managerialist ends, as a way of persuading workers to accept changes that might otherwise have been rejected in order that the organization can benefit from the increased efficiency that results from user involvement. The ideas promoted by the Tavistock were also taken up in Scandinavia, but with a stronger emphasis on democracy in the workplace. Ehn (1993) defines democracy as freedom from the constraints of the market economy and the power of capital. The desire to accumulate capital is the driver for changes in work practices – the result is intensification of work and the use of new technology.

Greenbaum (1995) has reviewed the development technology and changes in work in the twentieth century and reaches the conclusion that management objectives have not changed: the aim is to reduce cost and to increase productivity. This drive for efficiency gains can lead to the intensification of work practices, as is the case with an airline reservations call centre:

> There's AHU, that's After Hang Up time. It's supposed to be fourteen seconds. It just came down to thirteen. But my average is five seconds

AHU, because I do most of the work while the customer's still on the phone. There's your talk time, your availability, your occupancy – that's the per cent of time you're plugged in, which is supposed to be 98 per cent …. (p. 84)

You might think that routinization and intensification of work is restricted to clerical and production line work, and this was largely true up until the 1980s. With the introduction of 'business process redesign' initiatives Greenbaum argues that the intensification of work has spread to managerial grades, who have seen the clericalization of professional work (for example, they do their own word processing and answer the telephone) accompanied by greater productivity demands. The drive for profit and capital accumulation can now be seen to affect all levels of the organization.

The setting in Scandinavia is supportive of workplace democracy. Scandinavian countries tend to have highly educated workforces, strong trade unions, centralized negotiation mechanisms, social democratic parties in government, regulated relations between trade unions and employers, and a positive attitude to technology (Ehn, 1993). Throughout the 1970s and the 1980s participative design projects were initiated in Scandinavian countries. One of these was UTOPIA (Ehn & Kyng, 1987), a collaborative project between the Nordic Graphic Workers' Union and research institutions in Sweden and Denmark to investigate computer support for integrated text and image processing. In projects such as UTOPIA the potential for dehumanization of work was put centre stage as an issue to be addressed when introducing new technology. System developers and researchers worked with a group of typographers to understand how computer technology might be used to enhance the typographers' skills and to improve the typographic quality of the newspaper. These projects focused jointly on the quality of work-life *and* the quality of the product.

7.3.1 Participative design principles

Following Bodker et al. (1993) we can summarize the participative design approach to computer applications (p. 158):

- Computer applications should enhance workplace skills rather than degrade them;
- Computer applications are tools that should be designed to be under the control of the people who use them. The computer systems should support flexible work practices – not make them more rigid;
- The introduction of computer applications changes the organization of work. The interplay between computers and work needs to be addressed directly in design;

- Computer applications are often implemented to improve productivity, but they can also be used to improve the quality of the product.

7.3.2 The participative design process

To support the design process Bodker et al. (1993) propose a phased structure (figure 7.5) that we will adapt to the Playhouse case study. In the first phase, developers learn about the work at the Playhouse through interviews and user demonstrations of how work is accomplished currently. The future workshop lasts around half a day and is facilitated (preferably by an independent third party) to ensure that all attendees have the opportunity to contribute. It is possible that managers won't be invited to the workshop so that workers can speak freely and without concern about management retaliation. The critique phase is a brain-storming session where current problems and issues are brought out and then categorized. The fantasy phase gives the participants the opportunity to think about 'what if' – how could the work and the workplace be different?

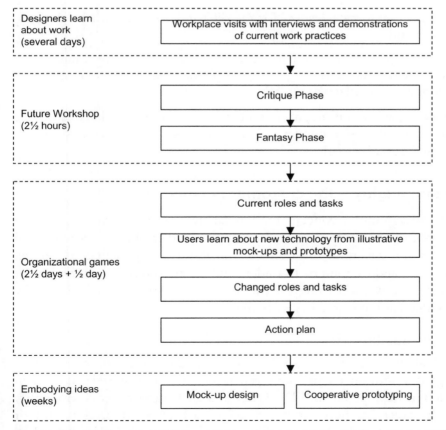

Figure 7.5: Participative design process (adapted from Bodker et al., 1993)

In the organizational game phase current roles and tasks are described and new possibilities explored using mock-ups and prototypes. This phase, for example, could involve a cardboard replica of the box office to allow users to play with the layout of work-stations, customer windows, etc. The mock-up might also be combined with theatre staff playing the role of theatre-goers. The organizational games phase should make a difference to the participants, produce results that are likely to be implemented, and be fun to participate in.

The action plan produced from the organizational games is taken forward into a continued process of cooperative design where the mock-ups and prototypes are developed further and tested by embodying them into new and modified work practices. Trying the prototypes in a true-to-life work situation is an important aspect of participative design; these are not merely user-interface prototypes produced by developers and then tested out of context by workers in laboratory conditions. The exploration and experimentation of cooperative design in the workplace provides the basis for making a detailed plan about the new box office information system and associated work practices.

However, to reinforce a respect for the difficulties of design Ehn & Kyng (1987) recommend:

> Designers should restrict their activities to a few domains of application, and they should spend at least a year or two getting acquainted with a new area before doing actual design. (p. 56).

Although organizations might not be in a position to take this advice literally, it is a salutary reminder of the difficulty for IS developers to understand and describe work.

7.4 Web site quality – the customer perspective

Participative design and a concern for job satisfaction and democracy in the workplace are important aspects of achieving user satisfaction. A more general concern is for the quality of the web site and the user experience, which will affect employees and customers. In understanding the subjective experience of the web site user we will draw on the WebQual instrument developed by Barnes & Vidgen at the University of Bath.

7.4.1 Web site quality

The WebQual instrument is a way of assessing the quality of web sites – particularly sites with an e-commerce aspect – and was inspired by work in quality function deployment (QFD). QFD is a structured process to identify and carry the voice of the customer through each stage of product and/or service development and implementation. Based upon a distinction of 'what' and 'how', a series of matrices are used to deploy customer-demanded qualities through design requirements, product functions, part characteristics, and manufacturing operations into production requirements. The starting point for QFD is the 'voice of the customer' – an expression of quality requirements from the perspective of, and in the words of, the customer (King, 1989).

One way to get access to the voice of the customer is to hold a quality workshop. In the context of the theatre this could involve getting a group of theatre-goers together and asking them: 'What are the qualities of an excellent theatre booking web site?'. In the workshop the attendees first work individually and write down everything they can think of on post-it notes (one idea per post-it). Some of the items will be qualities, such as 'easy to use' and some will be product functions, such as a 'restaurant booking facility'. At this stage we are interested primarily in qualities rather than characteristics and functions, but everything is collected ready for use in later stages of QFD, or as input to the requirements specification. The individuals now work together in teams of 3 or 4 and look for groupings in their qualities. Working quietly they move the post-it notes around a work surface bringing together qualities that seem to have an affinity. They can either promote one of the existing items in a group to be a header for that category or come up with a new header item that in some way describes the group. This process may seem rather vague and imprecise, but remember that the aim is to understand how the customer conceptualizes web site quality – not how the supplier (IS developer and theatre management) sees it. For further details of running a quality workshop see Bossert (1991).

Quality workshops were held at every stage of the development of the WebQual instrument. The findings were then checked against the literature to see where previous work might inform the development of an instrument for assessing web site quality. In WebQual 4.0 web site users are asked to rate offerings against a range of qualities (table 7.4) using a 7-point scale. The respondents are also asked to rate each of the qualities for importance (again, using a 7-point scale), which helps the web site supplier gain an understanding of which qualities are considered by the user to carry most weight. WebQual consists of three dimensions for assessing e-commerce website quality: usability, information quality, and service interaction quality.

Usability

Usability draws on the field of human computer interaction and is concerned with the pragmatics of how a user perceives and interacts with a web site: is it easy to navigate? Is the design appropriate to the type of site? It is not, in the first instance, concerned with design principles such as the use of frames or the percentage of white space, although these are concerns for the web site designer who is charged with improving usability.

Information quality

Assuming that a web site is usable, then the user's attention can turn to the content of the web site. Questions 9 through 15 address the quality of the information presented on the web site. There is a longstanding body of IS literature examining aspects of information and information quality. Most of this literature predates the explosion in web commerce and builds on the seminal work of Shannon and Weaver from the 1940s on communications. They proposed 'information' as the message in a communication system, from sender (S), via a communication channel, to receiver (R). This can be measured at a number of levels: technical, referring to the accuracy and efficiency of the system producing information; semantic, referring to the success of the system in conveying intended meaning; and, effectiveness, referring to the effect or influence of the information on the receiver. Such a conception is most poignant, particularly to web commerce, where organizations aim to transmit data efficiently and accurately over the Internet, such as product offerings, which convey a desired meaning and achieve a desired effect, such as ticket sales.

Category	WebQual 4.0 Questions
Usability	1. I find the site easy to learn to operate
	2. My interaction with the site is clear and understandable
	3. I find the site easy to navigate
	4. I find the site easy to use
	5. The site has an attractive appearance
	6. The design is appropriate to the type of site
	7. The site conveys a sense of competency
	8. The site creates a positive experience for me
Information	9. Provides accurate information
	10. Provides believable information
	11. Provides timely information
	12. Provides relevant information
	13. Provides easy to understand information
	14. Provides information at the right level of detail
	15. Presents the information in an appropriate format
Service	16. Has a good reputation
Interaction	17 It feels safe to complete transactions
	18. My personal information feels secure
	19. Creates a sense of personalization
	20. Conveys a sense of community
	21. Makes it easy to communicate with the organization
	22. I feel confident that goods/services will be delivered as promised
Overall	23. My overall view of this web site

Table 7.4: WebQual 4.0 instrument (Barnes & Vidgen, 2002)

Service interaction quality

Information quality is clearly important in conducting e-commerce, but it does not capture the interaction aspects. A service encounter is the period of time during which a consumer directly interacts with a *service*. This encounter may or may not involve a human interaction element and in the case of Internet transactions will probably not. The SERVQUAL instrument was developed as a means of assessing customer satisfaction with the service level of a firm (Zeithaml et al., 1990). SERVQUAL has been applied in many domains, including appliance repair, banking, dentistry, accounting, and department stores. There is a service element involved in the delivery of any product, whether it is intangible (such as opening a new credit card account), or tangible (such as buying a book). Although important, in many industries cost is not the sole determinant of competitiveness; the customer experience has come to be recognized as a significant basis for differentiating suppliers. SERVQUAL was developed in the context of a physical world of buildings and human service representatives, but many of the concepts underlying the instrument can be adapted for the Internet and e-commerce.

7.4.2 The application of WebQual to online bookstores

To illustrate the WebQual approach we will summarize an application of the instrument to online bookstores (Barnes & Vidgen, 2002). Buying books over the Internet is one of the early applications of B2C e-commerce and has matured to become relatively stable, at least in Internet terms, with 5.4% of total global book sales in 1999. In the fall of 2000 we conducted a survey of the three largest UK online bookshops: Amazon, Bertelsmann Online (BOL) and the Internet Bookshop (IBS).

Amazon.com was launched in July 1995. However, although Amazon.com is accessible from all over the world, in the last few years the company has also established a localized presence in other international markets – including the UK, Germany, France and Japan – to comply with publishers' territorial rights while minimizing shipping costs. Amazon established a UK presence in 1998, Amazon.co.uk, with headquarters in Slough, a town 25 miles west of London.

Owned by the media conglomerate Bertlesmann AG, BOL (Bertelsmann Online) is the newest of the sites examined – launched in 1999. The launch of BOL follows Bertelsmann's acquisition of a 50% share in US-based Barnes and Noble's online book retailing subsidiary BarnesandNoble.com for $200 million in October 1998. Barnes and Noble is one of the World's largest booksellers with around 1000 bookstores.

The Internet Bookshop was established in 1993, making it one of the UK's longest-established Internet bookstores. The owner of the IBS web site, WH Smith, is a traditional UK high-street business, selling newspapers, books, music and stationery. WH Smith have an estimated £330 million (19.4%) of the UK book market and is estimated to be in second place for Internet sales behind Amazon.co.uk, although there are no accurate figures for its web operations.

Data collection

The WebQual approach to data collection is to use an online questionnaire targeted at real users of an e-commerce offering. In the case of Internet bookstores the students and staff of a university make excellent subjects given that both groups buy books as a matter of course and have considerable experience of this area of e-commerce.

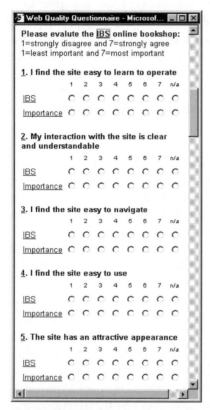

Figure 7.6: WebQual interface

The questionnaire was administered online and resulted in 280 usable responses. Respondents were directed to the start page for the survey, where they could read a set of brief instructions and then click the 'start' button. This button opened a second window that was used to collect questionnaire data (see figure 7.6). By clicking on the question number the user could see a dictionary entry for that item – a paragraph of text expanding on the quality and giving examples as appropriate. A random number was generated to pick which of the three sites would be presented to any given respondent. Questionnaires were checked online prior to submission to ensure that valid responses had been entered for all questions (an option 'not applicable' was included to ensure that responses were not forced).

To ensure a deeper level of commitment to the evaluation of the site the respondents were asked to find a book on the site that they would like as a runners-up prize. Respondents were asked to supply the title, price, and delivery cost. These are 'facts' that the respondent is asked to determine, which made it more likely that they would engage in searching and navigating the site. Furthermore, in setting a task we aimed to maintain a more natural and representative flow of interaction between the user and the web site.

The results

Table 7.5 shows the top 6 and the bottom 6 questions in terms of importance to respondents. Those questions considered most important by the respondents are heavily tied to information accuracy, usability and issues of trust. Such questions concern security and reliability regarding completion of transactions, receipt of goods and personal information, accuracy of content, as well as ease of site use and navigation. Conversely, when examining those items considered least important there is a quite different variety of questions. This group revolves around empathy with the user (communication, community and personalization), as well as site design issues (site experience, appropriateness of design and aesthetics). Given the high profile given to Amazon.com's reader reviews of books, it is interesting to note that respondents rate the community aspects as low in importance. Perhaps the basic building blocks of e-commerce – accurate information and safe to complete transactions – are still uppermost in web site users' minds.

Most important (top 6 qualities)	
9	Provides accurate information
17	It feels safe to complete transactions
22	I feel confident that goods/services will be delivered as promised
18	My personal information feels secure
3	I find the site easy to navigate
4	I find the site easy to use
21	Makes it easy to communicate with the organization
6	The design is appropriate to the type of site
8	The site creates a positive experience for me
5	The site has an attractive appearance
19	Creates a sense of personalization
20	Conveys a sense of community
Least important (bottom 6 qualities)	

Table 7.5: importance ranking of the questions

Weighted results for each of the sites can be calculated by multiplying the score given to the site for an item by the importance attached to that item by the individual. However, the individual weighted scores for each question make it difficult to give an overall benchmark for the sites. One way to achieve this is to index the total weighted score for a site against the total possible score (i.e. the total importance multiplied by 7, the maximum rating for a site). This allows a WebQual Index (WQI) to be calculated for the overall site. The results of the WQI analysis are:

Amazon	72%
BOL	70%
IBS	67%

Factor analysis is a statistical method for finding 'natural' groupings of questions in the data. Factor analysis showed five constructs to be present in the data. The usability questions contained two constructs, which the authors labeled usability and design, and service interaction, which subdivided into trust and empathy. Information questions grouped together in a single construct. These five dimensions give a statistically verifiable indication of how web site users perceive quality in the online bookshop domain. To summarize the performance of the three cyber bookshops the data was organized around the five questionnaire subcategories. Then, and similarly to the overall WebQual Index, the total score for each category was indexed against the maximum score (based on the importance ratings for questions multiplied by 7). Figure 7.7 is the result – a comparison of the three sites in graphical form showing how each performed in terms of the five constructs of web site quality. Note that the scale has been restricted to values between 0.4 and 1.0 to allow for clearer comparison.

Figure 7.7 demonstrates very clearly that the Amazon UK site stands 'head and shoulders' above the two rivals. The indices for the Amazon subcategories make a clear circle around the other two sites, with Trust rating particularly well. Other areas are less strong, in relative terms, although clearly ahead of the nearest rival. Empathy had the lowest WQI for Amazon, with other categories somewhere in between. The scores of the two other bookshops are very close, with IBS edging only slightly ahead of BOL for three of the subcategories. Information quality presents the largest discrepancy with IBS leading BOL. IBS also score marginally higher for empathy and usability, with the remaining categories containing almost equal scores.

Interpretation of the results

The survey indicates that the differences in usability between the three sites are relatively small, suggesting that once a basic level of usability is achieved then the design of the web site is unlikely to be a differentiating competitive factor. With regard to design, the difference is more marked, indicating that the design of the Amazon site is preferred, although this may be due in part to respondents being more likely to be familiar with the Amazon site. It is a relatively straightforward task for an organization to benchmark the usability of its web site, for example by holding a usability workshop where users are given tasks to complete and are monitored while doing so.

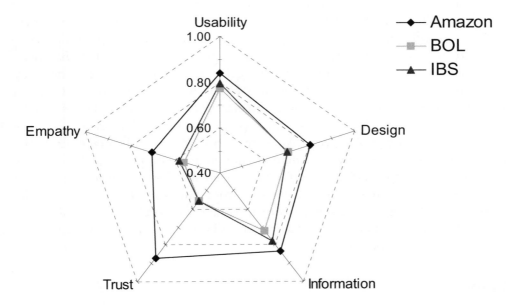

Figure 7.7: Radar chart of web site quality

Respondents rated 'accurate information' as the most important item in the WebQual instrument. This indicates that e-commerce businesses need to pay particular attention to the content of their web sites. Lack of control over content is evident when, for example, organizations do not remove special offers that have expired, or, more seriously, when pricing errors are introduced, such as a dishwasher being offered at £2.99 rather than £299. Managing information quality is likely to be rather more difficult than improving web usability since the content management cycle needs to manage web documents from creation through publishing to archival and, eventually, destruction. Whereas usability can be evaluated quickly, information quality is likely to require an enterprise-wide approach that addresses all the sources of content, encompassing authors, existing systems and databases.

While usability and information quality might be addressed largely through internal changes, interaction quality requires a stronger external perspective. The greatest differentiator of the sites is 'trust', where Amazon is a long way ahead of its competitors. Yet the concept of 'trust' has a degree of ambiguity; a variety of definitions of trust have been proposed, including those related to benevolence, integrity, competence and predictability (McKnight & Chervany, 2001). Interestingly, in the online bookshop application of WebQual, of the four questions that comprise 'trust', three of the questions were rated as second, third, and fourth most important by respondents (only 'accurate information' rated more highly in terms of customer importance).

It is unlikely that excellent web site design and judicious use of new technology will increase the perception of trust by customers, since trust is affected by external factors, such as the strength of the brand, the customer's previous experiences, and the whole range of communications generated by the brand-owner, the media, and word of mouth. There are web site design implications for 'trust', such as making sure that the privacy policy is visible, and displaying the logo of a third party for accreditation of security mechanisms. However, given Amazon's first-mover advantage and the switching costs incurred by customers in moving to a competitor, BOL and the Internet Bookshop need to go further than web site design considerations and offer something that distinguishes them from Amazon. In the case of the Internet Bookshop this might involve integration of online activity with the physical high-street network of its owner, WH Smith, and for BOL with its partner Barnes and Noble.

Summary

- A successful web-based information system will typically need to meet the requirements of at least two sets of stakeholder: employees and customers.
- Employee job satisfaction can be enhanced through participative design and sociotechnical approaches such as ETHICS and the Scandinavian School.
- Customer satisfaction requires a marketing approach and can be assessed through instruments such as WebQual.

Exercises

1. How might an ETHICS-based development be applied to the creation of a new research student admission process (appendix B)?
2. How would you safeguard against a sociotechnical design process being used in a managerialist way in the single-minded pursuit of profit?
3. Conduct a web site quality workshop for your organization to elicit your customers' quality requirements. How closely do the qualities map to the WebQual instrument?

Further reading

Bancroft, N., (1992). *New Partnerships for Managing Technological Change.* Wiley, New York.

Barnes, S. and Vidgen, R., (2002). An Integrative Approach to the Assessment of e-Commerce Quality. *Journal of Electronic Commerce Research,* 3(3).

Bodker, S., Gronbaek, K. and Kyng, M., (1993). *Cooperative Design: techniques and experiences from the Scandinavian Scene.* In: Schuler, D., and Namioka, (1983).

Bossert, J. L., (1991). *Quality Function Deployment: a practitioner's approach.* ASQC Quality Press, Wisconsin.

Bravo, E., (1993). *The Hazards of Leaving out the Users.* In: Schuler, D. and Namioka, (1983).

Ehn, P., (1993). *Scandinavian Design: on participation and skill.* In: Schuler, D. and Namioka, (1983).

Ehn, P. and Kyng, M., (1987). The Collective Resource Approach to Systems Design. In: Bjerknes, G., Ehn, P. and Kyng, M., editors, *Computers and Democracy. A Scandinavian Challenge.* Avebury, Aldershot, England.

Greenbaum, J., (1995). *Windows on the Workplace.* Cornerstone Books, NY.

King, R., (1989). *Better Designs in Half the Time: implementing QFD.* GOAL/QPC, Methuen, Massachusetts.

Land, F., (1982). Notes on Participation. *Computer Journal* 25(2).

McKnight, D. H. and Chervany, N. L., (2001). Conceptualizing Trust: A Typology and E-Commerce Customer Relationships Model, *Proceedings of the Hawaii International Conference on System Sciences*, Maui, Hawaii.

Mumford, E., (1995). *Effective Systems Design and Requirements Analysis – the ETHICS approach.* Macmillan Press, Basingstoke, UK.

Mumford, E., (1983). *Designing Human Systems.* Manchester Business School.

Sachs, P., (1995). Transforming Work: collaboration, learning, and design. *Communications of the ACM*, 38(9): 36–44.

Schuler, D. and Namioka, A., (1993). *Participatory Design: principles and practices.* Lawrence Erlbaum Associates, NJ.

Zeithaml, V., Parasuraman, A. and Berry, L., (1990). *Delivering Quality Service: balancing customer perceptions and expectations.* The Free Press, New York.

8

Information Analysis

8.1 Introduction

In this chapter we introduce the traditional methods for the analysis of information system requirements. There are many methods for expressing requirements. We will use the Unified Modeling Language (UML), which is an established and widely used method for system development. Using the UML notation we can express IS requirements in a formal way, providing a platform for software system designs and software construction.

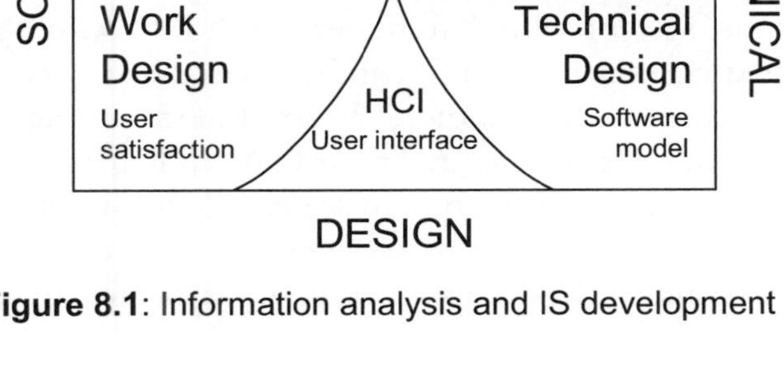

ANALYSIS

Organizational Analysis		**Information Analysis**
Value creation		Requirements specification
Work Design	HCI	**Technical Design**
User satisfaction	User interface	Software model

SOCIO — TECHNICAL

DESIGN

Figure 8.1: Information analysis and IS development

8.1.1 The theatre booking system

Imagine that the Barchester Playhouse decides to start up an Internet ticketing facility in conjunction with a software house, Nimbus Information Systems. The plan is to make the theatre booking system an Internet application available to the two other theatres in Barchester, both of which rely currently on in-person and telephone ticket bookings. Once the system is operational it would be a relatively small step to make the service available to theatres in any part of the country. And why stop there? With appropriate user interfaces and a ticketless system, as introduced by budget airlines in Europe, the theatre booking system could provide a booking service for theatres in any country.

This would be a radical departure for the Barchester Playhouse, raising issues concerning the identity of the theatre and its core competencies – if the online ticketing service is a success it is possible that its revenues and profitability will exceed those from staging theatrical productions. In this imagining the Barchester Playhouse is transformed – the core business of the Playhouse would be better seen as ticketing operations with the staging of theatrical productions as a separate, but possibly complementary activity. In such a scenario, the Playhouse could discontinue the staging of productions and still be viable – i.e., capable of a separate existence – as an online ticket sales operation.

This scenario is the 'American Airlines story', whose CEO was reported as saying that he would sell the airline before selling the flight reservation system, SABRE. The SABRE flight reservation system, which takes bookings for many different carriers, was indeed spun off at a later date as a separate business. This is perhaps the most likely scenario for a successful online ticketing service, since there are likely to be low synergies between staging theatrical productions and operating an online ticketing service.

The competencies of the Playhouse are in selecting, promoting, and staging theatrical productions, not in the development of online ticketing systems, although these may be competencies of the software house, Nimbus. The strategy for the Playhouse ticketing system would have been decided as part of the *organizational analysis* (chapters 4, 5, 6). For the purposes of *information analysis* we will tackle the establishment of a ticket booking system from the perspective of the software house, Nimbus, who are interested in co-developing the theatre booking system with Barchester Playhouse with the intention of making it sufficiently general so that it can be offered as a service to other theatres. The booking system will be a multi-theatre Internet ticketing system that takes payment for ticket sales by credit card. Assuming that an Internet connection is available operators in the box office could also use it for processing in-person ticket sales. If the application were extended to cater for cash and cheque payments it could indeed become the single source of all ticket reservations and ticket sales.

8.2 Information system modeling

In response to the question 'why do we model?' Booch et al. (1999) propose a fundamental reason: so that we can better understand the system we are developing. Booch et al. argue that:

- Models help us visualize a system as it is or as we want it to be
- Models allow us to specify the structure or behaviour of a system
- Models provide a template to guide us when constructing a system
- Models document the decisions we have made.

The choice of what to model and how to represent the situation using a modeling notation are not neutral decisions. A model is indeed a simplification of a complex reality, but models do not merely reflect reality (as is) – they are also implicated in the construction of new realities (to be). If we choose to model work practices using only box and line diagrams then our model is unlikely to be able to show, for example, personal, political, and cultural aspects of the work situation. The analyst should be ever aware that a complex reality is best approached using a range of modeling approaches that capture and help shape different aspects of the problem situation. Over-reliance on any one modeling approach is likely to lead to blind spots in the developer's view of the domain.

When producing information models that will guide us in the development of software artefacts it is common to focus on structure and behaviour. A structural model describes the types of thing that will be represented in software and for which data must be held. For example, in the case of a motor vehicle some of these types might be wheels, engine, and gearbox. The structural model will also describe relationships between the types of thing; a motor vehicle typically has four wheels and an engine. Behaviour describes what the system does, often in response to some external stimuli. A motor vehicle can, for example, turn, accelerate, and go forwards and backwards. Depressing the accelerator pedal will cause the engine to turn more quickly – a behaviour. Structural and behavioural models provide a template to guide the developer in specifying, designing, and constructing software artefacts. The models also act as documentation, helping to record both decisions and the rationale for the decisions at each stage of a development project.

8.2.1 Analysis and design

Analysis is often presented as '*what* the application will do' and design as '*how* it will be achieved'. In analysis we are trying to understand and represent the problem situation, or domain – we are not concerned at this stage with the technologies that will be used to achieve a software implementation.

Structured systems analysis and design

Structured systems analysis and design came out of the structured programming methods of the 1970s and reached its zenith in the United Kingdom with SSADM (structured systems analysis and design method) in the early 1990s. In the US popular structured methods included the Yourdon method and James Martin's Information Engineering. A common theme in structured methods is to view the system from three perspectives: data, process, and dynamics. The principal models used in systems analysis are the entity relationship diagram (data), the data flow diagram (process) and the entity life history (dynamics). However, the separation of data and behaviour meant that a lot of effort had to be expended in keeping the models synchronized; it also made reuse of software objects difficult. In the 1980s object-oriented programming using languages such as Eifel and Smalltalk gained in popularity, largely because of claims of faster development times, reuse, and extensibility. In the 1990s the principles of object-oriented programming were migrated up-stream and adopted in systems analysis.

Object-oriented analysis and design

Many benefits have been claimed for an object-oriented approach to systems development, including reusability, reliability, scalability, faster development, easier maintenance, greater extensibility, a closer correspondence with the real world, and a more effective way of handling complexity. One of the attractive features of an object-oriented approach is that the same paradigm can be used throughout analysis, design, and construction. This means that the same diagramming notations can be used at each level and refined as the models become more physical, finally evolving into an executable specification from which software can be generated.

8.3 The unified modeling language (UML)

As object-oriented (OO) programming rose in popularity during the 1980s the ideas were taken from software development upstream into systems design and systems analysis. In the early 1990s a number of OO analysis and design methods were proposed. All had strengths and weaknesses: the Booch (1994) method was strong on design and real-time applications, the object modeling technique (OMT) of Rumbaugh et al. (1991) on analysis and data-intensive applications, and the use case approach of Jacobson (1994) on business process modeling.

In 1994 Booch, Rumbaugh, and Jacobson got together and pooled their ideas in a unified modeling language (UML), taking the best ideas from each and bringing some standardization to the wide range of methods and notations for OO analysis and design. We adopt UML here as it is fast becoming an industry standard, has OMG (Object Management Group) acceptance, and a rich set of resources and software development tools available (e.g., the Rational Rose modeling software). This chapter is concerned with information system analysis, i.e., with what is required, and the UML is therefore used at the conceptual system level to support analysis.

The core UML techniques used in information analysis are:

- Use cases
- Class diagrams
- Interaction diagrams
    - Sequence diagrams
    - Collaboration diagrams
- State transition diagrams
- Activity diagrams.

We will illustrate these modeling techniques using the theatre booking system. As the UML is grounded firmly in object-orientation it will be useful to first lay out the ideas that characterize the object-oriented paradigm.

8.3.1 Fundamentals of object-orientation

Fundamental concepts of object-orientation include classes and instances, encapsulation, communication by messages, inheritance, and polymorphism.

Objects

An object is perhaps best defined simply as a 'thing'. An object could be a physical thing such as one of the seats in the stalls of the theatre. In software terms, objects are used to represent things of interest in the problem domain, such as customers, theatre seats, and ticket sales. Objects have identity, state, and exhibit behaviour.

Objects have **identity**, which means that each object is distinct, even if they happen to look the same to the naked eye or happen to have exactly the same attributes. Identity persists even though the characteristics of the object may change. For example, imagine a motorcar that has been painted a different colour, had a new engine, and been re-registered with a new vanity plate. The motorcar has a continuing existence that is not dependent solely on the values of its attributes. In practice, identity can pose difficulties. We might like to identify our customers by name, but a customer can change his or her name and still be the same person, although they might have a new legal 'identity'. Identity is therefore not just about attributes. An old broom might have had three new heads and two new handles – is it still the same broom? In a physical sense it is clearly not the same broom, but if the broom has been in the corner of the kitchen for the last 25 years, then in a contextual and historic sense it is in some way the same broom.

Objects have **state**. The state of an object is given by the sum of its attributes. For example, a training course booking could be provisional or confirmed. Objects exhibit **behaviour** in response to stimuli. When a customer pays in full a provisional booking becomes a confirmed booking, i.e., it undergoes a state change. The training course booking object can receive and respond to messages. How it responds will depend on the values of its attributes; if the booking object receives a message requesting confirmation and it is already in the state 'confirmed' it might return an error code to the sender of the message.

Classes and instances

A class is a category that defines common characteristics, structure, and behaviour of objects. For example, 'Person', 'Vegetable', and 'Motor Vehicle' are classes that we would recognize as a way of perceiving things in the world. An object is an instance of a class, such as an individual person, a particular carrot, or the motorcar parked outside my house. The instances of a class have shared attributes, such as the height of a person, the weight of a carrot, or the recorded mileage of a motorcar. To underline the importance of distinguishing between classes and instances one OO trainer has been known to hold up a banana and proclaim: 'this is an object – it is a member of the class banana'.

We will use the terms 'object' and 'instance' interchangeably. However, the word 'instance' makes it clear that we are talking about *this* or *a* customer rather than the general class of Customer, especially when we come to look at UML class models and need to be able to differentiate between the class and the object.

Encapsulation and communication by messages

Encapsulation requires a service view of data (what does the object do?) to be adopted rather than an implementation view (how is the object constructed?). The representation of the object is hidden and therefore the only means of accessing and modifying an instance of a class is via the external interface operations defined for that instance's class. The external interface supported by a class is implemented as a set of operations. To get an object to do something, i.e., exhibit behaviour, we need to send it a **message** invoking an operation. An **operation** specifies the way in which the object will behave when it receives a message. For example, we would expect the Motor Vehicle class to support an operation such as 'accelerate', which when invoked will cause a motor vehicle to increase its speed. How the operation is implemented is hidden from the sender of the message. The class of which the object is a member defines the operations that the object supports and therefore the messages to which it can respond. The packaging of behaviour and data structure such that they are hidden behind an interface is referred to as **encapsulation**.

The concept of encapsulation (or information hiding) therefore requires objects to communicate via narrowly defined interfaces using messages. To change the bodywork colour of a motor vehicle requires that a message be sent with a colour as an argument (note that the colour used as an argument is an object that is a member of the class Colour – *everything* is an object and therefore a member of some class). The operation invoked is responsible for changing the representation of the motor vehicle object. To find out what colour interior a motor vehicle currently has also requires a message to be sent because direct inspection of an attribute value would violate the requirement for encapsulation. As usual in OO, how the operation is executed and how the representation of motor vehicle objects is maintained is hidden from the sender of the message.

Inheritance

A class can inherit both structure and behaviour from another class, known as a supertype class. For example, if the attribute bodywork colour is defined for the class Motor Vehicle, then all subtype classes of Motor Vehicle, such as Public Passenger Vehicle and Private Vehicle, inherit that characteristic. The operations supported by the class structure can also be inherited. If the operation 'calculate road tax' has been defined for the class Motor Vehicle then it will be inherited by the subtype classes of Motor Vehicle.

Where the basis for calculation of road tax is different by class then the subtype classes might need to re-implement the operation 'calculate road tax'. For example, it may be that Public Passenger Vehicle calculates road tax based upon the number of passengers the vehicle is licenced to carry and Private Vehicle on the basis of engine size. Any other vehicles that are instances of the supertype class Motor Vehicle will use the original 'calculate road tax' operation. When a new type of motor vehicle is needed it can be added to the class structure and inherit the common attributes and operations of existing classes (generalization) and add new attributes and operations as needed to differentiate it from existing classes (specialization).

Polymorphism

Because an object knows which class it belongs to it knows which messages it can respond to. The same operation can apply to many classes and result in different behaviour depending upon the class of the object. For example, assume that the class Clock has the subclasses AnalogueClock and DigitalClock. Clocks of both types will respond to the message 'display time' but will behave differently. The sender of the message need not be aware of the type of clock the recipient is when sending the message 'display time' – the recipient will respond according to its class. New types of clock can be added, e.g., Sun Dial, and as long as the new subclasses support the generic operation 'display time' then no further changes will be needed to the clock system.

Encapsulation, inheritance, and polymorphism are the fundamentals of OO that help reduce the complexity of large software systems, promote flexibility, reuse, and extensibility.

8.4 Requirements gathering and use case diagrams

8.4.1 Requirements gathering

In an ideal world, requirements should be expressed in terms that are testable and verifiable, justifiable, unambiguous, consistent, modifiable, and traceable. For example, it is not a testable requirement of the theatre booking system to say that theatre yield must be increased. The requirement is testable if annual theatre yield is defined as the total available seats in a year divided by the number of seats sold with a target increase of 8.5% for the first year of operation of the booking system.

Traditionally, the system analyst would gather requirements through interviews with individuals, questionnaires, observation of work practices, and by studying business documents. All of these can be useful in understanding the current situation, although they tend to focus on the current situation and run the risk of reinforcing incremental change rather than creative thinking and radical change. A more participative approach to requirements analysis is joint application design (JAD), where key users, managers, and systems developers come together in a workshop setting to discuss system requirements. These sessions are typically intense, lasting from a few hours up to several days and are often run off-site to ensure the participants focus on the task free from the distractions of the office. JAD workshops combined with the development of prototypes – possibly a throw-away – to deliver an executable specification make a particularly powerful combination for understanding and agreeing requirements. Where the prototype develops iteratively into the final system then the requirements specification is in a process of continuous refinement and can be adapted to changes in the environment. In chapter 7 we took the notion of participation beyond JAD and considered how users can be empowered to participate fully and genuinely in the system development process.

Further sources of requirements include external research, such as an investigation of industry best practices. For example, in developing a theatre booking system it would be advisable to carry out a review of existing Internet theatre booking systems and also industry leaders from other industries (e.g.,

Amazon.com) to see how things are done and to find out what constitutes best practice.

Requirements are often categorized as functional and non-functional. For a theatre booking system, we would expect to find a functional requirement such as 'take payment for online ticket booking'. The functional requirements of the theatre booking system will be captured in use case diagrams and use case descriptions. A non-functional requirement might be for booking enquiry pages to load quickly. The non-functional requirements also need to be recorded and specified in terms that can be tested and verified, e.g., 'maximum page load time of 8 seconds with an average load time of 3 seconds using a 56k dial-up modem'.

8.4.2 Use case notation

Use case diagrams are a formalized notation for modeling the system from the perspective of the user. The focus is on what the system does – its behaviour – rather than how it achieves it. A use case typically represents some functionality of the proposed system as perceived by a user. Use cases will add business value, such as 'process ticket returns', and have a business outcome, such as 'returned tickets reallocated'. In the early stages of a development project it is important that use cases focus on business goals rather than system goals.

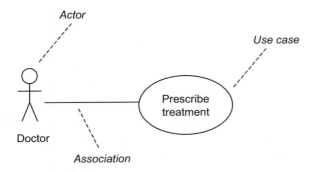

Figure 8.2: Use case diagramming notation

The use case notation comprises actors, use cases, and associations (figure 8.2). An actor reflects a role that is played by a human (or non-human) with respect to a system. A role can be played by many people, e.g., doctor, and one person can play many roles, e.g., the theatre manager could play the role of box office clerk during busy periods and a box office clerk might also attend a performance as a member of the public. It is therefore important to think in terms of actors and roles rather than individuals and job titles. Actors execute use cases, such as a doctor prescribing treatment. The link between actors and use cases is shown by an association (figure 8.2), which indicates that there is communication between the actor and the use case, such as the sending and receiving of messages.

Figure 8.3 shows a use case diagram for the box office of a theatre, such as the Barchester Playhouse. Human actors (we are not talking here about the actors in a play!) include customers and telephone sales operators. The accounting system is a non-human actor. It is external to the box office domain but it has requirements of the box office and is therefore shown as an actor.

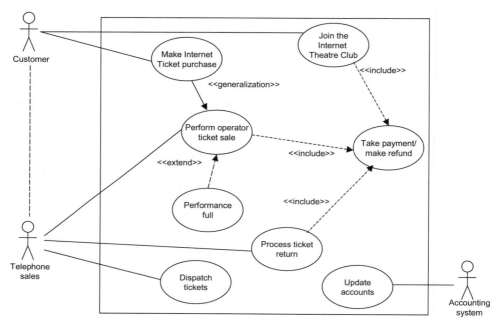

Figure 8.3: Use case diagram for Theatre operations

Customers are associated with two use cases: 'make Internet ticket purchase' and 'join the Internet Theatre Club'. These will be activities that the customers can perform for themselves online via the Internet. It might be argued that the inclusion of a technology, the Internet, is misplaced in a conceptual model of the box office. However, although we might remove the word 'Internet' or replace it with 'online', from a business perspective it may be appropriate to make it absolutely clear that these will be Internet services available to customers. When developing a use case diagram it is important that the use cases are described from the reference point of the actor – for example, operators sell tickets, but customers purchase tickets on the Internet (from the Playhouse's perspective they are both ticket sale mechanisms).

8.4.3 Extension, inclusion, and generalization

Extends

The extends relationship is used where there are similar use cases but one use case does more than the other. For example, a ticket sale where the performance is full (figure 8.3) requires that a variation on the ticket sale use case be carried out. For an extends relationship:

First capture the simple, normal case, e.g., operator ticket sale.

Then, for each step in the use case ask what could go wrong, e.g.,

Check seat availability (performance full)

Take payment (credit card not authorized)

These variations can then be modeled as extensions of the base use case. An extends relationship models the part of a use case that the user may see as optional behaviour, such as the situation in figure 8.3 where the requested performance is full.

Include

If multiple use cases require the same chunk of functionality then it can be made into a separate use case and referred to with an 'includes' relationship. For example, ticket sales and ticket returns both need to use the take payment use case, as does join Internet theatre club. This functionality can be separated out into a single use case rather than being duplicated in multiple use cases.

With 'extends' the actor will deal with the base case and the variations – the same operator will deal with ticket sales that can be fulfilled and ticket sales that cannot because no seats are available. With an 'includes' relationship a different actor might be responsible for making a refund for returned tickets (e.g., box office supervisor) from the actor involved in an operator ticket sale (e.g., box office operator).

Generalization

The Internet ticket purchase, where the customer interacts directly with the ticket booking system rather than using a telephone operator or box office clerk as an intermediary, can be modeled as a specialization of the more general case of ticket sale. This would allow the Internet ticket purchase to inherit some of the general characteristics of the operator ticket sale and to add refinements as needed. For example, the operator would be able to see the theatre layout with available seats in one colour and booked seats in another colour. The Internet customer might not be allowed to see exactly which seats are booked (an empty theatre might put them off booking) and be allocated seats automatically by the system.

8.4.4 Describing a use case

Each of the use cases in the diagram should be elaborated with a use case description. This is the starting point for a process of elaboration that will eventually lead to a software implementation.

Use case name	Make Internet ticket purchase
Use case intent	To satisfy customer request for seats at a performance
Use case description	

1.   Establish the customer's seat at performance requirements
2.   Find available seats
3.   If seats available calculate the price of the seats
    3.1 Where the customer is not a member of the Internet Theatre Club charge full price
    3.2 Where the customer is a member of the Internet Theatre Club give discount
4.   Get customer details and take payment <<include>>
5.   If customer requested ticket delivery then mail tickets

Table 8.1: Use case description for 'make Internet ticket purchase'

The use case description in table 8.1 provides a high-level description of the Internet ticket purchase use case. Figure 8.3 addresses the operations of the box office with respect to ticket sales, but there is a range of administrative activities needed to support the ticket sales activities (figure 8.4).

8.5 Class diagrams

Booch et al. (1999) define a class as 'a description of a set of objects that share the same attributes, operations, relationships, and semantics' (p. 49). A class diagram is a model of the things that are of interest in the problem domain being studied. In different domains there will be different things of interest; in modeling a university the developer might find classes such as 'Student', 'LectureCourse', and 'LectureRoom'. In the context of a theatre classes for consideration could be 'Actor', 'Star', 'Theatre', 'Seat', 'Production', and so on. These are the conceptual categories that help us make sense when structuring our perceptions about the theatre situation. In UML classes are shown as rectangles (figure 8.5).

The class name should be a short noun or noun phrase and begin with a capital letter. The class model typically represents things that last over time – the functionality of the system may change often, but a good class model will either cope with new functionality as is or be capable of being extended without being the subject of a major redesign. It is very unlikely that a 'correct' class diagram will be produced at the first attempt. The class diagram will evolve as the developer understands the domain and the requirements better and, despite our best attempts to separate out analysis and design, it will in all likelihood be impacted by the technical design and the software construction phases of the project.

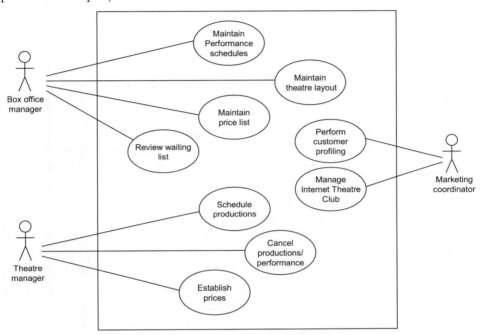

Figure 8.4: Use case diagram for Theatre administration

Classes can represent tangible things, such as the seats in a theatre, and intangible things, such as an account balance in an accounting system. Classes can also be used to model roles, such as the box office manager in a theatre. To find classes in a domain, two approaches are typically used: modeling the vocabulary and modeling the responsibilities of the system. In taking a *vocabulary* (or data-driven) approach the developer looks at the things that users already use to describe their system (good sources for these things are the use case analyses) and highlights nouns and noun phrases. This is a seemingly simple technique, but experience is needed to decide on what should be kept in, what excluded, and how to rename and restructure the candidate classes. Responsibility modeling of classes is concerned with how *responsibility* will be divided between a group of classes; the aim is to achieve a balance of responsibilities. In a group of classes we do not want one class that is large and complex with too many responsibilities while other classes have trivial responsibilities. The design heuristic is to look at how the classes collaborate and to redistribute responsibilities evenly. In practice, the OO developer will tend to use a combination of data-driven and responsibility based modeling, although they might struggle to explain exactly how they do this! However, the stereotypes of vocabulary and responsibility are useful as they are a reminder that a good class model will represent the things of interest as well as their collaborations and responsibilities.

Figure 8.5: Classes

It is important to note that the objects being modeled are going to be represented in software. We cannot represent every characteristic of the real-world object being modeled, even for seemingly simple objects. The architect Christopher Alexander (1964) gives the example of the difficulty of modeling the characteristics of a button. Characteristics of a button include the shape, size, colour, number of holes, and the material it is constructed from. However, further characteristics might include weight, oil-resistance, and flammability. Weight might be relevant for sport or space travel; oil-resistance for engineers and anglers; flammability for the fire service. A software model is an abstraction of the problem situation and the developer must understand the context and purpose of the model to know what is relevant and what is not.

In software terms, the system is a collection of collaborating objects. However, there is a connection between the software representation and the things in the problem domain. As a minimum, the software representation needs to be consistent with the things in the problem domain. For example, an asset register of personal computers in the organization might involve stencilling a bar code onto each physical computer so that it can be matched to an object in the software system that holds details of the computer's location, specification, service record, and original purchase price. The development of location aware and context-sensitive devices will lead to a closer integration of software and real-world things. Imagine that each seat in the theatre is made intelligent and can report on its status – 'I need cleaning', 'I have been removed for repair'. In this scenario the act of removing a seat would result in a message to the software system indicating that the seat was no longer available for bookings. The growth in mobile communication will see more and more intelligent devices and therefore a stronger link between the software and the things being modeled or controlled in the problem domain. This suggests that software systems will not only have informational implications, but will have a more immediate and direct physical impact on our world.

8.5.1 Relationships: associations

Classes represent things; relationships represent the connections *between* things. UML caters for three types of relationship: association, generalization, and aggregation. An association is a structural relationship between things showing that one can navigate from the instances of one class to the instances of another (and possibly vice versa).

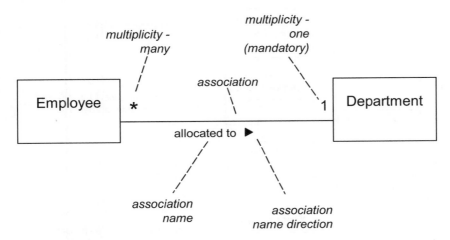

Figure 8.6: Classes and associations

Associations are shown as solid lines that connect the same or different classes. In figure 8.6 the association might reflect the real-world business rule in the ABC Company that 'each employee *must* be allocated to a *single* department'. The association can be read in two directions – the inverse to figure 8.6 would be that 'each department may have many employees allocated to it'. Each of the directions represents a *role* of the association; connections between two classes, known as binary associations, have two roles. Just as classes have instances, so do associations. Instances of the Employee/Department association could be 'employee Tom Smith is allocated to the Marketing department' and 'employee Sue Jones is allocated to the Finance department'.

Multiplicity

In the case of figure 8.6 the '1' indicates that an employee must have one – and only one – department. Tom Smith can work for the Marketing department, but cannot work for the Personnel department at the same time. If Tom moves from Marketing to Personnel then a new instance of the Employee/Department association is made, linking Tom Smith (employee instance) to Personnel (department instance). In the XYZ Company it may be possible for employees to have split posts, in which case there would be a many to many association between Employee and Department. Such an association might have an attribute specifying the percentage of time that each employee is allocated to a particular department with a constraint that the total for each employee must equal 100.

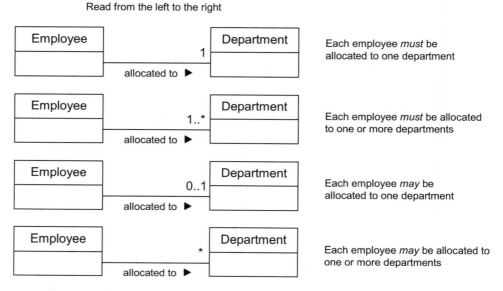

Figure 8.7: Multiplicity of associations

Reading from left to right, figure 8.7 shows the most common association multiplicities. Each of the examples of association multiplicity could reflect the policies of an organization and therefore none is correct or incorrect in an abstract sense – correctness is decided by reference to the problem domain.

8.5.2 Attributes and operations

Attributes

Booch et al. (1999) define an attribute as 'a named property of a class that describes a range of values that instances of the property may hold' (p. 50). More intuitively, an attribute describes the instances of a class. For example, every employee would be expected to have a name, address, and date of birth. An instance of the class Employee could have the values 'Tom Smith', '1 Oak Street', and '20-Jun-1970'. Attributes are shown below the class name and each compound word should begin with a capital with the exception of the first word, e.g., productionType (figure 8.8). Some attributes will be mandatory, such as title, while others are optional, e.g., videoClip. Optionality is not usually shown on the class diagram, although it can be, e.g., videoClip(o).

Operations

'An operation is the implementation of a service that can be requested from any object of the class to affect behaviour' (Booch et al., 1999, p. 51). Operations are listed in the bottom compartment of the class box (figure 8.8). To invoke behaviour in an object, another object sends that object a message. For example, instances of the class Production support the operation 'assessViability'. A production object receiving this message will assess its viability and, let us assume, return a binary value: 'viable' or 'non-viable'. How the Production class implements this method is not the concern of the object sending the message. The production class might carry out the equivalent of flipping a coin, or it might make a forecast of bookings and compare this with production costs such as stage set design. The complexity of the implementation is hidden; the sender of the message invoking the operation need only know how the public interface is defined for the class Production.

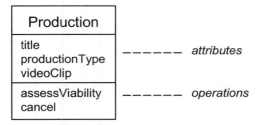

Figure 8.8: Attributes and operations

8.5.3 Relationships: generalization

Generalization is a relationship between a general thing and a more specific thing. The more general thing is of a supertype class and the more specific thing is of a subtype class. For example, in the Nimbus web development agency, staff can be subtyped into graphic designers and technical staff (figure 8.9). The technical staff work in systems development or in support operations (e.g., database administrator, UNIX specialist). Common characteristics are inherited by subtypes; all IT staff will inherit the properties of their supertype, such as employee number and name and all staff instances will respond to a message invoking the changeSalary operation. However, subtypes must also be different in some way. For example, development staff may hold certification qualifications, such as Microsoft's Certified Professional. The bonus calculation for graphic designers is different from the calculation for technical staff, so the subtypes re-implement this operation as appropriate. The bonus calculation is also different between development and support staff, reflecting the different basis on which they will be assessed. In this case the subtypes implement the bonus calculation differently from their supertype, technical staff.

The class Technical Staff is an abstract class, which is indicated by the class name being in italics. This class does not have instances; its role is to provide an abstraction for technical staff, allowing common attributes such as 'certification' to be inherited by the instances of Support Staff and Developer. The operation 'calculateBonus' is also shown in italics, because it is abstract and incomplete and needs its subtypes, Support Staff and Developer, to implement the operation. Since the supertype class 'Staff' has not been modeled as an abstract class it may be instantiated, perhaps with administrative and managerial staff.

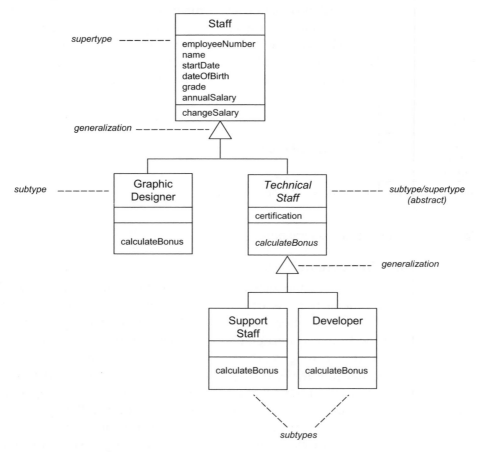

Figure 8.9: Generalization

8.5.4 Relationships: aggregation

The third type of association is the aggregation. The aggregation represents a 'whole/part' relationship. In practice it is often difficult to distinguish between associations and aggregations; in many cases the aggregation is just a strong form of association between two classes and is shown by an open diamond (figure 8.10). A composition, shown by a filled diamond, is a stronger form of aggregation. With a composition the parts live and die with the whole and cannot be transferred. For example, it does not make sense to move part of one theatre to another theatre. If a theatre is deleted then the parts of that theatre must go as well. But, one could move seats from one part to another or to another theatre altogether.

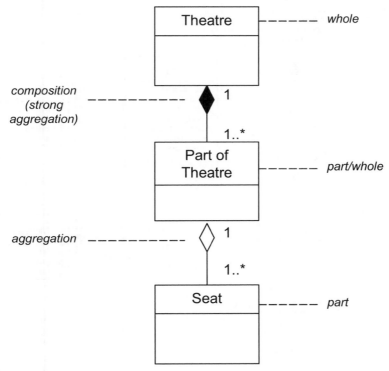

Figure 8.10: Aggregation

8.5.5 The theatre booking system class model

The conceptual class diagram for the theatre booking system is shown in figure 8.11. This diagram will form the basis for design and implementation in later chapters. The model is basic but it does support the core requirements of a simple ticketing system. At the heart of the model is the class SeatAtPerformance. Instances of this class tie together a performance and a part of a theatre, e.g., 'Hamlet' at 8.00 pm on 5 March 2003 in seat B15 of the circle of the Barchester Playhouse. Because seats can be reserved prior to payment, the association with Transaction is optional. A transaction is simply a device for grouping together seats at a performance for the purposes of payment. A transaction must have a customer, but some of the customers will be members of the theatre club and qualify for a discount on the ticket price.

Because it is possible to get to the class theatre via two routes – performance and part of theatre – a constraint is needed to ensure that the theatre is the same via both routes for a given 'seat at performance'. This situation arises because in the early life of a production no seats have been sold and therefore an association with Theatre is needed via Performance and Production.

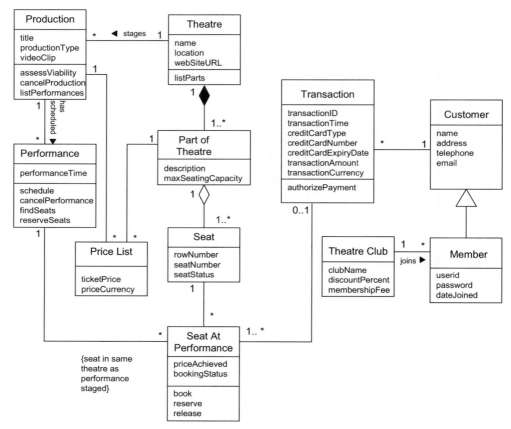

Figure 8.11: Conceptual class model for theatre booking system

Note that the class model includes a Theatre class. This could be instantiated with a single theatre, e.g., the Barchester Playhouse, but it could also be instantiated with multiple theatres and therefore forms the basis for the theatre booking system – a generic multi-theatre booking system suitable for a theatre industry portal site. The model in figure 8.11 provides a basic facility for making Internet ticket sales, but little more. A more sophisticated system might allow customers to go onto a wait list for performances or productions that are full (figure 8.12). The wait list would be for one customer and would specify the number of seats required; the part of theatre preferred would be optional. The wait list is then subtyped into a wait list for a specific performance and a wait list for a production (any performance will be considered).

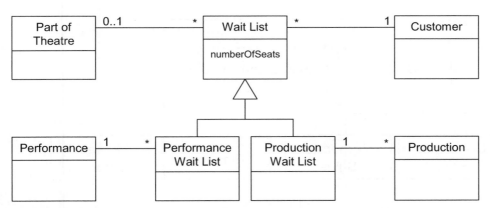

Figure 8.12: Theatre booking system class diagram – adding wait list classes

8.5.6 Navigability

We will assume that the default for a class diagram is that associations are navigable in both directions. Therefore, in the theatre booking system class model it is possible to find all the seats at a performance for a given performance and for a given seat at performance it is possible to navigate to that seat's performance. As the conceptual class diagram is refined into a design specification and software implementation model then navigation is added. The arrow in figure 8.13 shows that a performance knows about the seats at performance and that it is possible to navigate from a specific performance to the seats at the performance. Conversely, it is not the responsibility of a seat at performance to know about the performance. The design implication of this is that one of the attributes of Performance might be implemented as a collection of seats at performance.

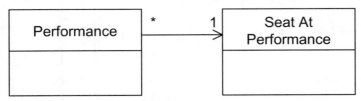

Figure 8.13: Navigability

8.5.7 Recursion

A common modeling situation is the hierarchy, where each part is made up of further parts through a number of levels. In figure 8.14 (a) the ABC Company is organized into divisions and departments, which can be modeled as in figure 8.14 (b).

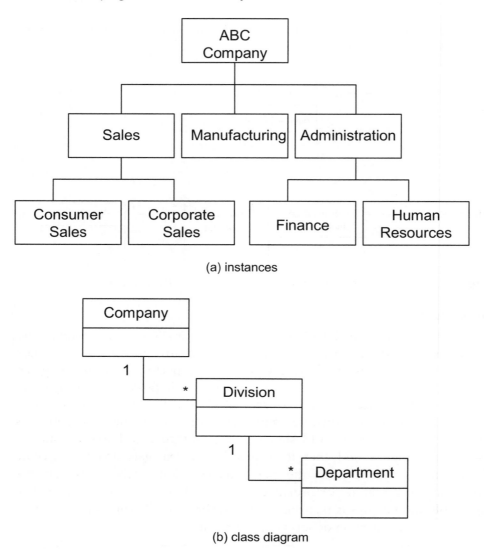

(a) instances

(b) class diagram

Figure 8.14: Organization structure

The system has been built using the class structure in figure 8.14 (b) and is running smoothly for a number of months until the ABC Company decides to reorganize and add another tier to its structure in response to fast growth of its business (figure 8.15 (a)). This would result in the class model of figure 8.14 (b) being redesigned to show that departments are made up of sub-departments. A more robust solution that will cater for changes to the organization structure without requiring accompanying changes to the class diagram is a recursive class structure. Figure 8.15 (b) shows that organizational units are made up of further organizational units. It is optional at both ends as one unit – the company – does not have a parent and some units (sub-departments) do not have children. The aggregation shows that there is a strong association between the parts and the wholes and the specialization allows the company to be represented with its specific attributes and operations.

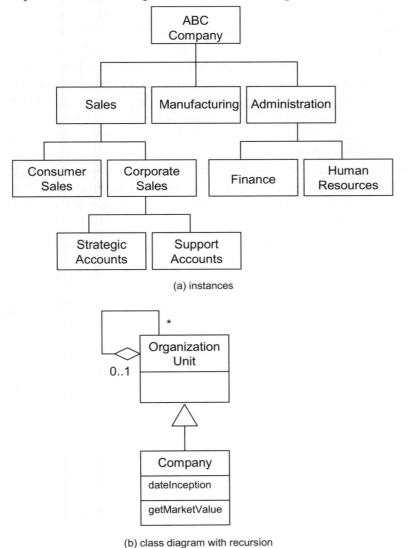

(a) instances

(b) class diagram with recursion

Figure 8.15: Revised organization structure

8.6 Interaction diagrams

There are two types of interaction diagram in UML: the sequence diagram and the collaboration diagram.

8.6.1 Sequence diagram

The sequence diagram models the collaboration between objects and actors, showing the exchange of messages needed to accomplish a specific purpose. Typically, a sequence diagram is prepared to represent a single use case. As with class diagrams, sequence diagrams are elaborated throughout the development process with design detail. At the conceptual level the sequence diagram should be consistent with the use case and the conceptual class model.

Figure 8.16 is a sequence diagram for the use case 'Internet ticket sale'. The dashed vertical line represents an object's lifeline, with time moving from the top of the diagram to the bottom. Objects are spread out across the page. Note that the class name is shown after a colon – this indicates that we are referring to an instance of the class, a particular production or performance rather than the class itself. Arrows represent the passing of messages from object to object. When a message is sent to an object it invokes an operation supported by that object's interface. The period of time that the operation is active is shown by a rectangle on the object's lifeline.

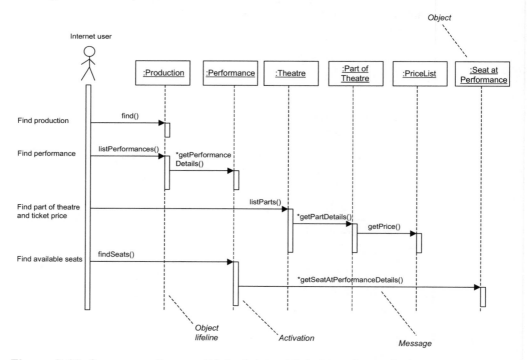

Figure 8.16: Sequence diagram 'Make Internet ticket purchase: find seats at performance'

In figure 8.16 the collaboration begins with the Internet user finding a production. The production responds to the user by returning the details of the selected production (the return message is not shown, although it can be where it aids understanding). The user then requests a list of performances for the production by invoking the listPerformances() operation of the production object. The production object satisfies the request by sending the message [for all of the production's performances] getPerformanceDetails(). The iteration is shown by an asterisk. The Internet user then finds the prices for the different parts of the theatre by sending a message to the theatre. The next stage of the process is to find available seats.

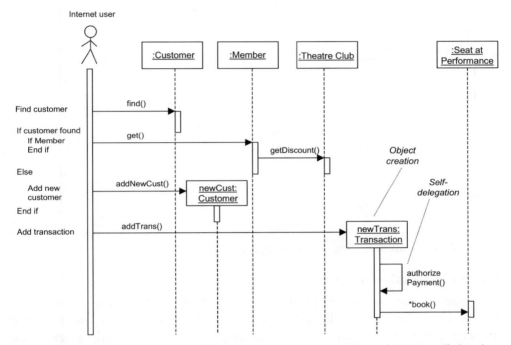

Figure 8.17: Sequence diagram 'Make Internet ticket purchase (continued): book seats at performance'

In the second part of the Internet ticket sale use case (figure 8.17) the sequence is to check for an existing customer (and add a new one if needed), to check if the customer is due a discount on the price as a member, take payment and write the transaction, and finally to change the seat at performance status to booked. Note that instances are created for new customers and for the transaction class. The creation is shown at the point in the timeline they are created.

Separating the use case into two parts is rather useful since the find seats and book seats parts of the use case could be reused. As well as creating new objects, a message might invoke the destruction of an object. In the use case 'cancel performance' the performance object then sends messages to invoke the object destruction operation for the seats at performance associated with that performance object (figure 8.18). The performance then sends a message to itself (reflexive) to destroy the performance instance.

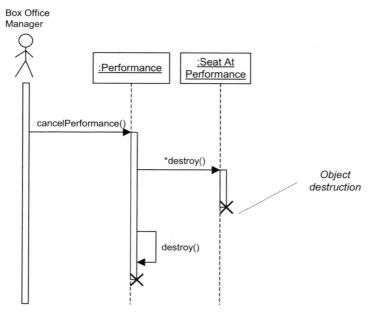

Figure 8.18: Sequence diagram with object destruction

8.6.2 Collaboration diagram

Collaboration diagrams are the second interaction modeling technique in the UML. They are strongly linked to sequence diagrams. Again, arrows show messages, but in the collaboration diagram numbers are used to show the sequence of messaging.

Both forms of interaction diagram show collaboration between objects. From an analysis and conceptual modeling perspective it is probably sufficient to prepare a sequence diagram. As the diagrams are refined for design purposes then the collaboration diagram becomes more useful, allowing packages of processing to be identified from clusters of interactions. We have introduced some conditional behaviour into the second part of the sequence diagram (figure 8.17) to branch for customers who are members. As more conditional processing is added the interaction diagrams get more and more convoluted and it is wise to consider developing different diagrams for different scenarios, e.g., 'Internet ticket purchase by member' and 'Internet ticket purchase by non-member'.

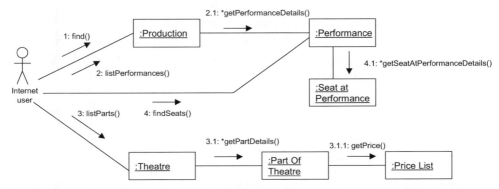

Figure 8.19: Collaboration diagram 'Make Internet ticket purchase: find seats at performance'

8.7 State transition diagrams

The class model has defined the structural aspects of the system and interaction diagrams show how objects interact to achieve a specific purpose, as defined by a use case. As we have seen already, an object can take on a number of states at different times – is the seat at performance available, reserved, or booked? More formally, a state is a 'condition or situation in the life of an object during which it satisfies some condition, performs some activity, or waits for some event' (Booch et al., 1999, p. 333).

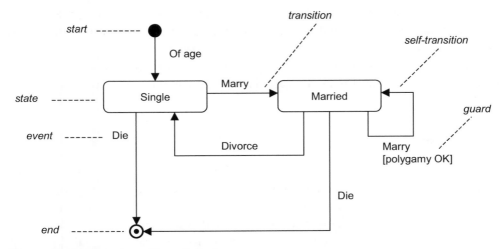

Figure 8.20: State transition diagram

An event is something that happens in space and time: 'user clicks on button', 'it begins to rain', 'I've been waiting for 5 minutes in a telephone queue'. It is events that trigger changes in the state of objects – a state transition. When a user clicks on a button the result might be to maximize a window on the screen, i.e., a state change for the window from minimized to maximized. If it starts to rain then person changes to person with open umbrella; if I have been waiting for 10 minutes I will cancel my call and become a dissatisfied customer.

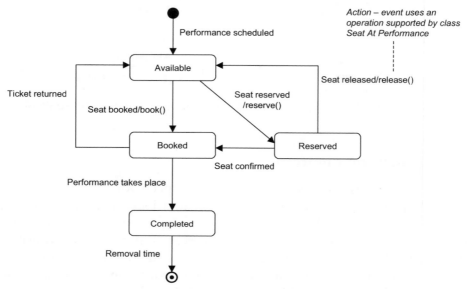

Figure 8.21: State transition diagram for class Seat At Performance

A state transition diagram shows the different life-cycles that an object of a class can undergo. The state of an instance is given by the attributes and associations it has. For example, a seat at performance that has been booked will have an association with a transaction object. States are shown as rounded rectangles and transitions as arrows. The labels on the transitions are of the form:

event [guard]/action

In figure 8.20 the transitions are labelled with events, such as 'Die', 'Marry', and 'Divorce'. In the United Kingdom it is necessary to get divorced before remarrying. If polygamy is allowed then a married person can get married again without being divorced. This is shown as a self-transition in figure 8.20 and a guard has been added to ensure that this transition can only take place if 'Polygamy OK' (of course, although our model is accurate from a legal standpoint, it does not stop people committing bigamy). The state transition diagram is a template. It describes the possible paths that an object might take. For example, some people will be born and die without getting married.

Others will marry once and others might marry multiple times. By definition, an object must have a state and can only be in one state at any one time.

State transition diagrams are prepared for those classes that have sufficiently complex states and transitions to warrant modeling. Some classes will have simple states and transitions going directly from creation to destruction. Others will have more complex behaviour, such as objects in the class Seat At Performance (figure 8.21).

The state transition diagram therefore represents the possible life-cycle of objects of a given class. It is closely related to the sequence diagram, which shows the message passing that will result in state changes in objects.

8.8 Activity diagrams

An activity diagram, at the conceptual level, shows a set of tasks that need to be accomplished to achieve a business outcome. Activity diagrams are useful for modeling business processes and work flows, especially where there is parallel activity and interaction between different actors.

In an activity diagram an activity is represented by a rectangle with rounded corners. Arrows are used to show sequential activities, such as 'receive ticket orders' and 'check ticket order details' (figure 8.22). Although activity diagrams look like flow charts they are, more formally, extended state diagrams. Once the activity 'receive ticket orders' completes a state change takes place (this could be written against the arrow coming out of the activity box): the process is now in the state 'ticket order received'. The completion of the activity also triggers the next activity; this is a multiple activity (indicated by an asterisk) that involves the box office clerk checking each line of the ticket order to see if all of the information needed has been provided (e.g., performance time) and whether it is valid. The allocation of seats leads to a synchronization bar, in this case a fork. If there are insufficient seats available for a performance then the request is put on the wait list. In parallel to allocating seats the payment is checked. The diamond is a control condition indicating that a decision is taken. If all goes well, all the requests for seats are satisfied, payment is authorized and the tickets are dispatched. If not, then the order is held pending seats becoming re-available. Ticket returns are received by the box office clerk and the box office manager allocated the returned tickets to those on the wait list.

A particularly useful aspect of activity diagrams is the swim lane notation. These are vertical lines that show not only what is done, but who does it. For complex business processes there will be multiple interactions between actors (classes, people, departments, computer systems, etc.) to achieve a business process outcome. The activity diagram might be for a single use case, such as 'perform operator ticket sale', or it might span a number of use cases (this activity diagram also includes the use case 'process ticket return').

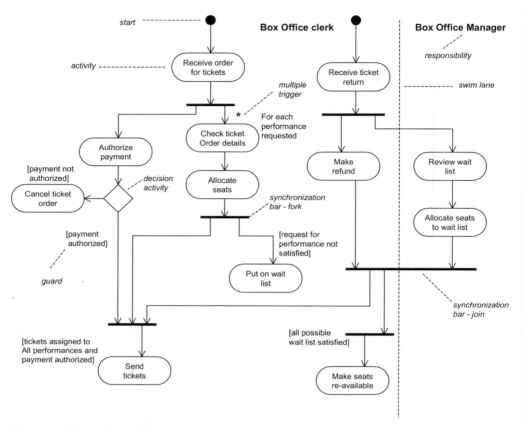

Figure 8.22: Activity diagram

Summary

- UML use cases are used to model the information requirements from the user, or business, perspective.
- Class diagrams are used to model the data structures of the information system and their behaviours (operations).
- The interactions between structural objects are modeled using interaction diagrams (sequence and collaboration).
- The internal states and state transitions of a structural class are modeled with state transition diagrams.
- Business processes are modeled using activity diagrams to show how business areas interact.

Exercises

1. Develop use cases for the *current* research student admission application (appendix B) taking into account the needs of applicants, administrators, academic supervisors, the research director, and interfacing information systems.
2. Develop a range of scenarios for how the admissions business process could be transformed through the novel use of the Internet and other communication technologies.
3. Develop use cases for your proposed research student admission application.
4. Draw an activity diagram with swim lanes showing how the various parties would work together to process research applications.
5. Develop a class diagram to meet the data requirements of the proposed research student admissions application. Show how one of the use cases can be satisfied by the classes and operations in the class diagram by developing a sequence diagram and a collaboration diagram.
6. Which class is central to the admissions application? Model the state transitions of this class.

Further reading

Alexander, C., (1964). *Notes on the Synthesis of Form.* Harvard University Press, Cambridge, MA.

Booch, G., (1994). *Object-Oriented Design with Applications.* Second edition. Benjamin Cummings, Redwood City, CA.

Booch, G., Rumbaugh, J. and Jacobson, I., (1999). *The Unified Modeling Language.* Addison Wesley, Reading MA.

Rumbaugh, J., Blaha, M., Premerlani, W., Eddy, F. and Lorensen, W., (1991). *Object-Oriented Modeling and Design.* Prentice-Hall, Englewood Cliffs, New Jersey.

Jacobson, I., Ericsson, M., and Jacobson, A., (1994). *The Object Advantage: business process reengineering with object technology.* Addison-Wesley.

9

Technical Design

9.1 Introduction

This chapter is concerned with building a bridge between the problem situation requirements, as reflected in the UML information models, and an information system implementation. It is apposite to view technical design as a bridge, rather than a transition, since the analogy of a bridge suggests a bi-directional movement between information system requirements and implementation in software.

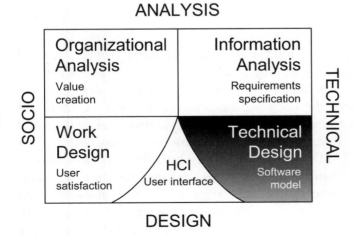

Figure 9.1: Technical design and the methods matrix

9.2 Information system design

The metaphor of time's arrow suggests a one-way path from requirements to design to implementation. Feedback loops and arrows can be added to give the impression of iteration, but this is a weak depiction of the complex relationship between requirements and design. The idea of mediation in IS development means that the social and technical aspects are mangled together and whether we like it or not, technical design should not and cannot be reduced to an exercise in techno-rationality. The technical design process must be considered within the context of organizational analysis and work design, and not simply as a scientistic refinement of the requirements specification. However, despite this caveat, in order to illustrate technical design in a clear way we will work within a techno-rational paradigm in this chapter.

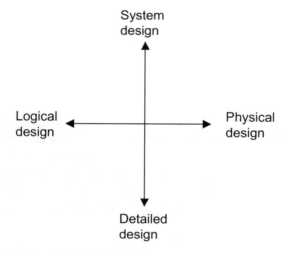

Figure 9.2: Dimensions of design

Analysis is often defined as the 'what' of IS development, being concerned with what the system can do, e.g., find available seats, process a ticket sale transaction, rather than how it achieves this end. In moving to design we are more concerned with 'how' the ends will be achieved in software terms. In practice the boundaries between 'what' and 'how' are blurred and analysis and design are difficult to disentangle. With traditional approaches to IS development, such as SSADM (Structured Systems Analysis and Design Method), there are clear cut-off points where the deliverables from one stage are signed-off, ready to move to the next stage where new notations and techniques are introduced. For many developers, the appeal of OO and UML is that the developer is not forced into making a hard, once-and-for-all, break between analysis and design. With UML the principal diagrams are elaborated in greater detail until they become sufficiently detailed to become an executable specification, or for a human programmer to implement them by hand in program code. In the UML approach design is not a one-off activity. It is an iterative process of elaboration of detail, moving back and forwards between a logical, implementation-independent design and a physical, implementation-specific design (figure 9.2). The design process also entails a movement between a high level system or architectural design and the detailed design of software components, such as the individual classes and operations (figure 9.2).

9.3 System design overview

Any large and complex system needs to be divided into layers if it is to be comprehended and managed. The system design for the theatre booking application will follow a three-tier client-server architecture. A client-server architecture links computers such that some computers – servers – perform functions for other computers – clients (usually end-user PCs). Indeed, this is how the worldwide web works. The user browses the web using a client PC that can request web pages (a service) from Internet web servers.

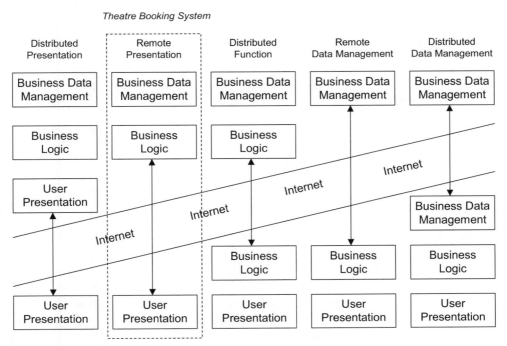

Figure 9.3: Client–server computing models (adapted from Gartner Group, 1995)

The three layers of the application can be configured in different ways (figure 9.3), ranging from server-intensive (distributed presentation) to client-intensive (distributed data management). For the Theatre Booking System we will take a straightforward approach: remote presentation. The presentation layer will be handled by the user's web browser. The business logic layer will reside on the server, but some of it could be distributed to the client (distributed function) to reduce network traffic and server load. For example, form validation and simple calculations, such as VAT (sales tax), could be handled using JavaScript or a Java applet downloaded by the client. Data management will reside on the server. Although cookies will be used to store data on the client, for example, to identify returning customers, client-side cookies are only used for transient data. Permanent data will be stored on the central server since cookies are ephemeral and specific to individual client PCs.

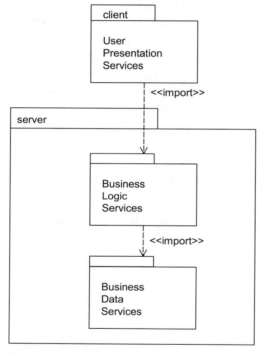

Figure 9.4: UML package diagram for a three-tier client–server architecture

The architecture of the theatre booking system consists of three layers: business data services, business logic services, and user presentation services (figure 9.4). In UML notation, each of these layers is represented as a package. The user presentation services are the responsibility of the client, while business logic and business data services will reside on the server. The business logic services will handle business functions such as 'find available seats at performance', and the business data services layer will be responsible for maintaining details of productions, performances, ticket transactions, etc.

The UML stereotype <<import>> in figure 9.4 indicates that one layer has access to the contents of another layer, for example the user presentation layer can access the business logic services, but not the other way around. This architecture will make the application easier to maintain and extend in the future; changes to the databases or the addition of new business logic can be localized to individual layers such that they are transparent to the invocating layer. So, if the way the seat allocation algorithm works was re-specified, then the change is localized to the business logic layer – no changes are required to the user presentation services, assuming that the interface exported by the seat allocation business logic is unchanged.

9.3.1 Design constraints

In some situations the development team start with a blank sheet of paper and choose technologies for the project based on the system requirements. In other cases, the project team is mandated to use specified technologies, perhaps because these are the house standards for the organization or even just the favoured technical platform of a senior manager. In practice both of these scenarios – the blank sheet and the mandated platform – have their drawbacks. A too restrictive approach can result in the project team being forced to use inappropriate technologies, i.e., differences between this project and previous projects have not been recognized. But, what could be wrong with the project team being given carte blanche? Unless it is carefully managed, too much choice can be problematic as well as it can lead to endless evaluations and the introduction of new technologies for which the organization has inadequate infrastructural support (skills, experience, operating procedures, quality assurance, etc.). We want to avoid the situation where everything looks like a nail – our only tool is a hammer – but we also want to minimize search costs and capitalize on the existing skill base.

The major constraint on the design of the theatre booking system is that it must be publicly available via the Internet. This immediately places technology constraints on the project: some variant of HTML (and possibly XML) is going to be needed to serve up pages on the client's browser and an Internet server is going to be needed to host the web pages. Application development will require a database technology that can be accessed via the Internet server and a server side programming or scripting language will be needed to develop the system functionality. Within this broad constraint there are still plenty of technology platform decisions to be made before physical design can be completed:

- What operating system will the web server run on (Linux, Windows/NT, Unix)?
- What database will be used (Microsoft SQL Server, Oracle, mySQL)?
- How will the server-side business logic be developed (Active Server Pages (ASP), ColdFusion, Perl, Java, C++)?

For logical design the choice of technology platform should be irrelevant – that's why it is called logical. However, as the design becomes more physical and detailed (figure 9.2) then the choice of technology impinges more and more. For example, the physical database design needs to take account of performance issues, and as a result the physical design will in all likelihood differ from one database management system to another.

9.4 Logical database design

The business data will be stored in a *relational* database. Most organizations will have implemented a relational database, such as Microsoft Access, for end-user computing and an industrial-strength database server for enterprise applications, such as Microsoft SQL Server, Oracle, or Sybase. There are also Open Source database management systems (DBMS) available, such as MySQL. It is quite likely that the organization already has software licences for a relational database and some expertise in this technology. One of the benefits of a three-tier architecture design is that the database management system can be replaced with a minimum of disruption to the business logic layer and with no changes to the presentation layer.

Before looking at how the theatre booking system might be implemented in a relational database we will look briefly at the underlying principles of the relational model (see Date (1999) for a thorough introduction to database theory).

9.4.1 Relational databases

The relational model requires data to be stored as a series of two-dimensional tables known as relations. A relational table consists of columns and rows (figure 9.5). The tables (or relations) in a database must conform to the following rules:

- Entries in a relational table are single-valued. In figure 9.5 each of the cells of the table is atomic – a cell cannot contain a collection. For example, if it is a requirement to store multiple telephone numbers for employees then extra columns or tables must be created
- Each column has a distinct name (the attribute name). For example, empName, salary
- All of the values in a column are values of the same attribute, i.e., they share the same domain. All of the values in the salary column are from the salary domain – there won't be a telephone number or a bonus mixed in for one of the rows in the table
- The order of the columns is immaterial. The relational table will mean the same whatever the order of the columns. The table in figure 9.5 would not

be affected if the columns were reordered, for example, as telNo, salary, dateOfBirth, empID, empName (although the column(s) constituting the primary key are shown first for ease of reading)

- Each row is distinct. There must not be two rows with the same attribute values in each column. The attribute, or combination of attributes, that ensure that each row in the table is unique are known as the *primary key*. In the Employee table the primary key has been defined as a single column – empID. We have shaded the column header in figure 9.5 to make its role as primary key stand out clearly
- The order of the rows is immaterial. There is no implied order to the rows. To retrieve records in a given order a table must be sorted by one or more of the attributes of that table. For example, to present a list of employees in descending order of salary it is necessary to sort the rows first by the salary column.

Primary keys

The distinctness, or uniqueness, of the rows in a table is achieved by the definition of a primary key. Clearly, a primary key cannot have empty (or null) values, which means that the attribute telNo is not a candidate for the role of primary key since it is possible for an employee to exist without a telephone number (e.g., Gupta in figure 9.5).

Employee

empID	empName	salary	dateOfBirth	telNo
1000	Smith	45,000	1-Jan-80	3872
0892	Jones	30,000	23-Dec-65	2876
3091	Gupta	20,000	30-May-54	
2011	Jones	24,000	23-Nov-66	1722
0034	Singh	35,000	14-Jun-75	3442
2001	Costello	50,000	18-Jul-76	1982

Figure 9.5: Relational table populated with data

It is also possible for two employees to share the same telephone number. It might be tempting to use the field empName, but this has problems since there are two employees called Jones. This might lead us into a compound key, such as empName + dateOfBirth, but does this guarantee uniqueness? It *is* possible, although unlikely, that there will be two employees in an organization with the same name and same date of birth and therefore we could not reliably use this as a key. The typical response is to assign an artificial identifier, such as empID, that is guaranteed to be unique (because it is system generated). Look around any organization and you will see the attempts of organizations to impose artificial identifiers on its members, whether it is a student number, an employee number, or a customer number. You will see these on library cards, employee identification cards, and supermarket loyalty cards respectively. Although these identifiers are somewhat artificial, they often become engrained in the real world, as is the case with National Insurance numbers.

Relationships

The distinctness of the rows in the table, and hence the primary key, is an essential aspect of the relational model, since it is through the primary key that one table is related to another. Relationships are implemented through matching the columns in one table with the columns in another table (figure 9.6).

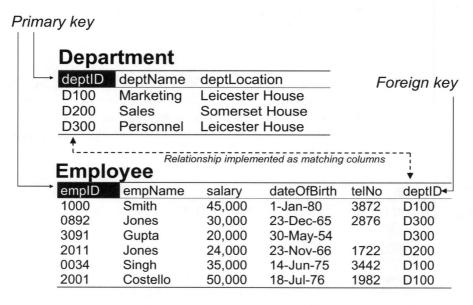

Figure 9.6: Implementing a relationship between two tables

In a many-to-one relationship, one occurrence of a table (such as Department) can be associated with many occurrences of another table (such as Employee). The relationship between Department and Employee is implemented by adding another column to the Employee table to house the key of the Department table. Thus, we say that the key of Department is a *foreign* key in Employee. The column deptID in table Employee does not represent an attribute of Employee – it represents and implements the relationship between Department and Employee and reflects the business requirement that each employee is allocated to one department (and the inverse, each department may have allocated many employees). Intuitively, we can imagine scanning down the Employee table, making a note of the value of the deptID and then going off to look up the details of the department in the Department table using the deptID as our direct access point. This is, in effect, what a database management system (DBMS) does using the structured query language (SQL).

The table layout of figures 9.5 and 9.6 is useful because it can show occurrences of the tables and is therefore helpful in visualizing the data structures. The design of a relational table can also be shown as a list, which is more useful for generating a database design. In the list presentation, the name of the table begins with an upper case letter and is followed by an indented list of attributes (columns), which begin with a lower case letter:

Department

        <u>deptID</u>
        deptName
        deptLocation

Employee

        <u>empID</u>
        empName
        salary
        dateOfBirth
  (o) telNo
        deptID
  Foreign: deptID → Department

The primary key of the table is underlined and optional attributes are marked by '(o)'. The relationship between Department and Employee is represented by the Foreign clause in the Employee table, which indicates that the attribute deptID is from the table Department (i.e., it is foreign to Employee). Graphically the tables can be represented as boxes and lines with multiplicity in similar fashion to the way the UML class model is drawn (figure 9.7). The boxes represent entities (tables) and the lines represent relationships and the diagram is known as an entity-relationship model.

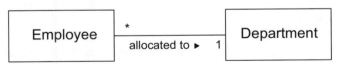

Figure 9.7: Graphical presentation of a relational schema (entity-relationship model) in UML-style notation

Normalization

Relational databases have a strong theoretical foundation in set theory and implement a relational algebra that specifies the operations that can be carried out on relations in mathematical terms. The aim of breaking a data structure down into a set of two-dimensional tables is to remove data redundancy and to ensure data integrity and consistency. The fact that an employee has a salary is held only once, and if the salary of an employee changes then the changed salary is reflected automatically in all the reports and applications that use that database.

The process for ensuring that a set of tables in a database design conforms to the relational model is called normalization. This is a process for taking a complex data structure and breaking it down into a set of tables that conform to the rules of normal form. The database designer moves in stepwise fashion through different stages of normalization, from first normal form to third normal form (at least) and on to fifth normal form (ideally). It is outside the scope of this book to include details of the normalization process, which we leave to specialist books on database design (Date, 1999). However, an experienced data modeler will intuitively develop normalized models.

9.4.2 Moving from UML class model to relational schema

The design of a relational database using an entity-relationship model that shows primary and foreign keys is a logical design activity. Although it is often used as an information modeling technique (e.g., in SSADM) for analysis it is more rightly seen as a design activity since it is predicated on a specific database model, namely the relational model. The UML class diagram is less implementation dependent and is therefore more suitable for expressing information requirements of the problem situation.

UML/OO	Relational theory	Logical database design	Physical Database	Physical file system	Spread sheet
Class	Relation	Entity	Table	File	Spread sheet
Instance/ object	Tuple	Occurrence	Row	Record	Row
Attribute	Attribute	Attribute	Column	Field	Column
Association	Relationship	Relationship	Relationship	Pointer	Lookup

Table 9.1: Loosely allied concepts

The move from analysis design has involved the introduction of new terminology and it will probably help to clarify the terms used and show how they are loosely allied (table 9.1). Table 9.1 is not a direct comparison of terms. An entity is NOT directly equivalent to a class. One of the appeals of an object-oriented approach is that objects are not flat and two-dimensional as they are in a relational database. An object can hide complex data structures behind an interface of publicly declared operations. As we will see, it is possible to break complex objects down into relational tables, but those tables will need to be recombined to reconstruct them as equivalent objects. There will be an overhead involved in doing this and for that reason an object-oriented database will often be greatly more efficient at dealing with applications that require complex objects, such as the three-dimensional graphical design software packages used in the aerospace industry. However, for maintaining business data in the theatre setting and for satisfying management reporting requirements from that data a relational database is a suitable implementation environment. It is also relatively cheap, tried and tested, and has a large skill pool available.

A relational database does not typically support operations, although these can be approximated using database triggers, which are rules that fire whenever a given event occurs. For example a database trigger could be written to check that when an employee is added the salary is within the range stipulated by the grade of the employee. The business logic of the application will, most probably, be implemented using a programming language such as Java, COBOL, C++, or a scripting language such as Microsoft's active server pages (ASP) or ColdFusion (and possibly a combination of these approaches).

Other specific aspects of the class model that need to be worked around in the relational database schema are many-to-many associations and inheritance (generalization/specialization structures).

Implementing many-to-many relationships

Many-to-many associations in the class model must be resolved, as these cannot be represented in a relational database (at least, not without violating the rules of the relational theory outlined above). Figure 9.8 shows a class diagram with a many-to-many relationship between stores of a supermarket chain and the items stocked in those stores: a store may stock many items and an item may be stocked by many stores. The relational tables for Store and Item are:

StoreItem

       storeID
       storeName
       storeAddress
       storeTelephoneNo

Item

       itemID
       itemDescription
       itemPrice
       ifOwnBrand

The many-to-many relationship in the class diagram is resolved by the table StoreItem, which is defined relationally as:

StoreItem

<u>storeID</u>
<u>itemID</u>
Foreign: storeID → Store
Foreign: itemID → Item

Notice that there are two Foreign clauses in the StoreItem – one for each of the relationships in figure 9.8. Although the StoreItem table has no attributes of its own, this need not necessarily be the case. An attribute of the resolving table might be qtyStockLevel – this belongs to neither Store nor Item but to them both and is therefore located in StoreItem. The primary key of the resolving entity StoreItem comprises the primary key of the contributing tables Store and Item. This is a *primary* foreign key relationship because the keys of Store and Item contributes to the identity of the entity StoreItem. The primary foreign key relationship is shown diagrammatically by the relationship line entering the top of the entity box. Non-identifying relationships, such as that between Dept and Employee (e.g., figure 9.7), are shown entering the side of the box.

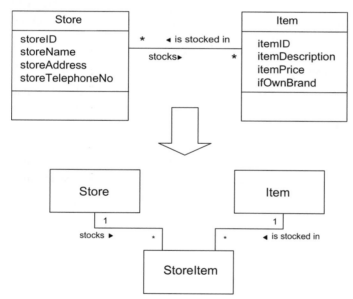

Figure 9.8: Many-to-many association in UML class diagram resolved into a relational schema

Implementing supertype and subtype classes

The basic relational model does not support inheritance and generalization/specialization directly. However, a supertype/subtype class structure can be approximated using one-to-one relationships (figure 9.9).

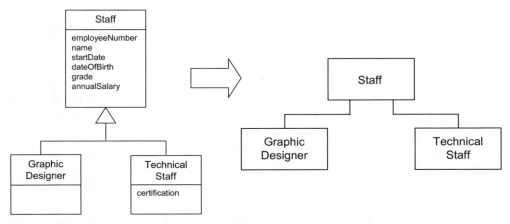

Figure 9.9: Supertype/subtype modeled using one-to-one relationships

The table specification for figure 9.9 is as follows:

Staff

           employeeNumber
           name
           startDate
           dateOfBirth
           grade
           annualSalary

GraphicDesigner

           employeeNumber
      Foreign: employeeNumber → Staff

TechnicalStaff

           employeeNumber
           ifCertified
      Foreign: employeeNumber → Staff

All three tables have the same key, employeeNumber. This is because they are all members of staff. An occurrence of GraphicDesigner or TechnicalStaff *must* have a corresponding occurrence in Staff. Assuming that it is acceptable for some members to be neither technical nor graphic designers then it is permissible for occurrences of Staff to exist without corresponding entries in the sub-tables. To access all the graphic designers all we need do is join the Staff and GraphicDesigner tables on their common column (employeeID).

There is no mechanism for aggregation in the relational model, which is modeled using one-to-many and one-to-one relationships.

9.4.3 Theatre booking system database design

We now bring together the threads and show how the theatre class model of chapter 8 can be represented as a logical database design.

Entity-relationship model

The entity relationship model for the Theatre is shown in figure 9.10. Where a relationship is identifying (primary foreign key) then the relationship line is shown entering the top of the entity box. For example, the logical key of a performance is a productionID and a performanceTime; as productionID, which comes from the Production entity, is part of the primary key of Performance it is a *primary foreign* key relationship. By contrast, theatreClubID is not part of the primary key of Member; it does not contribute to the identity of member and is therefore a *foreign* key relationship and is shown visually by the relationship line entering the side of the entity box.

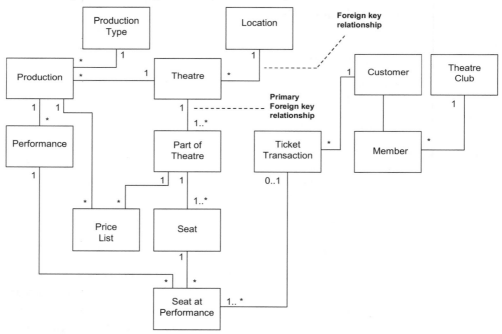

Figure 9.10: Relational database schema for the Theatre

Extra tables have been introduced to control the values that location and productionType can take on. The Location table is a list of locations that can be used to define where a theatre is allocated, e.g., Birmingham, Manchester, and Penzance. This table will ensure that only a valid location is entered against a theatre. The ProductionType table contains a list of production types, e.g., comedy, drama, and musical, to ensure that all productions can be searched reliably. In the absence of an agreed list of production types productions might be given types, such as comedy, humour, light entertainment, etc., making it difficult for customers to perform accurate searches.

The subtype relationship between Customer and Member has been implemented as a one-to-one relationship.

Entity and attribute list

The natural key of the table Performance is productionID plus performanceTime. However, with one eye on the UML class diagram and the other eye on implementation, each table will be allocated an artificial identifier that will be used to uniquely identify each occurrence of a table. This is analogous to an object identifier and helps provide a pseudo-OO dimension to the design – in a true OO implementation the object identifier, or OID, remains hidden from the user (including the system developer). Assigning a single field to act as an identifier is also a useful tactic for software development since any row in a table can be identified by a single value, thus avoiding the need to pass around long and complicated keys made up of multiple attributes. However, we must maintain the integrity of the database by ensuring that the 'real' key is enforced. Using an artificial identifier, such as an automatically incremented counter, means that it would be possible, for example, to add two rows to the performance table with the same productionID and performanceTime but different performanceIDs. This would allow the performance to be booked twice over, which would clearly be a major problem. To ensure this cannot happen all that needs to be done is for a unique index to be added to the Performance table to make the combination of productionID and performanceTime unique. This will ensure that a duplicate performance cannot be added while allowing us to use the object identifier performanceID for implementation purposes. Thus, performanceID and the combination of productionID plus performanceTime are alternate keys – either could serve as the primary key of the table. The Unique clause is used in the table definitions to show and enforce primary foreign key relationships while retaining the sense of an OO implementation with an object identifier (the ID attribute).

Therefore, each of the relationships that enters the top of the entity box in figure 9.10 is a primary foreign key relationship and will be accompanied by a Unique clause in the dependent table. The Member subtype of Customer is implemented with a one-to-one relationship and has an attribute 'user id' that would make a useful alternate key for the Member entity. The full entity attribute list for the Theatre database is as follows:

ProductionType

       <u>productionTypeID</u>
       productionType

Location

       <u>locationID</u>
       location

Theatre

       <u>theatreID</u>
       theatreName
       webSiteURL
       locationID
  Foreign: locationID → Location

Production

       <u>productionID</u>
       productionTitle
       videoClip
       productionTypeID
       theatreID
  Foreign: productionTypeID → ProductionType
  Foreign: theatreID → Theatre

Performance

       <u>performanceID</u>
       performanceTime
       productionID
  Foreign: productionID → Production
  Unique: productionID, performanceTime

PartOfTheatre

       <u>partOfTheatreID</u>
       theatreID
       partOfTheatreDesc
       maxSeatingCapacity
  Foreign: theatreID → Theatre
  Unique: theatreID, partOfTheatreDesc

Seat

       <u>seatID</u>
       partOfTheatreID
       rowNumber
       seatNumber
       seatStatus
  Foreign: partOfTheatreID → PartOfTheatre
  Unique: partOfTheatreID, rowNumber, seatNumber

PriceList

> <u>priceListID</u>
> partOfTheatreID
> productionID
> ticketPrice
> priceCurrency

Foreign:	partOfTheatreID → PartOfTheatre
Foreign:	productionID → Production
Unique:	partOfTheatreID, productionID

TheatreClub

> <u>theatreClubID</u>
> clubName
> membershipFee
> clubDiscountPercent

Customer

> <u>customerID</u>
> name
> address

(o) telephoneNumber
> email

Member

> <u>customerID</u>
> dateJoined
> userID
> password
> theatreClubID

Foreign:	theatreClubID → TheatreClub
Foreign:	customerID → Customer
Unique:	userID

TicketTransaction

> <u>ticketTransactionID</u>
> ticketTransactionTime
> creditCardType
> creditCardNumber
> creditCardExpiryDate
> transactionTotalAmount
> transactionCurrency
> customerID

Foreign:	customerID → Customer

SeatAtPerformance

> <u>seatAtPerformanceID</u>
> performanceID
> seatID

(o) ticketTransactionID
> priceAchieved

Unique:	seatID, performanceID
Foreign:	ticketTransactionID → TicketTransaction
Foreign:	seatID → Seat
Foreign:	performanceID → Performance

9.4.4 Object-oriented databases

The technical design has assumed that the implementation will take place in a relational database environment. This is largely because relational database management systems (RDBMS) are the most-widely used form of DBMS today and are therefore the most likely environment that the reader will have ready access. A more consistent approach with the UML-based information modeling might have been to implement the Theatre system using an object-oriented DBMS. An OODBMS, such as GemStone, Ontos and ObjectStore, can store complex objects – objects that contain other objects, encapsulate behaviour, and have explicit support for inheritance (of attributes *and* behaviours). An OODBMS is often a suitable implementation environment for multi-media intensive applications and applications that rely heavily on complex objects (e.g., computer aided design). However, for business transaction processing and management reporting a relational DBMS is usually an appropriate choice.

Object-relational hybrids

Although at the extremes there are relational and OODBMS, in the middle ground hybrids are common – the 'object-relational' database. These DBMS, such as Oracle 8*i*, retain the power and simplicity of the relational DBMS but add facilities to store complex objects and to encapsulate behaviour.

9.4.5 Physical design

Figure 9.2 shows that design covers a spectrum of logical to physical design. The normalized database design presented here (figure 9.10) can be implemented as it is into any relational DBMS product. However, there are valid reasons for compromising the logical design through denormalization. The main reason for denormalization is to improve system performance. For example, if it is necessary to achieve sub-one second response times at peak periods of usage then some denormalization might be needed to reduce the number of database accesses and the number of tables that need to be updated when making online updates and queries. Other motivations for denormalization are archiving and security. In the interests of maintenance and simplicity denormalization is best avoided wherever possible – we shall implement the Theatre data model in its logical form.

Database transactions

Imagine that a web page is updating a record in the database for each of the four seats allocated to customer A pending payment. At the same time another customer, B, has been trying to reserve seats and has managed to lock onto one of the seats that is required by customer A. If the database accepts two of the three reservations but then fails on the third seat reservation then the system will be in an inconsistent state. This is likely to happen in a booking system with lots of users trying simultaneously to make ticket bookings and safeguards must be in place to handle it. In database terms a transaction is a logical grouping of database operations that must all succeed if the transaction is to be committed, i.e., written permanently to the database. If any part of the transaction fails, then all of the transaction is abandoned and the database is rolled back to the state it was prior to the transaction beginning to execute. Technical design should allow updates to be grouped into transactions and for the DBMS to instigate remedial action should a transaction fail.

9.5 Application design

The business logic layer of our theatre application will be implemented using business objects developed in ColdFusion. ColdFusion is produced by Macromedia (www.macromedia.com) and consists of an Application Server and a Markup Language (CFML). The ColdFusion server takes files containing CFML and HTML and converts them into pure HTML web pages for delivery to the user's browser. The ColdFusion Server is an extension to the web server, which could be Microsoft's Internet Information Server (IIS) on a Windows NT platform, or an Apache server on a Unix platform. The ColdFusion Markup Language (CFML) is similar in style to HTML, being tag-based, but has all the facilities and power of a programming language such as Visual Basic as well as database connectivity and many web-specific tags, such as email and file upload. We will look at how ColdFusion works in more detail in chapter 10, software system construction.

Web pages do not fit comfortably with an object-oriented approach to design. In converting the sequence diagram to web pages a rather functional feel to the design is introduced. To preserve an OO approach to the design we will use ColdFusion components to handle the business logic layer of the three-tier architecture. A component is a package of ColdFusion code that will implement the operations of one or more classes. For example, a component called production.cfc will be used to implement the operations of the Production class. This component will implement functions to add, change, delete, and list productions in the database. Components are new to ColdFusion MX (note that they are not available in ColdFusion version 5) and are stored with the file suffix ".cfc".

As long as components are used throughout the application for all types of access to the database then the three-tier architecture can be preserved and the OO analysis of chapter 8 can be carried through to the design of the business logic. By preserving the three-tier architecture we could change the database vendor, e.g., from Microsoft's SQL Server to Oracle, by modifying the components in the business logic layer – the presentation layer would not be affected. This approach also makes it easier and safer to change the business logic. For example, changes to the seat allocation algorithm need only be made in the performance.cfc component since this is the only way that seats can be allocated to bookings (using the method 'findSeats'). The complexity of the seat allocation logic is hidden from the presentation layer – we don't care how it works, just as long as it returns a set of available seats.

9.5.1 Sequence diagrams

In figure 9.11 the UML sequence diagram from chapter 8 is mapped directly into web pages (figure 9.11). Each web page will interact with the business data via the business logic that has been encapsulated in the ColdFusion components.

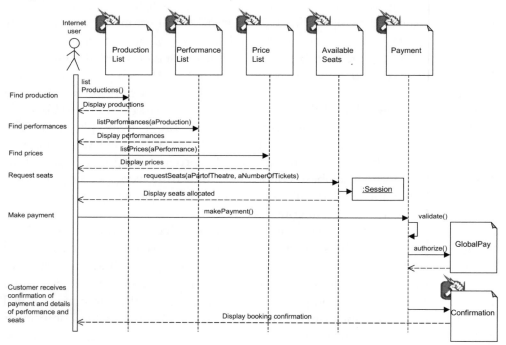

Figure 9.11: Web page sequence diagram for use case 'Make Internet ticket purchase'

The sequence diagram shows the web pages across the page and the interactions between the user and the pages running down the page. The icon on the web pages is the Allaire logo and indicates that these pages will be ColdFusion templates (different symbols should be used for standard HTML pages, active server pages, etc.). The dashed lines on the diagram show the return values from an interaction.

User registration

Cookies are a useful way of tracking customers, but they do not work in all situations, as is the case if a user refuses to allow cookies to be placed in their browser. Furthermore, the cookie is specific to a computer, not to a person, so if a user accesses the web site from another machine (e.g., at work or from a cyber café) then the cookie will not be on that computer and the web site will not be able to match the person with a customer record. One way round this is to encourage customers to register with the ticket booking site (figure 9.12) so that when a user logs in with a user id and password it will be possible to build a profile of their activity and preferences. Why should users register with the theatre booking system? There may need to be an incentive, such as discounted ticket prices, 'theatre miles', special offers such as member-only ticket auctions, or just a sense of a vibrant theatre-going community.

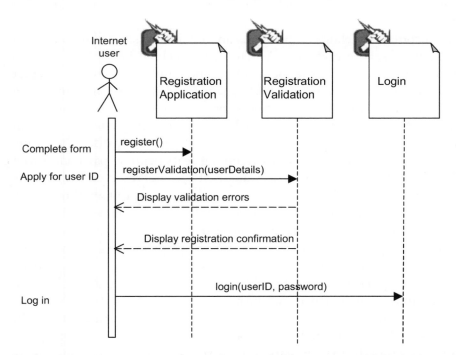

Figure 9.12: Web page sequence diagram for the use case 'Join the Internet Theatre Club'

Payments

The credit card processing is shown as being handled by a third party, GlobalPay (figure 9.11). The benefit of this approach is that credit card details need never be held by the Theatre. GlobalPay will authorize payment and return processing to the page nominated by the Theatre, i.e., confirmation.cfm. This page then commits the seat transaction and confirms the booking to the user. If the theatre booking takes details of credit cards then there must be encryption of the communication while in transit between user browser and server as well as secure (encrypted) storage of the credit card details on the server. By displaying prominently on its site that a large and trusted third party will process credit card transactions the Theatre can mitigate concerns of customers about transacting via the Internet.

9.5.2 Seat reservations - locking strategy

With physical products many web sites will simply carry on taking orders for products as they arrive and worry about fulfilment off-line in back office systems. Of course, this can lead to situations where the product ordered is out of stock and result in dissatisfied customers, so more sophisticated operations link their Internet sales systems to their back office inventory systems. With a product like theatre tickets we are selling *this* seat, not just *any* seat for a performance.

The conceptual modeling of the classes and interactions was not concerned with the details of seat reservations. As part of the technical design we need to consider how specific seats will be held in the time between an Internet customer being allocated seats at a performance and the customer making a payment. Clearly, we do not want a customer to be allocated four seats for a performance of Hamlet only to find that by the time their payment has been processed the seats have been sold or reserved by somebody else. Therefore, the system must have a mechanism for reserving seats pending payment. From the theatre's perspective we do not want seats to be reserved indefinitely because a customer could be allocated seats but never follow through to payment. Therefore, there must be a mechanism for releasing seats that have been allocated but never committed by a ticket transaction.

A simple strategy for seat reservations will be implemented. Seats will be held for 10 minutes. The time limit of 10 minutes is arbitrary and would be established as an application-wide variable that can be changed as appropriate to balance customer convenience and theatre occupancy. After the hold period of 10 minutes is up, reserved seats can be reallocated to other customers. In simplified form the algorithm for seat bookings is, for a given part of the theatre and a given performance, start at the first seat and:

```
DO UNTIL sufficient seats at performance are found
        IF the seat at performance is not connected to a transaction (i.e., seat is unsold)
        THEN

                IF the seat at performance is not reserved OR (time now − reserved time)
                is more than hold_period THEN
                        reserve the current seat
                ENDIF
        ENDIF
NEXT seat
```

This is a very simple seat allocation and reservation algorithm. Seats are allocated in blocks starting with the first seat in the part of the theatre requested. If sufficient seats are found then setting the attribute reserve time to the current time reserves them for the customer. A customer is guaranteed a minimum period, such as 10 minutes, between being allocated seats and paying for them. During this period no other booking transaction will attempt to allocate these seats. After 10 minutes it is possible for another customer to place a hold on the seats. Once the customer pays for the seats then a connection is made with a transaction and the seats will be ignored in future seat allocations.

A weakness of the algorithm is that seats are filled starting at seat A1 and filled in sequence. This might not be ideal since singletons might be left at the end of each row and performances with low occupancy levels would end up with all the theatre-goers bundled together at the front of the theatre! In practice the seat allocation and reservation algorithm is likely to be considerably more sophisticated, but at least all of the complexity of the seat allocation algorithm can be hidden within the business logic of the performance component.

9.5.3 State transition diagrams

A seat at performance must be in one of the following states: available, reserved, or booked. In the database we can tell the state of a seat at performance as follows:

- *Available*: there is no row in the table for this combination of performance and part of theatre. If we try to find a seat and the set returned has zero rows then we can add the seat to the database and reserve it
- *Booked*: if the seat at performance exists and has a value in the transactionID field then it has been paid for and cannot be rebooked
- *On hold*: if the seat at performance exists but the transactionID is null then it has been reserved. This is why the transactionID field in the SeatAtPerformance table is marked as optional – in the early life of a seat at performance there will not be an associated transaction. If the reservation has timed out, i.e., older than 10 minutes, then it can be reserved by another customer.

It must be possible to distinguish the different states of each of the classes in the database, using a combination of attribute values and relationships. Although it is often done, it is not always necessary to add an attribute such as seatStatus since the seat status can be derived from other data in the database. To add a redundant attribute represents an unnecessary denormalization of the database design.

The table SeatAtPerformance needs to be modified to allow a seat to be held pending the completion of a ticket transaction. This means that the attribute ticketTransactionID needs to be optional and a new attribute, seatHoldTime added to record when the seat was put on hold:

```
SeatAtPerformance
            seatAtPerformanceID
            performanceID
            seatID
     (o)    ticketTransactionID
            priceAchieved
            seatHoldTime
     Unique:       seatID, performanceID
     Foreign:      ticketTransactionID → TicketTransaction
     Foreign:      seatID → Seat
     Foreign:      performanceID → Performance
```

This design is simple but has the benefit of ensuring that any locked seats can be reclaimed as soon as the lock times out, avoiding the business damage of the application reporting seats as reserved when they are in fact available.

9.6 User interface design

Although the design of the human computer interface (HCI) has long been a fundamental activity in the system development process (figure 9.13), the area of graphical design for the Internet represents a significant departure for the traditional IS developer. IS development can indeed be a creative and innovative activity, but it is of a different type from graphical design. Creativity in IS development in the past has been characterized by novel applications of IT to business problems and opportunities, and in the production of elegant technical solutions such as database structures and program algorithms. Graphic design is intensely visual – it is about the surface rather than the deep and hidden aspects of IS design. It takes training, application, and many years to become a skilled database designer and programmer – becoming a graphical designer is no different and we should not expect a traditional developer to have in-built graphical design sensibilities and skills or to pick it up on the job over a period of weeks. To build a web site that is appealing and usable for customers and employees it is clear that an injection of graphic design skills will be needed for a web-based IS development project. Three options at least should be considered:

- Include an experienced web graphic designer as part of the development project team
- Train a traditional IS developer in web graphic design
- Buy a web site template off the shelf.

The first option is the recommended route to take for a commercial and business-critical web development projects. The second option might appear to be cheaper but is likely to be risky (does the IS developer have an aptitude for graphic design?) and time-consuming (how long will it take to become proficient?) and may well turn out more expensive in the long run (the developer was not comfortable with graphic design so the training was wasted, the project is delayed and the project has to hire a professional designer anyway). The third option – buy a web template – is not recommended for a business critical web development project where it is essential to communicate the organization's identity and brand image, but it can be worth considering where time and budget are constrained (see www.projectseven.com for DreamWeaver web site templates for under $100). All in all, the most likely route is the appointment of a professional web designer to the IS development team.

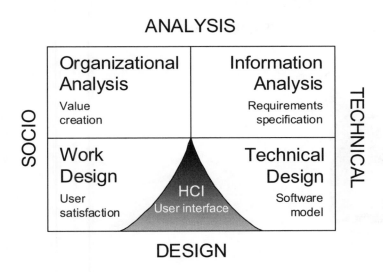

Figure 9.13: Human computer interface design

However, a basic knowledge of design principles is invaluable for any developer involved in web projects, particularly internal applications such as an Intranet where speed and cost are key criteria. Although an in-depth study of graphic design principles is outside the scope of this book, we will provide some basic guidelines here to help the new designer or traditional developer get started.

9.6.1 Page layout guidelines

The web page layout in figure 9.14 is poor – it is difficult to read and hard on the eye. Simple changes to the layout can improve this page significantly (figure

9.15). Some simple but effective guidelines for page layout are (these are taken from Williams & Tollett, 2001):

- Use one alignment – the mix of centred text and left justified text is messy
- Centred text can look weak. The left justification of text and image in figure 9.15 creates an imaginary ruler and interior cohesion to the layout. Centred text can be used effectively, but requires more advanced graphic design expertise to pull it off
- Tables are an essential layout device. The layout of figure 9.15 is controlled with a table; you can't see the table because the borders have been turned off. Tables with borders are another sign of amateurish design, although an experienced designer can use them effectively

PHILOSPHERS ARE US

GREAT MINDS OF THE TWENTIETH CENTURY

MICHEL FOUCAULT 1926-1984
POST-STRUCTURALIST

Best viewed with Internet Explorer 4.0 and up

Figure 9.14: A poor web page design (with unintentional spelling error)

- Don't get too close to the edges of the browser window – again, the table allows the spacing to be controlled
- Avoid major headings in all capitals – they are hard to read and look ugly
- Don't italicise words in capitals
- Remove screen junk, such as 'Built with Internet Explorer'
- Create a focal point; if all of the text is in the same font size then it is hard to see what is important

- Don't mix too many fonts – two should be enough (figure 9.15 uses just one serif font, Times Roman)
- It is usually best to keep the traditional blue underline for links as this is universally recognized – if you do change the link appearance make sure it is obvious that it is a link and that it stands out on the page, otherwise the user has a trial and error exercise of 'spot the link' mouse-over
- Don't underline text unless it is a clickable link
- Use a spell-checker! Bad spelling and bad grammar, such as abuse of the apostrophe, create an unprofessional image. The misspelling of 'philosophers' in figure 9.14 was a genuine error, made harder to see due to the text being all capitals and underlined.

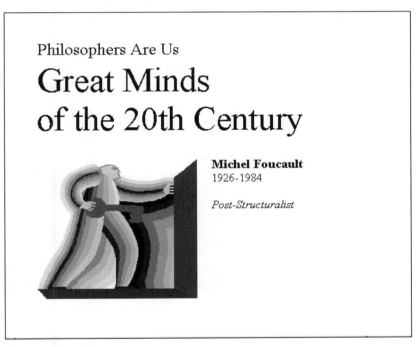

Figure 9.15: A better web page design

Some further guidelines for web page design culled from Nielsen (2000), Spool et al. (2000) and the authors' practical experience include:

- Don't use complicated background images that interfere with the readability of the body text
- Never have a splash screen, especially if it has long-winded Flash animation
- Don't use animations. Animated images (GIFs) can be amusing first time but they tire quickly and then become intensely annoying. If you must have an animation, set it to run once and then turn off

- Don't require the user to have a plug-in and don't use grandiose Flash animations unless there is a good reason to do so
- Keep multi-media file sizes to a minimum and where they are used give the file size or clip time to give an idea of download time. Don't use photos unless they add value and think about providing thumbnails to speed up page loading time
- Open links in the current window rather than a new one; users don't like you cluttering up their screen and can feel trapped on your site
- Don't use pop-up windows, especially if they contain advertising
- Don't create images that look like buttons but are just decoration as this will confuse navigation
- Avoid white on black or white on blue if the aim is maximum readability – black on white is still the best. Don't compromise readability for visual impact
- Don't make the user scroll sideways. To be absolutely safe design for a 600 pixel width since the full 640 is never available due to the frame borders of the browser window
- Scrolling vertically is acceptable. Some designers keep the pages short so that nothing is 'below the fold' but this can lead to too many pages with low content. Users don't necessarily mind scrolling downwards
- A clean serif face is most readable for large amounts of text, such as Times Roman. Sans serif fonts create a pleasing image and can be used effectively for headings and diagrams
- Don't be too tied up with traditional measures of readability – users scan web pages more than they read them, so busy pages that are hard to read might actually be good for scanning
- Think about providing printer-friendly versions of web pages that users might want to print out (e.g., a programme of theatre events) or creating Acrobat pdf files
- To get the user experience at its ugliest, make sure you test your site with a dial-up connection and a 486 PC with a 14 inch monitor
- Check the site regularly for dead links.

The basic message is 'simple is usually better' – especially if your design skills are limited. However, these are only rules (remember to challenge 'universals', as we did in chapter 5) and with experience the developer will come to know how and when to break them.

9.6.2 Navigation schemes

The key to good navigation is to make the flow from page to page as easy as possible for the user. Navigation and content are inseparable, the navigation scheme should reflect the style and aims of the site. Most navigation schemes are hierarchical, where high-level categories are broken down into sub-categories and sub-categories further broken down as needed. The hierarchical structure might be 'narrow and deep' with multiple levels of hierarchy but few items at each level. Alternatively, it might be 'broad and shallow' with few levels (perhaps just two) but many items at each level. Broad and shallow makes for faster navigation from the home page (fewer clicks) but the screen will be more cluttered with navigation buttons. An often-quoted rule of thumb for navigation design is that any piece of information should be accessible within three clicks. Valuable screen real estate should not be wasted on non-content such as navigation and advertising. As a rule of thumb, navigation should account for no more than 20% of the potential content space.

Nielsen (2000) advises that 'deep-linking' be allowed, so that users can access a detailed page of information on a web site directly rather than being forced to navigate via the home page. Nielsen succinctly expresses the key aims of navigation as enabling users to know: 'Where am I? Where have I been? Where can I go?'. On any given page in a site the user should know where they are, relative to the site structure. A useful device is to display a location on each page, such as

home>products>software

When buying from Amazon.com the user can see where they are in the purchasing cycle – this helps them see where they are going and where they have already been. A site structure map is another way that users can get a feel for where they might go. An essential aid to navigation is a good site search facility, prominently displayed and easy to find (the top right hand corner of the page is a popular location). It is important that the site is consistent; the navigation menu should be in the same place on every page and the buttons presented consistently. The site should also cater for users with disabilities, such as the visually impaired, who may be accessing the site via a speech synthesiser. International and cultural aspects can also play a part, requiring local versions of the site to be prepared in different languages and styles.

Frames

If you see scroll bars anywhere than along the bottom or the righthand side of the page, then it is a frame set. If part of the web page stays still while another part scrolls, then it is a frameset. Frames are sometimes a more elegant solution to web design because the menu options stay on the screen in a frame while the user scrolls down the page of a content frame, as might be the case in a directory listing, where clicking on an item in one pane changes the content of another pane. If you must use frames then make them borderless. Because a frame set contains multiple individual web pages there are often problems with search engines indexing a site's content – sometimes only the home page will be indexed. Most search engines work best with non-frames sites, but if frames must be used then provide <NOFRAMES> content to help with search engine indexing or, even better, have two versions of the site, one with frames and one without. Referencing frameset web pages is not only difficult for search engines but also problematic for users. If a page in a frameset is bookmarked then it will load without the frameset that gives the page its context and may be confusing for the user who expected to see the full frameset. There are ways of working around this with JavaScript to force the pages of a frameset to open the frameset rather than the individual page, but it is all extra work for the developer.

Although Nielsen (2000) suggests that frames be avoided (and most web designers would argue the same), Spool et al. (1999) consider that users do not find that frames necessarily hurt navigability. Perhaps it is web designers who feel most strongly about the frames issue? Generally, however, if a similar layout can be achieved using a single templated page then avoid frames unless there is a sound and compelling design reason for using them.

Summary

- Design ranges from an overall system design (architecture) to a detailed component design (software classes) and from a logical view to a physical view (software specific).
- A three-tier architecture allows the design to be divided into business data, business logic, and presentation – this allows work to be allocated to different developers and leads to a more robust and maintainable application.
- The UML class diagram is implemented as a relational database. This is a close approximation to the close diagram rather than a seamless transition.
- The business logic is separated from the database and the user interface using components in ColdFusion.
- The application flow of web pages is modeled using sequence diagrams – these are an implementation of the way objects collaborate to achieve use cases.
- User interface design principles need to be adhered to in order to create a web site that is visually appealing and easy to navigate.

Exercises

1. Translate the UML class diagram of the research student admissions system into a relational database design.

2. Create a set of sequence diagrams to show how web pages are used to implement one of the use cases developed for the research student admissions system.
3. Create a layout of how the web pages in the Research Student Admission System will appear and justify your choice of navigation strategy.

Further reading

Date, C. J., (1999). *An Introduction to Database Systems*. Seventh edition. Addison-Wesley.

Gartner Group, (1996). Discover the Fountain of Youth: How to Revitalize Host Systems for Client/Server Computing. "Attachmate" advertising section, *DATAMATION Magazine*, April 1.

Nielsen, J., (2000). *Designing Web Usability*. New Riders Publishing, Indiana.

Spool, J., Scanlon, T., Schroeder, W., Snyder, C., and DeAngelo, T., (1999). *Web Site Usability: a Designer's Guide*. Morgan Kaufmann, San Francisco.

Williams, R. and Tollett, J., (2001). *The Non-Designers Web Book*. Peachpit Press, Berkeley, Ca.

10

Software System Construction

10.1 Introduction

The technical design has taken us to the stage where the design can be implemented into software. The three layers – business data, business objects, and presentation – will be preserved in the implementation. Strictly speaking, this chapter falls outside of the WISDM methods matrix, which addresses analysis and design as opposed to software construction. Many systems analysis and design texts stop at the construction phase, but this cut-off can be unsatisfactory because it fails to give a sense of closure to the analysis and design work. We will therefore demonstrate how the theatre booking system can be implemented as a working software system. We will call this software implementation of the theatre booking system design 'TicketManager'.

The construction of the TicketManager application requires three areas of technical expertise:

- Databases and Structured Query Language (SQL) (Microsoft Access 2000 for demonstration and Microsoft SQL Server 2000 for production operation) to implement the business data layer
- Web server-side programming (Macromedia ColdFusion) with the option of client-side JavaScript for added functionality and efficiency to implement the business logic layer
- Web authoring (Macromedia DreamWeaver and HTML) and graphics preparation (Macromedia Fireworks) to implement the user presentation layer.

Each of these topics deserves a complete text in its own right – and many are available in various degrees of thickness. In appendix C resources for these three aspects of web development are supplied and interested readers are encouraged to download evaluation copies of the software and to experiment for themselves. Furthermore, the database and complete source code for TicketManager can be downloaded from the WISDM site, www.wisdm.net, for installation on a local PC running the Microsoft Windows family of operating systems. One of the best ways to learn how to develop web applications is to look at the code of a working application, understand how it works, and then adapt (play with) the application. You will often learn more from looking at a well-designed DreamWeaver web site, such as the templates available from projectseven.com, than from any number of books on DreamWeaver and HTML, however exhaustive these texts might be.

10.2 Software implementation overview

The three-tier client–server architecture developed in the technical design is preserved in the implementation (figure 10.1).

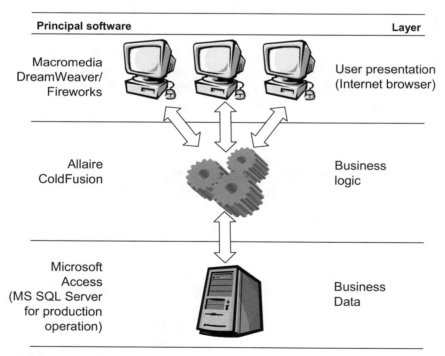

Principal software		Layer
Macromedia DreamWeaver/ Fireworks		User presentation (Internet browser)
Allaire ColdFusion		Business logic
Microsoft Access (MS SQL Server for production operation)		Business Data

Figure 10.1: Software implementation – layers and software tools

The business data will be implemented in the live system with Microsoft SQL Server, but for the purposes of rapid prototyping and ease of software availability we will use Microsoft Access to illustrate the TicketManager application. Microsoft Access is intended as an end-user database; although it can cope with a small number of concurrent users (around 10), it is not recommended as an industrial-strength database server for the Internet. An up-sizing wizard is supplied with Access to allow the database tables to be migrated to Microsoft SQL Server for use in a production environment. The business logic will be implemented as business objects using ColdFusion components, creating an insulating layer between the presentation layer and the business data. This introduces a degree of technical complexity that the developer new to ColdFusion would typically come across under one of the later 'advanced' chapters in a ColdFusion textbook. However, it is important to start with – and preserve – a three-tier architecture if the system is to be capable of being worked on by multiple developers concurrently and for the application to be maintainable and scalable in the future. The presentation layer will be developed using Dreamweaver. The graphical images will be prepared using Fireworks.

10.3 Business data implementation

The logical database design developed in chapter 9, Technical Design, will be implemented into MS Access without change, i.e., the logical design and the physical design will be the same. Although Access has sophisticated reporting and form-building facilities we will not use these, as the TicketManager application will be delivered purely for the Internet, with the assumption that any internal accesses will be made via an Intranet. Input forms and reports will instead be generated using ColdFusion. Where more sophisticated web interfaces are needed, such as a theatre seating plan, then the recommended approach would be to use a 'heavier' programming language such as Java or C++ (which are outside the scope of this book). We will therefore be concerned purely with the basic Access facilities of database building and query generation.

Object	Prefix
Table	tbl
Query	qry
Indexes	idx
Fields	fld

Table 10.1: Naming convention for MS Access database objects

Although there are numerous types of Access objects, we are concerned only with tables, fields (the columns in a table), queries, and indexes. To avoid confusion it helps greatly to use a naming convention for Access objects (table 10.1). Agreeing naming conventions before work commences is essential to the development of code that is maintainable; it helps the original programmer and is essential when maintaining code developed by someone else.

10.3.1 Defining tables

The physical database implementation is a simple copy of the physical design in chapter 9 with the naming conventions added for tables and fields, including the seatHoldTime attribute in the SeatAtPerformance table needed to support the seat locking strategy:

tblProductionType
<u>fldProductionTypeID</u>
fldProductionType

tblLocation
<u>fldLocationID</u>
fldLocation

tblTheatre
<u>fldTheatreID</u>
fldTheatreName
fldWebSiteURL
fldLocationID
Foreign: fldLocationID → tblLocation

tblProduction
<u>fldProductionID</u>
fldProductionTitle
fldVideoClip
fldProductionTypeID
fldTheatreID
Foreign: fldProductionTypeID → ProductionType
Foreign: fldTheatreID → tblTheatre

tblPerformance
<u>fldPerformanceID</u>
fldPerformanceTime
fldProductionID
Foreign: fldProductionID → tblProduction
Unique: fldProductionID, fldPerformanceTime

tblPartOfTheatre
<u>fldPrtOfTheatreID</u>
fldTheatreID
fldPartOfTheatreDesc
fldMaxSeatingCapacity
Foreign: fldTheatreID → tblTheatre
Unique: fldTheatreID, fldPartOfTheatreDesc

tblSeat

> <u>fldSeatID</u>
> fldPartOfTheatreID
> fldRowNumber
> fldSeatNumber
> fldSeatStatus

Foreign: fldPartOfTheatreID → tblPartOfTheatre
Unique: fldPartOfTheatreID, fldRowNumber, fldSeatNumber

tblPriceList

> <u>fldPriceListID</u>
> fldPartOfTheatreID
> fldProductionID
> fldTicketPrice
> fldPriceCurrency

Foreign: fldPartOfTheatreID → tblPartOfTheatre
Foreign: fldProductionID → tblProduction
Unique: fldPartOfTheatreID, fldProductionID

tblTheatreClub

> <u>fldTheatreClubID</u>
> fldClubName
> fldMembershipFee
> fldClubDiscountPercent

tblCustomer

> <u>fldCustomerID</u>
> fldName
> fldAddress
> (o)   fldTelephoneNumber
> fldEmail

tblMember

> <u>fldCustomerID</u>
> fldDateJoined
> fldUserID
> fldPassword
> fldTheatreClubID

Foreign: fldTheatreClubID → tblTheatreClub
Foreign: fldCustomerID → tblCustomer
Unique: fldUserID

tblTicketTransaction

> <u>fldTicketTransactionID</u>
> fldTicketTransactionTime
> fldCreditCardType
> fldCreditCardNumber
> fldCreditCardExpiryDate
> fldTransactionTotalAmount
> fldTransactionCurrency
> fldCustomerID

Foreign: fldCustomerID → tblCustomer

tblSeatAtPerformance
              fldSeatAtPerformanceID
              fldPerformanceID
              fldSeatID
(o)   fldTicketTransactionID
              fldPriceAchieved
              seatHoldTime

Unique:	fldSeatID, fldPerformanceID
Foreign:	fldTicketTransactionID → tblTicketTransaction
Foreign:	fldSeatID → tblSeat
Foreign:	fldPerformanceID → tblPerformance

The first step is to open up Access and create a blank database, theatre.mdb. Once the empty database has been created then tables can be added. Let's start by adding the table tblTheatre (figure 10.2). The primary key field, fldTheatreID, is denoted by the key symbol and is of type 'AutoNumber'. Fields of this type are incremented automatically by the database every time a new record is added. This is useful as it ensures that every record has a unique identifier and it saves the developer the work of finding out the last value of the field fldTheatreID and then incrementing it before adding a new record.

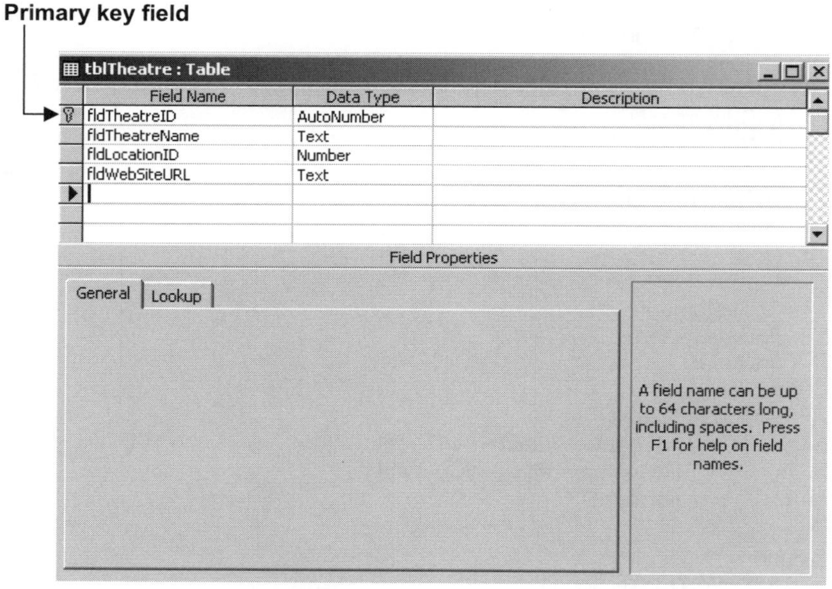

Primary key field

Figure 10.2: Creating tblTheatre in MS Access

The remaining fields in tblTheatre are given data types as appropriate: theatre name is text, but location ID is a number as it will refer to the key field in the Location table. The key field in the Location table will be of the type autoNumber, as is the case with all the tables in the database, and is therefore numeric.

Some of the tables require that unique indexes be added to ensure the integrity of the database. For every UNIQUE clause in the entity and attribute list there should be a corresponding unique index in Access. For example, tblPerformance has a primary key of fldPerformanceID. This field is indexed automatically by Access since it is the primary key and must be unique (figure 10.3). In the interests of system performance, Access will automatically index fields that are foreign keys, such as fldProductionID. However, Access does not know that the combination of fldProductionID and fldPerformanceDate must be unique. We ensure that duplicates cannot be added to the database by adding a unique index, idxProdPerf, to the table tblPerformance.

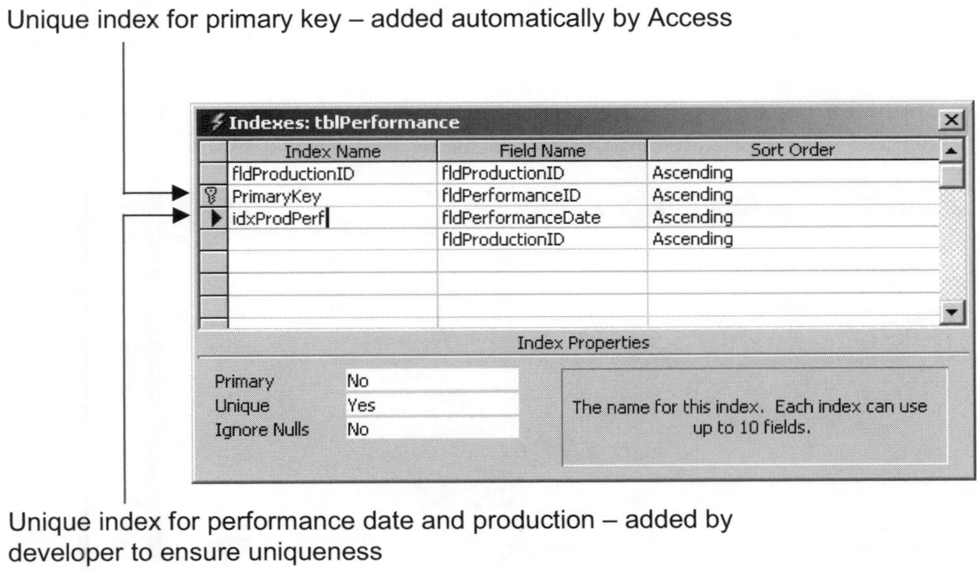

Unique index for primary key – added automatically by Access

Unique index for performance date and production – added by developer to ensure uniqueness

Figure 10.3: Defining a unique index in MS Access

All of the tables in the TicketManager are added in similar fashion. In practice, the development team may be using a computer-aided software engineering (CASE) tool, such as Computer Associates' ERWin or Rational Rose for UML (see appendix C). Many software development toolsets will generate SQL statements automatically from the graphical database design, thus enabling a seamless transition from design to construction.

10.3.2 Defining relationships

We have dealt with the object identifiers that ensure uniqueness through the primary key and have addressed the data integrity aspects of the UNIQUE clause through adding unique indexes. But, how does Access know about the FOREIGN clauses in the entity and attribute list? By using the relationship window we can define the relationships visually using drag and drop. One benefit of this approach is that Access will add indexes automatically to improve performance. A more significant benefit is that it allows referential integrity rules to be defined. Referential integrity rules will ensure that, for example, a performance cannot be added to a non-existent production. It will allow a rule to be established so that a production cannot be deleted without all the performances for that production having been deleted (cancelled) first. Figure 10.4 shows a subset of the relationships in the TicketManager application.

The '1' symbol and the infinity symbol represent one-to-many relationships. By right-clicking on the relationship line the properties can be examined (figure 10.5). Figure 10.5 shows the relationship between the Production and Performance tables. The field has the same name in both tables (this is not a requirement but it is a good guideline) and the 'enforce referential integrity' option is ticked. This will ensure that all performances are associated with a production that exists in the Production table.

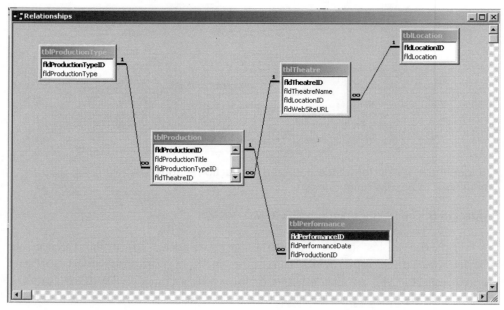

Figure 10.4: Microsoft Access relationship window (partial database design)

Notice in figure 10.5 that it is possible to specify a referential integrity option for update and delete. If a production is deleted and the option box to cascade delete related records is not checked then the delete will fail if there are any related records. For example, if a production has performances scheduled then it would be necessary to delete the performances first. As some of these performances might already have seats booked it would then be necessary to delete the bookings before the performance could be deleted. If the cascade delete option has been checked in all the subsidiary tables then a single delete of a production will cascade down and delete all the performances and all the bookings for that production – a powerful facility indeed and one to be used with caution.

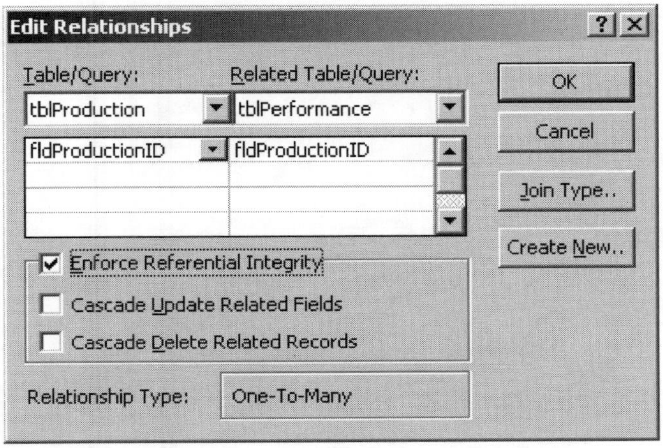

Figure 10.5: Setting referential integrity

10.3.3 Subtypes

The entity Member is a subtype of entity Customer. These are recognized as one-to-one relationships by Access because they share the same primary key, fldCustomerID (figure 10.6), and can therefore only be associated on a one to one basis. Using a query we can join Customer to Member to get a list of members and their attributes. Such a query would ignore Customers who are not members as these records would not have a corresponding record in the Member table. This query represents a user view of the database, a view in which only members exist and the user of the view is unaware of the fact that the data is actually stored in the database as two separate tables.

10.3.4 Populating the database

The database design is implemented directly from the entity and attribute list, with each UNIQUE clause becoming a unique index and each FOREIGN clause being defined as a relationship to Access with appropriate referential integrity rules. The end result is a set of empty data structures. The next task is to populate the database with test data, e.g., a few theatres, productions, and performances. In the early stages of development small volumes of data with high variety are needed to test and develop the application. Later on, larger volumes of data for system testing will be needed. To avoid having to re-key the data in every time the database design changes (and it will) it is worth investing some time in building a test data bank that can be imported into the empty database structure as needed. A little bit of effort in the early stage will save a lot of time later on.

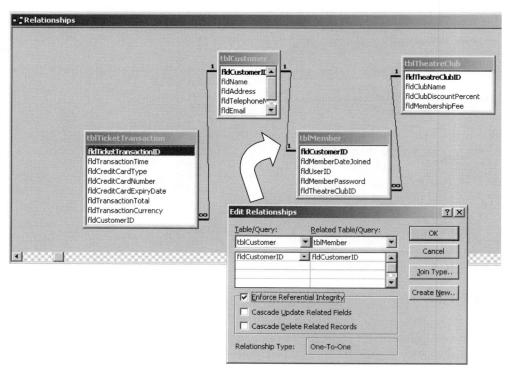

Figure 10.6: Subtypes as one-to-one relationships

10.3.5 SQL and queries

SQL can be used to build the theatre database structure using the data definition language (DDL) to CREATE tables. Typically, DDL will be generated automatically by the developer's toolset (e.g., ERWin), thus avoiding the need to hand-build the database. This is usually a better way to build a database since it allows the database to be deleted and rebuilt from SQL DDL statements at a single stroke. As anyone who has hand-built an Access database will know, rebuilding the database each time the design changes is a labour-intensive and error-prone activity. The SQL DDL statement that could be generated by a development toolset (or written by hand) to add the location table is as follows:

```
CREATE TABLE tblLocation
        (fldLocationID          INTEGER         NOT NULL,
        fldLocation             CHAR (40)       NOT NULL,
    PRIMARY KEY (fldLocationID))
```

SQL is also used as a data manipulation language (DML), to add, change, and delete records in the database and provide read access. Having established a database we will want to access the data in different ways. Consider a requirement to list all of the productions by theatre. This can be written as an Access query, such as qryListTheatreProduction. The SQL code can be written by hand or generated through an Access query wizard. Either way, a SQL SELECT statement will be the result:

```
SELECT fldTheatreName, fldWebsiteURL, fldProductionTitle
FROM tblTheatre, tblProduction
WHERE tblTheatre.fldTheatreID = tblProduction.fldTheatreID
ORDER BY fldTheatreName, fldProductionTitle
```

In the above example we have performed a join of the Theatre and Production tables where only those Theatres with one or more productions will be output by the query. This is known as an inner join. The join condition is specified in the WHERE clause, which is used to match the column values in one table with the column values in another table. This query can be thought of as traversing the relationship from Theatre to Production. Joins can involve many tables and can be written in different ways. The above example is intended as a simple illustration only. Remember that it is a requirement of the relational model that the rows in a table are not in any pre-existing order. To get the output in the sequence of theatre name the ORDER clause is used (table 10.1).

fldTheatreName	FldWebsiteURL	fldProductionTitle
Adelphi Theatre	www.adelphi.com	Anyone For Dennis
Barchester Playhouse	www.barchesterplayhouse.com	Hamlet
Barchester Playhouse	www.barchesterplayhouse.com	Oliver
Everyman Theatre	www.everyman.com	Cats
Globe Theatre	www.globe.com	Hamlet

Table 10.2: Results of the query qryListTheatreProduction

10.4 Business logic

10.4.1 Using ColdFusion to publish a database on the Internet

Allaire's ColdFusion is used to implement the functionality of the application. ColdFusion is a scripting language that involves writing tags that are then converted to HTML for delivery to the client browser. In simple terms, any page that has the extension '.cfm' will be intercepted by the ColdFusion Application Server and processed on the server before being handed back to the web server as straight HTML for return to the client (figure 10.7). In ColdFusion, web pages with the extension .cfm are known as ColdFusion

templates. There is a potential for confusion between a ColdFusion template –
which is used to generate HTML content for delivery to the user browser –
and a DreamWeaver template, which is used by the web site designer to create
a design layout for the 'real' web pages that will be served up to a client.

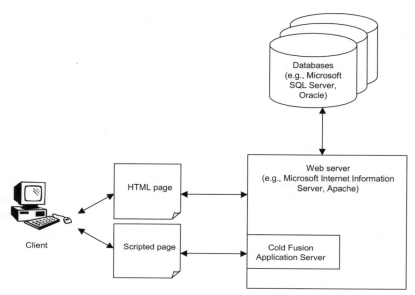

Figure 10.7: ColdFusion Server

To give a flavour of the power of ColdFusion, we will list the contents of
the table tblProductionType in a web browser using the MS Access query
qryProductionType. The ColdFusion template is a mixture of standard HTML
and ColdFusion tags. These tags are processed on the server to generate pure
HTML that is served up to the client browser. Assume that the ColdFusion
template, listprodtype.cfm, is as follows:

```
<html>
<head>
<title>Production Type list</title>
</head>
<body>
<cfquery name="productionTypeList" datasource="theatre">
select *
from qryProductionType
order by fldProductionType
</cfquery>
<h1>ProductionType List</h1>
<cfoutput query="productionTypeList">
#fldProductionTypeID#: #fldProductionType#<br>
</cfoutput>
</body>
</html>
```

The ColdFusion tags used in this example are <CFQuery> and <CFOutput>; one executes a SQL statement to query the database and the other presents the results back to the browser. The <CFQuery> tag accesses the MS Access database (theatre.mdb) via the parameter 'datasource'. The datasource 'theatre' is established and tuned using the ColdFusion administrator interface, keeping the code free from the details of database connectivity. The <CFOutput> tag cycles through the records returned by the query replacing the fields surrounded by '#' characters with the actual database content. To achieve the same result with Active Server Pages (ASP) would require a lot more code – explicit code to loop through the records and provision of full details of the database connection. The HTML delivered to the browser by the server and the browser output are shown in figure 10.8.

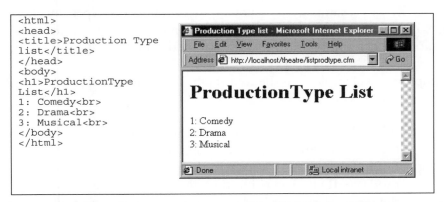

Figure 10.8: HTML source generated by ColdFusion for delivery to user browser

Queries and the three ANSI three-level architecture model

By defining a query in MS Access it is possible to achieve a degree of insulation from the underlying database structure. A general rule is to use queries (known as views in MS SQL Server) so that changes to the underlying tables do not necessarily result in changes to the business logic. This preserves the ANSI three-level architecture where the external or user view (implemented as queries in Access), the conceptual view (implemented as tables in Access), and the internal or physical view of the database (implemented using the JET database engine in MS Access) are kept separate. Users, who can be people and programs, should only access the database via a user view, i.e., using a query in MS Access. If one user is allowed to see the details of employees but not their salaries then their view will not contain this field – it is as though this field does not exist in the database. Another user might be able to access all the employee details, including salary, but only for box office staff. The three-level model also means that changes to the physical storage of data in the DBMS do not lead to changes in the database tables. Furthermore, changes to the conceptual view (the Access tables) do not necessarily mean that the programmes using that view need to be rewritten – it may be sufficient to rewrite the query.

This three-level database model should not be confused with the three-tier application architecture adopted for the TicketManager application. The business logic tier of the application architecture should only access the database via user views, i.e., MS Access queries. We would therefore expect all of our SQL statements in ColdFusion templates to refer to MS Access query objects (prefixed 'qry') and never to MS Access base tables (prefixed 'tbl'). This is another good reason for implementing and adhering to naming standards.

10.4.2   Developing ColdFusion components for the business logic

In the technical design we proposed that the operations of each of the classes would be implemented using components, a new feature introduced in ColdFusion MX. For example, to maintain the production types business objects we will build a component called productionType that is stored in the file productiontype.cfc and will support the methods 'add', 'change', 'delete', and 'get'.

The component will implement the four methods as functions:

add	a new record is added to the database with value of fldProductionType set to the argument prodType
change	the value of fldProductionType in the record with fldProductionTypeID equal to the argument prodTypeID is changed to the value of prodType
delete	the record with a fldProductionTypeID value equal to the value of the argument prodTypeID is deleted
get	a query containing all the records in the qryProductionType view is returned

In figure 10.9 the form completed by the user to add a new type of production is shown, in this case a new type called 'Stand-up Comedy' is to be added. On clicking submit, the template maintainprodtype.cfm is invoked. This template calls the component productiontype.cfc using the method 'add' and then uses the method 'get' to list the updated contents of the database.

In the productiontype.cfc component there are four functions, each of which is defined by the <CFFunction> tag. Depending on the method called, different SQL statements are executed by the productionType component. To add a new record the SQL Insert statement is executed, to change a record SQL Update is executed, to delete a record SQL Delete is used, and to get a set of records the SQL Select statement is used. Each of the functions requires different inputs, which are specified using <CFArgument>. For example, to delete a production type from the database only the value of the fldProductionTypeID to be removed from the database need be passed to the function. Three of the functions – add, change, delete – alter the contents of the database and could be written such that they do not return a result to the caller. In the code listing above, they actually return a Boolean value, which is set to TRUE to indicate the operation on the database was completed. Additional code should be added to the component to check that the database operation was indeed successful, to catch any errors, and in the event of a problem, return a Boolean value of FALSE to the caller. The 'getProdTypes' function is slightly different because it does not alter the database contents but returns a result of type 'query' – a recordset containing the results of running the SQL Select statement.

The code listing for component productiontype.cfc is as follows:

```
<!---
Comment: ColdFusion Component to manage production type data
--->
<cfcomponent>

<!---
Comment: function to add a new production type to the database.
--->
<cffunction access="public" name="addProdType" output="false" returntype="boolean">
        <cfargument name="prodType" type="string" required="true" default="">
        <cfquery datasource="theatre">
         Insert into qryProductionType (fldProductionType)
         values ('#prodType#')
        </cfquery>
                <cfset resultAdd=TRUE>
                <cfreturn resultAdd>
</cffunction>

<!---
Comment: function to delete a production type to the database
--->
<cffunction access="public" name="deleteProdType" output="false" returntype="boolean">
        <cfargument name="prodTypeID" type="numeric" required="true" default="">
        <cfquery datasource="theatre">
         Delete from qryProductionType
         Where fldProductionTypeID = #prodTypeID#
        </cfquery>
                <cfset resultDelete=TRUE>
                <cfreturn resultDelete>
</cffunction>
```

```
<!---
Comment: function to change a production type from the database
--->
<cffunction access="public" name="changeProdType" output="false" returntype="boolean">
        <cfargument name="prodTypeID" type="numeric" required="true" default="">
        <cfargument name="prodType" type="string" required="true" default="">
        <cfquery datasource="theatre">
          Update qryProductionType
          Set fldProductionType = '#prodType#'
          Where fldProductionTypeID = #prodTypeID#
        </cfquery>
                <cfset resultChange=TRUE>
                <cfreturn resultChange>
</cffunction>


<!---
Comment: function to retrieve recordset of all production types
--->
<cffunction access="public" name="getProdTypes" output="false" returntype="query">
        <cfquery datasource="theatre" name="productiontype">
                select *
                from qryProductionType
                order by fldProductionType
        </cfquery>
                <cfset outputData="#productiontype#">
                <cfreturn outputData>
</cffunction>

</cfcomponent>
```

To invoke a method in a component from a ColdFusion template (such as maintainprodtype.cfm) the <CFInvoke> tag is used. For example, to add a new production type the following code can be used:

```
<cfinvoke
 component="theatremx.cfc.productiontype"
 method="addProdType"
 returnvariable="addSuccess">
 <cfinvokeargument name="prodType" value="Stand-up comedy">
</cfinvoke>
```

In practice, the value of the prodType argument will be retrieved from a form (as in figure 10.9) and a variable then passed to the component:

```
<cfinvokeargument name="prodType" value="#form.prodType#">
```

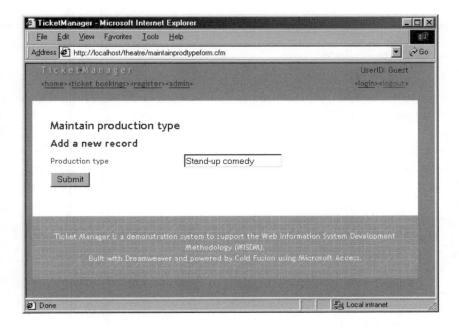

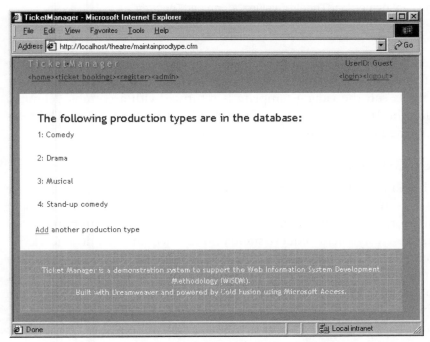

Figure 10.9: Form for collecting the new production type and the form result

To obtain a recordset containing all the production types in the database the calling ColdFusion template invokes the function 'getProdTypes':

```
<cfinvoke
 component="theatremx.cfc.productiontype"
 method="getProdTypes"
 returnvariable="prodTypeRecSet">
</cfinvoke>
```

The recordset returned in prodTypeRecSet is then used in conjunction with a <CFOutput> tag to display details of the production type query in the user browser.

If all applications use components to interface with the business data layer for add, change, delete, and read operations then changes to the business logic, such as the seat allocation algorithm can be made, secure in the knowledge that the change will be implemented in all areas of TicketManager and any other Internet applications that use the tag. For example, the seat allocation routine contains a considerable number of lines of code, but to invoke it from the user presentation layer is simple:

```
<cfinvoke
 component="theatremx.cfc.performance"
 method="findSeats"
 returnvariable="allocatedSeatList">
 <cfinvokeargument name="partTheatre" value="#form.partTheatre#">
 <cfinvokeargument name="performance" value="#form.performance#">
</cfinvoke>
```

The calling template of the method 'findSeats' simply specifies the identifiers for the user-selected performance and part of theatre. When the invocation tag is run the calling template is returned with a comma-delimited list containing the IDs of the seat numbers that have been allocated. The seats can now be presented to the user for confirmation of purchase.

10.4.3 State management

The ticket booking system requires us to be able to manage the state of the clients. There is no easy way for a server to manage the state of the client sessions, due to the inherent statelessness of client and server communications on the Internet. Every client request stands on its own and has no knowledge of prior interactions. This means that a variable set during one request, such as the productionID of the production a customer wants to find seats for is not available to the next processed request (e.g., the next web page). There are three main ways of addressing state on the Internet: URL parameters, cookies, and session variables. The TicketManager application will make use of all three approaches.

URL parameters and form fields

The simplest way of remembering state is to pass parameters between pages using the URL string, for example the web page productionlist.cfm might have the following link:

http://www.wisdm.net/theatre/performancelist.cfm?productionID=6

The value of the production is now accessible to the ColdFusion page performancelist.cfm, which can display the performances associated with the production where the production ID is equal to 6. This is simple and convenient and works best where the navigation is fixed, as is the case when users navigate from productionlist.cfm to performancelist.cfm. Form fields can also be used to pass values between pages and hidden form fields can be used to pass parameters from page to page to page. All of these techniques are used in the TicketManager application.

Cookies

Passing parameters from page to page works fine, but it becomes cumbersome, particularly where a parameter has to be passed through numerous intermediate pages. It would be nice to store the parameter somewhere so that all the pages invoked afterwards can access the parameter. One way of doing this is to set a cookie. A cookie is a variable that is stored on the client's browser and accessible by the web server. Cookies are often used to keep track of visitors, to know who they are and where they have been. However, not all browsers support cookies and some users will not allow cookies to be written to their browsers due to concerns about how the data collected will be used, and concerns about possible breaches of security.

In the theatre booking system cookies will be used to write the customer ID to the client browser of any visitor who has bought a ticket or has registered for membership. This will allow the application to identify and welcome back previous customers. When the user visits the site, if a cookie is found in their browser then the customer id is looked up in the database and a message can be displayed such as 'Welcome back Fred Jones!'. Marketing can now be targeted on a one-to-one basis. We might look at the purchase history of the customers and make them a special offer based on their theatre-going preferences. This is possible because every customer who purchases a ticket is set up in the Customer table and the cookie allows us to invisibly recognize a returning customer. This is what supermarket loyalty cards attempt to do, but they rely on the customer having their card with them – on the web it is more like slipping a token into their pocket as they leave the supermarket. We can do the same thing for members and therefore recognize them regardless of whether or not they log in. Of course, if they access the Theatre web site from a different machine, say from a CyberCafe, then the cookie will not be available and we will not be able to recognize the customer unless they log in.

Session variables

A session can involve many executable web pages and various interactions with the business logic. For example, one customer might carry out multiple searches for productions and available seats and could be allocated seats at many different performances before finally deciding to make a confirmed booking – or they might just wander off leaving the seats allocated but unpaid for. Cookies are one way of achieving the processing of a use case, another is to use session variables. The primary difference between a cookie and a session variable is that the session variable is held on the server rather than on the client's browser. The sequence diagram in figure 9.11 (chapter 9) shows the creation of a session variable following the allocation of seats. A session variable is used to hold details of the seat booking, including the seat numbers that have been allocated. Regardless of which pages the customer visits on the theatre site, or even if they leave the site altogether, the session variable will still contain details of their provisional booking. Session variables do not last forever and are assigned a timeout – in the TicketManager application they are set to timeout after 10 minutes of inactivity.

10.4.4 Database transactions

As noted in technical design, a logical transaction is often made up of a number of database updates. To add a ticket transaction involves adding a customer, a ticket transaction, and one or more seat at performance rows. All updates should succeed or the whole transaction fail. Industrial strength databases, such as Microsoft SQL Server and Oracle, have transaction support and rollback built into them. ColdFusion has a tag <CFTransaction> that can give this facility to any database, including MS Access.

Using the tag, the transaction can be rolled back if any part of it fails, thus leaving the database in a consistent state.

10.5 Presentation layer – the user interface

In conjunction with building the business logic the developers will be developing the user interface so that they can test their work and allow users to play with the system. In developing the user interface part of a web site it will be easier if some basic organization is established at the beginning. We will be using DreamWeaver to build the web interface. There are two fundamental building blocks to building a web site with DreamWeaver:

- Make a DreamWeaver template for the web site to control the layout of the pages, e.g., the position and the content of the navigation buttons;
- Define styles for the site and store them in an external style sheet.

10.5.1 DreamWeaver Templates

The main benefits of the template are that (a) a common look and feel can be maintained for the site as a whole and (b) maintenance and site makeovers are made easier. Any pages that are attached to a given DreamWeaver template will be updated automatically when changes are made to the template, such as navigation bars, background colours, standard wording, and graphics. For complex web pages there might be multiple templates, perhaps one for each subsection of the web site; in the theatre site there might be different templates for Internet ticket sales, internal operator ticket sales, and site administration facilities. We will use a single template as the foundation for all the ticket sales processing in TicketManager (figure 10.10).

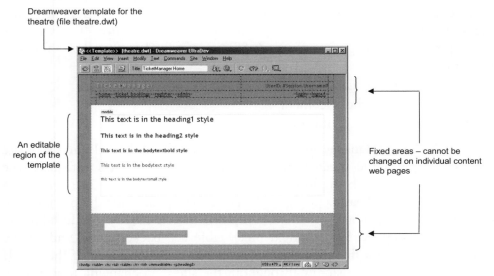

Figure 10.10: DreamWeaver template for the TicketManager application

The DreamWeaver template allows areas of a page to be locked, such as the header and the footer so that all the pages using that template must follow the same design. Furthermore, any changes to the template will be mirrored in all the pages that are attached to that template automatically by DreamWeaver. The fixed area at the bottom of the page is actually a library item – these can be shared site wide by all pages and any change to the content of the library item (e.g., the organization's telephone number) will be automatically updated on each of the pages using that library item.

The TicketManager design is rudimentary, but adheres to the tenets of good web page design. The template fixes the width at 600 pixels to cater for 640 pixel monitors (some pixels are always wasted with borders). This may be rather conservative, but the TicketManager is designed for usability rather than gratuitous style. A graphic designer could enhance the look and feel of the site at a later stage by modifying the template and the style sheet.

Navigation of the TicketManager site is in the header and will therefore be identical on every page in the application. Navigation has been deliberately kept simple and uses text links with a mouse-over defined in a style sheet. The only image in the template is the TicketManager logo above the navigation bar – this site should load quickly, although response time will depend in part on the ability of the server to handle database requests.

10.5.2 Style sheets

If you have used a word-processor you will be familiar with style sheets (you might also be rather confused by them). Style sheets are used on the web to achieve the same result as in word-processing – to have a consistent style and the ability to make site-wide changes at the click of a button. For web site development cascading style sheets (CSS) are used. These can be defined in three places:

- In the document against a specific section of content
- In the header of the document
- In a separate file (e.g., theatre.css)

For the TicketManager application, all the styles will be held in a separate file as this gives the greatest ease of maintenance and will safeguard the consistency of the web site look and feel. All the pages in the site will access the style sheet file, theatre.css (figure 10.11). Styles defined for the presentation of text include: heading1, heading2, bodytext, and smallbodytext. In addition, styles can be defined for hypertext links, table cell backgrounds, and so on, giving the designer a fine degree of control over the appearance of the site. If the styles are used consistently throughout the site then changing font weight, font colour, background colour, etc. and having the change affect every page on the site becomes a simple task.

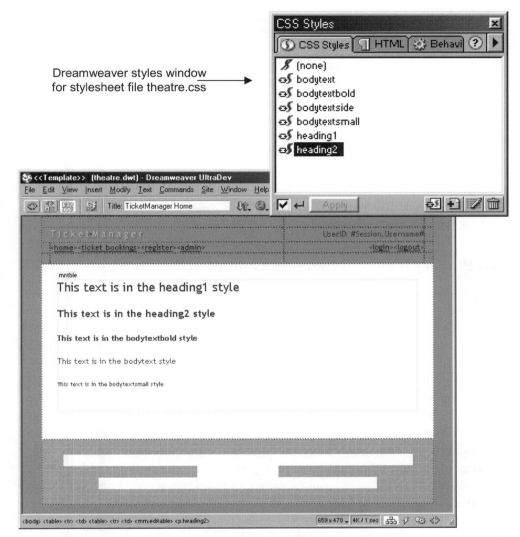

Figure 10.11: Defining a site-wide cascading style sheet (CSS)

10.5.3 Browser compatibility and bandwidth

Unfortunately, Netscape and Internet Explorer do not implement the various standards (e.g., cascading style sheets) in exactly the same way. If more sophisticated techniques are used, such as applying styles to tables, or using dynamic HTML to pop up windows, then there is the possibility that the site will work correctly with one browser, but not in others. The situation is further complicated due to older versions of browsers, such as Internet Explorer 3, that do not support the newer features (e.g., cascading style sheets) being still in use. One approach is to write for the lowest common denominator, avoiding anything but the most basic HTML code. Another approach is to add code to the web site to detect the type and version of the user's browser and to serve up the HTML accordingly. This can be done client-side using JavaScript, which DreamWeaver can generate automatically. A more sophisticated system would involve server-side code, such as ColdFusion or ASP, which delivers the HTML best suited to any particular client. The server-side solution affords the greatest flexibility and moves toward a proper separation of content and formatting, allowing delivery to different browser software and also to different platforms, such as a mobile telephone or a personal organizer.

Testing on different platforms with different browsers is therefore essential. It is also important to test the site using different monitors so that we may ask: 'how does it display on a monitor set to 640 by 480 pixel resolution?', 'using different connection speeds, how long does it take to load using a 24k modem?', and 'how does it look on an Apple Mac?'.

10.6 Putting it all together – the complete application

The complete theatre application can be accessed at http://www.wisdm.net. The Access database complete with test data and the HTML and ColdFusion web pages can be downloaded to allow local installation and the development of extensions to the functionality of the system. A few pages are shown here to illustrate how the site works. The menu options for the customer are to buy tickets or to register. Users that register can be tracked, their buying preferences noted, and used for one-to-one marketing. To get users to register may need an incentive, such as free membership of the theatre club entitling them to discounted ticket prices. Assuming that the theatre-goer can be enticed into registration then they are presented with the form in figure 10.12.

The registration system is implemented using session variables on the server. When a user logs in (using their user id and password) a session variable is created. Users that are logged in can be detected and served up with different content, such as price lists. When a user clicks on the <logout> button the session variable is destroyed and the user id returns to 'Guest'.

The first form in the 'ticket bookings' section of the site is a simple drop down list that allows the user to specify the location and type of production they would like to see (figure 10.13), such as comedy productions located in London. The results of the search are the productions shown in figure 10.14.

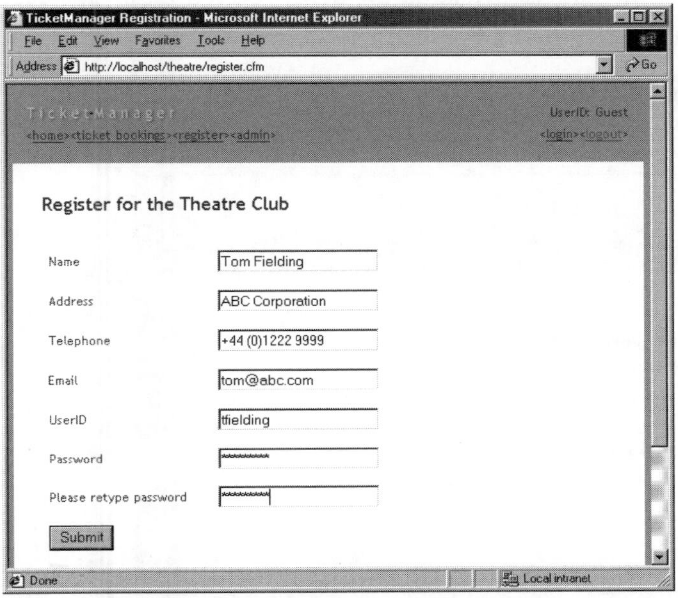

Figure 10.12: User registration (register.cfm)

Figure 10.13: Finding suitable productions (findproduction.cfm)

By clicking on 'more' against a particular production the theatre-goer is presented with a list of performances available for that production, in this case 'Anyone for Dennis'.

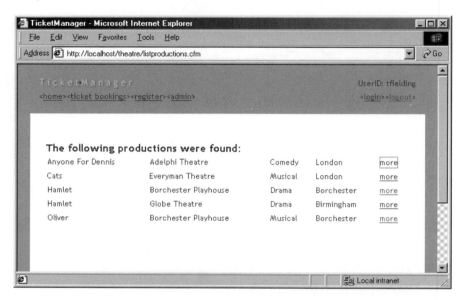

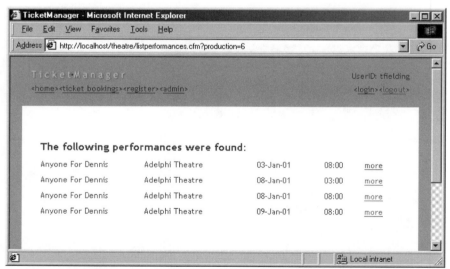

Figure 10.14: Productions and performances (listproductions.cfm and listperformances.cfm)

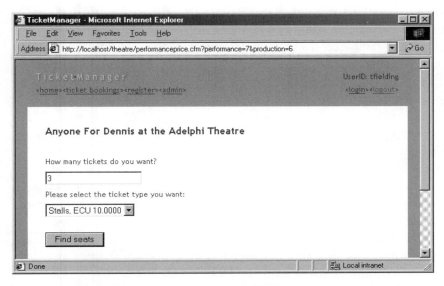

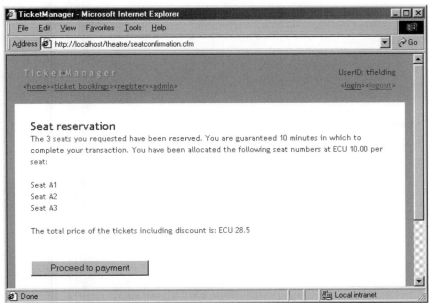

Figure 10.15: Seat allocation (performanceprice.cfm and seatconfirmation.cfm)

The theatre-goer is then asked how many tickets are required and to select the part of the theatre from a drop-down box (figure 10.15). Note that the drop-down box contains the price of the ticket for the selected part of the theatre. Once the tickets are selected, seat reservations are made. Because this user is a member of the theatre club and is logged in they are entitled to a discount of 5% off the total ticket price of ECU 30 (price with discount is ECU 28.5).

The seats are guaranteed for at least 10 minutes, after which time another customer can be allocated the seats. The time limit of 10 minutes is arbitrary and might be varied depending on demand; in busy times the time could be reduced to avoid seats being flagged as unavailable. The hold period of 10 minutes is set using an application-wide variable in ColdFusion and can therefore be changed easily and indeed automatically by the application itself, for example depending on the time of day.

Finally, the theatre-goer is asked for payment. As the user is logged in we only need collect payment details (figure 10.16). In a production system payment may well be handed off to a third party (GlobalPay) so that the Playhouse need never know the customer's credit card details, and therefore avoid trust-related issues and the responsibility of secure storage of credit card numbers. Customers that are not registered will be shown a different form, requesting them to complete their name and address details.

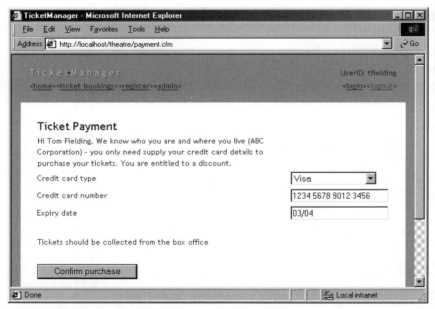

Figure 10.16: Payment for registered and logged in user (payment.cfm)

The 'admin' button would normally be hidden from the customer and is only provided here as an example of the type of administration facility that the booking office would need. The administration facility produces a simple list of ticket sale transactions (figure 10.17) – in all likelihood it would need to be developed with sophisticated search and ordering facilities to support the box office in dealing with queries and reconciling ticket sales for accounting purposes. As all the data is stored in the database, it would be a simple task to deliver a report to users showing their ticket-buying history (as is available on Amazon.com for book purchases).

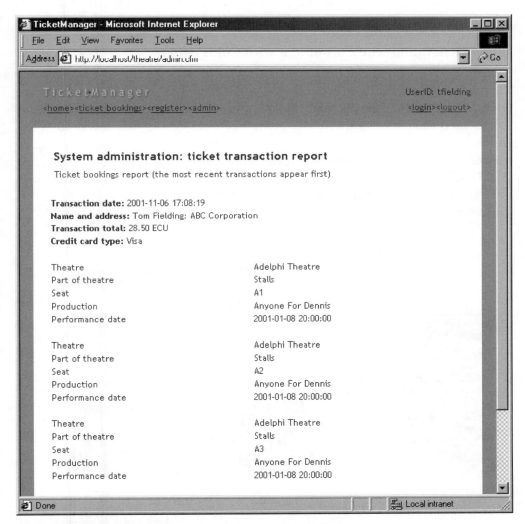

Figure 10.17: Administration report – transaction listing

10.7 Wireless application protocol (WAP)

As we discussed in chapter 2, the wireless access protocol (WAP) allows Internet content to be delivered to a mobile device, such as a phone. The wireless application protocol (WAP) deals with the transfer of data between a wireless device (such as a mobile phone) and a WAP gateway that can then use the hypertext transfer protocol (HTTP) to request services from web servers (figure 10.18). However, given the limitations of mobile telephones and WAP, rather than format content using HTML, WAP uses WML – wireless markup language – to format content for display on a mobile phone. A WML file is known as a deck, and contains one or more cards, where each card is a screen of information analogous to a web page on a web site.

10.6.1 Generating wireless content with ColdFusion

Before WML content can be accessed on a mobile device the web server must be configured to deal with requests for WML files. This is a simple task for the web server administrator and most Internet service providers will have configured their servers for WML, giving their customers free access to WML services. Files of content marked up using WML for delivery to a mobile device will normally have the extension '.wml', e.g., 'hello.wml'. Using ColdFusion we can serve up WML content to mobile devices from a database, just as we have already done for content targeted at HTML in a traditional PC browser.

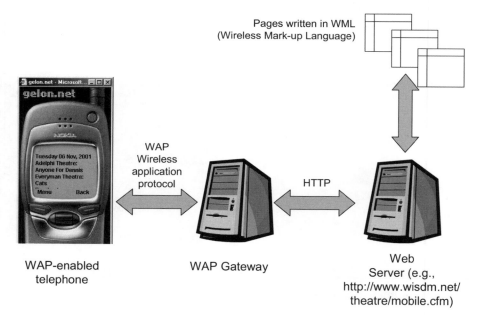

Figure 10.18: WAP and the mobile Internet

The ColdFusion server only looks at files with the extension 'cfm'. Therefore, mobile content must be in a file with a cfm extension. In order that the web server knows how to handle the wml content produced by ColdFusion the <CFContent> tag is used. This tag tells the web server that the content is WML rather than HTML. The following example shows how a ColdFusion template, mobile.cfm, can generate WML content from a database.

```
<cfcontent TYPE="text/vnd.wap.wml">
<?xml version="1.0"?>
<!DOCTYPE wml PUBLIC "-//WAPFORUM//DTD WML 1.1//EN"

"http://www.wapforum.org/DTD/wml_1.1.xml">
<wml>
<card id="Home">
<p>
<cfoutput>
#DateFormat(Now(),"dddd dd mmm, yyyy")#<br/>
</cfoutput>

<cfquery datasource="mydatabase" name="production">
select *
from qryProduction
order by fldProductionTitle
</cfquery>

<cfoutput query="production">
#fldTheatreName#:<br/>
#fldProductionTitle#<br/>
</cfoutput>
</p>
</card>
</wml>
```

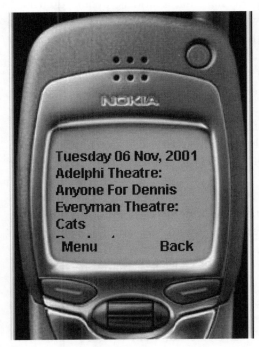

Figure 10.19: Sample output from the theatre database using www.wisdm.net/theatre/mobile.cfm on a WAP emulator (www.gelon.net)

As with the generation of HTML for a desktop browser, a CFQUERY tag is used to query the database to get a list of productions and CFOUTPUT is used to cycle through the record set 'production' outputting the theatre name and production title. We have also added a CFOUTPUT at the start of the deck to output the date and time. The output from mobile.cfm is shown in figure 10.19, which is produced using the gelon.net emulator on a PC browser. To see the theatre on a WAP phone create a bookmark on your mobile phone: http://www.wisdm.net/theatre/mobile.cfm.

10.8 Going live

10.8.1 Get a domain name

The simplest, cheapest, and fastest way to set up is to rent server space from an Internet service provider (ISP). In its most basic form this can be done free of charge using a free ISP service, which would provide a URL such as www.theatre.freeservice.co.uk or www.freeservice.co.uk/~theatre. It would be rather better for the theatre to register its own domain name, for example, www.barchesterplayhouse.co.uk. A domain name containing text as specific as Barchester Playhouse should be free, although there is no guarantee that someone has not already registered this domain name and is 'cyber-squatting'. If this were the case, the Playhouse would probably have a strong case for having the name returned, although this might involve a lengthy and costly legal process. Assuming that the desired domain is available then it is probably a good choice – it is informative and guessable since it contains the precise name of the organization, 'Barchester Playhouse', while the co.uk suffix indicates that it is a commercial concern. The 'co.uk' suffix might be used for ticket sales and an 'org' or 'org.uk' suffix used for publicising the community-based activities of the Playhouse. The downside is that it is quite a long URL to type. However, on balance, it is probably the best specific domain name for the Playhouse.

The TicketManager operations can cater for multiple theatres and is therefore not specific to the Playhouse. A generic domain name such as www.ticketsales.com or www.boxoffice.com would be rather nice domain names. Of course, these domain names are long gone and to buy one would be expensive. The lack of good domain names has led many to look for unconnected names, which often contain colours and animals: blue is particularly popular, e.g., www.blueferret.com (ferret is less popular). Sometimes it is better to have a disconnected name that is memorable and can be promoted through advertising, such as Egg.com, than a more pedestrian domain name that indicates the nature of the business but possibly projects a weak brand image.

The choice of a domain name is part of the Internet marketing strategy that needs to be developed for the Ticket Manager operation. This is a task that should not be left in the hands of the web site technical developers.

10.8.2 Hosting options

Once the site has been constructed, tested, and accepted by the user it needs to be out into live operation. There are three main options:

Host the site at an Internet Service Provider (ISP)

This is the quickest and cheapest option. As we have used Allaire's ColdFusion we will need to find an ISP that can host this platform. A number of ISPs offer these services, such as the www.advances.com, www.media3.net, and virtualscape.com. The costs of hosting at US-based Advances.com are shown in table 10.3.

Facility	Set up fee US$	Monthly charge US$
Registration of a new domain name	free	no charge
Basic hosting, including ColdFusion		15
Microsoft Access ODBC connections (each)	15	no charge
Remote Access database administration (optional)	no charge	10
Microsoft SQL Server	30	30

Table 10.3: Indicative hosting charges at Advances.com as at June 2002

For a set up cost of $15 for an Access database and a monthly ongoing charge of $15 any business can set up a database driven web site. However, an upgrade to SQL Server would be recommended since it will provide for scalability to meet higher transaction volumes and cope with a greater number of concurrent users.

Co-host a server with an ISP

As the TicketManager business takes off and transaction volumes grow there may come a time where a dedicated server is called for that can be administered by the Ticket Manager web support team to give greater flexibility and responsiveness. Many ISPs will host your server alongside their own. This gives the benefits of a dedicated service and high-speed access without the cost of a dedicated high bandwidth communication line between the TicketManager offices and an Internet Access Provider.

Host your own server

It is possible to host one's own server. For a large organization that already has the infrastructure in place this can make sense. For example, most universities have campus networks and high-speed access to the Internet (in the UK this is via JANET – Joint Academic Network). Many departments in a university can run their own dedicated Internet servers, as long as they have the resource and skills to administer them. Similarly, large commercial organizations, such as banks, have the necessary networking infrastructure and skills to run their own servers. This is not to say they should run their own servers; given the recent trend toward focussing on core business, many large organizations (commercial and non-commercial) have out-sourced their IT services to third parties. Similar arguments can be made for out-sourcing Internet service provision, regardless of the size of the organization.

For a small to medium enterprise, to host their own Internet server will most likely involve them in acquiring a dedicated high speed communication line from their Internet Access Provider to their office where the server is physically located. A dedicated line with suitable bandwidth will typically cost around £10,000 per annum. This is a significant overhead and unless the organization has good reasons, for example diversification into Internet development and consulting services, then careful thought should be given to as to whether this approach is justified.

10.8.3 Promoting the site

It is no use building the best Ticket sales web site in the world if nobody visits it and buys theatre tickets. Before theatre-goers can buy tickets from a site they need to find the site. Promotion of the site can be conducted online and offline.

The most common way of promoting a site online is to position it with the major search engines, such as Yahoo!, Lycos, and Excite. The aim is to have your site come up in the top 10 (i.e., on the first page of results) when a user performs a search containing a keyword relevant to your site. For the Ticket Manager this might include 'ticket booking', 'online ticket sales', and 'theatre'. These keywords are often added as meta tags to the web pages. Meta tags do not display in the browser window – they are data about data and are there to help search engines work out if the page is relevant to a particular search. Not all search engines use meta tags and it is a difficult task to keep up with the way in which the engines work. Google (www.google.com), for example, uses sophisticated algorithms to list a site on the basis of the links to that site. Some search engines are automated, with 'spidering' software crawling the web indexing pages as it comes across them. Other search engines use people rather than software (e.g., Yahoo!) to assess the quality and category of the sites submitted. Many companies specialize in offering services to improve your ranking in search engine results and software is available which will help tailor your web site and monitor its ranking. Possibly the simplest approach is to pay – Yahoo! introduced a scheme whereby for a fee (around $100) organizations can be fast-tracked for a listing.

Reciprocal links with related sites, online advertising banners, and online promotions can also promote traffic to the site and help with search engine placement. Affiliate programmes can be an effective way of getting high quality referrals. Amazon.com operate an affiliate program that gives a commission to the referrer. The more specific the referral, e.g., to a specific book, then the higher the commission. A similar model might be popular with ticket sales, whereby tourist information offices and other affiliates take a commission for referred sales, either as a result of an online link or an operator sale in person.

Off-line advertising should be designed in conjunction with the online campaign. This might include advertising banners on public transport and taxis and could extend as far as radio and national television. However, as the founders of the Internet failure Boo.com found, off-line advertising is not cheap and its effectiveness needs to be assessed carefully before hard cash is disbursed.

10.8.4 Monitoring the site

Monitoring the operation of the site is essential. Much can be learnt about user behaviour through analysing the web logs and many ideas for improvement can be generated. Software is available to analyse web server logs and any business serious about Internet commerce must monitor its web logs carefully. For example, how many users give up on their ticket purchase before reaching the payment stage? When the logs are combined with the customer relationship data stored in the database (preferences, ticket purchasing history) a powerful view of the user emerges that should inform future development of the site and support personalization and customization.

Summary

- The technical design of the theatre application is implemented in software using a three-tier architecture: the business data in MS Access, the business logic in ColdFusion, and the user interface in DreamWeaver/Fireworks.
- The implementation language for databases is Structured Query Language (SQL), which is used to define the database objects (tables, queries, indexes, etc.) and to add, change, and report on data in the database.
- The ANSI three-level model is maintained in the database, with the business logic only having access to data via user views (implemented as queries in MS Access).

- The business logic is implemented in the ColdFusion scripting language and operations encapsulated in components to promote reuse and maintainability of the application code.
- The user interface was implemented using DreamWeaver templates and HTML style sheets (with a graphics package such as Fireworks for image preparation).
- Database content can be delivered to mobile devices using WML in a ColdFusion template.
- To provide a live service attention must be given to where the site will be hosted, promotion to drive customers to the site, and monitoring of web logs to assess site effectiveness.

Exercises

1. Download the complete application from the WISDM web site (www.wisdm.net/theatre).
2. Extend the database to include a wait listing facility as described in chapter 8. Develop ColdFusion components and web pages to allow users to place requests for tickets.
3. Build an administration facility to allow the booking office to process ticket returns (free up seats at performance) and reallocate seats to the wait list.
4. Implement a prototype of the research student admissions system.

Further reading

The reading for this chapter is focussed on practical guides top using the core software technologies, i.e., ColdFusion, Access, and DreamWeaver. Be aware of new releases of the software to ensure that you refer to the appropriate guide.

Brooks-Bilson, R., (2003). *Programming ColdFusion MX* (second edition). O'Reilly, UK.

Catapult, Inc, (1999). *Microsoft 2000 Access Step by Step*. Microsoft Press International.

Forta, B., (2003). *Advanced ColdFusion X Application Development*. Macromedia Press.

Lowery, J., (2003). *DreamWeaver MX Bible*. Hungry Minds, Inc.

11

Web Information Management

11.1 Introduction

Organizations collect and organize data to support the process of management decision-making. Marketing managers have to make decisions about pricing, which requires data on competitor prices, market data (e.g., size, segmentation, historical trends), and an appreciation of the dynamics of the market and the intensity of competition. Data includes sound, pictures, and video as well as numbers and text. By using data in a context managers are enacting a process of creating information. The technology part of an information system can only ever hold data; it takes a human being in a specific context to interpret that data and make sense of it, i.e., to turn it into information. Knowledge goes still further and is often represented as competency – the ability to do something with that information. Creating and sharing knowledge within the firm and between firms was a major concern for the corporations of the late 20th century and continues to be high on the agenda in the 21st. Although we do not address knowledge management directly in this book, in this chapter we look at the technologies that can support the firm in developing its knowledge management processes.

We will look firstly at a technology that helps to codify data, the extensible Markup Language (XML) (this material is taken from Vidgen & Goodwin, 2000). Secondly, we will look at a broader class of emerging technology, content management systems (CMS), which help organizations manage large amounts of data in a web environment, whether it is support for e-commerce and external customers or an Intranet implementation of a knowledge base (Goodwin & Vidgen, 2002).

Knowledge, however, is an elusive concept and difficult to locate in practice, as Davenport and Prusak (1998) illustrate:

> Knowledge is a fluid mix of framed experience, values, contextual information, and expert insight that provides a framework for evaluating and incorporating new experiences and information. It originates and is applied in the minds of knowers. In organizations, it often becomes embedded not only in documents or repositories but also in organizational routines, processes, practices, and norms. (p.5)

Using data standards defined in XML we can support the process of knowledge codification and with a CMS we can manage the process of creating and publishing data. These technologies support knowledge management, but they are not by themselves a knowledge management *system*. A knowledge management system is always a combination of people and technology in some context and must cater for not only formalized knowledge that might in some limited sense be represented in software, but also the informal, tacit knowledge that cannot.

11.2 eXtensible Markup Language (XML)

The eXtensible Markup Language (XML) provides a notation for defining the content and presentation of data. It derives from the Standard Generalized Markup Language (SGML). SGML has been used for many years in document and specification-intensive industries such as pharmaceuticals and aerospace. However, although SGML is a powerful and general standard it is complex – XML is a simplified form of SGML that has been adapted to make it suitable for Internet applications.

XML is similar to HTML insofar as both are markup languages and both use angle-iron tags. Where HTML is concerned mainly with the presentation of data and not with what that data means, XML provides a blueprint of the data structure, just like an engineering drawing. For example, consider a web site that sells personal computers. There is a special offer on one of the Dill laptop computers. With HTML it is easy to emphasise a particular laptop, possibly by putting the price in a bold font, **£999**, making the font colour red, and increasing the font size so that it stands out to the human web user. There is no meaning associated with the price of £999; it is just text that is formatted for presentation in a browser. A search engine will struggle to find all the laptop computers on special offer on the web. It will be even harder to find a model with a given specification, e.g., an 800 MHz chip and 256 Mb of RAM.

Figure 11.1 shows how the HTML in figure 11.2 is rendered in an Internet browser. The HTML representation (figure 11.2) specifies how the data is formatted using tags such as **<h2>** for a heading and **<font>** for the font face. By inspection of the HTML source in figure 11.2 we can see that the code relates to PCs, but the data is not structured; it is just free-form text surrounded by formatting instructions. Each PC supplier will format their pages in different ways using different conventions, different phrases and abbreviations, and different levels of detail of content.

Figure 11.1: HTML document pcspec.htm displayed in a browser

```
<html>
<head>
<title>PCs for Sale</title>
<meta http-equiv="Content-Type" content="text/html;
charset=iso-8859-1">
</head>

<body bgcolor="#FFFFFF">
<h1>Personal Computers for Sale</h1>
<font face="Arial, Helvetica, sans-serif" size="3"
color="#336699">
<p><b>PC specification:</b><br>
<em>PC Type: </em>Notebook<br>
<em>Manufacturer: </em>Dill<br>
<em>Model: </em>Longitude CS<br>
<em>Disk: </em>5 GB<br>
<em>RAM: </em>64 MB<br>
<em>CPU: </em>500 MHZ<br>
<em>Price: </em>1500 ECU<br></p>
```

```
<p><b>PC specification:</b><br>
<em>PC Type: </em>Notebook<br>
<em>Manufacturer: </em>Dill<br>
<em>Model: </em>Longitude LS<br>
<em>Disk: </em>8 GB<br>
<em>RAM: </em>128 MB<br>
<em>CPU: </em>650 MHZ<br>
<em>Price: </em>2500 ECU<br></p>

</font>
</body>
</html>
```

Figure 11.2: HTML document, pcspec.htm

With XML the laptop can be coded with meta, or user-defined, tags such as **<price>£999</price>** and **<ram>128 Mb</ram>**. Using XML we can define a standard set of tags for describing personal computers (or any other class of object) that will enable engines to search more intelligently (figure 11.3).

```
<?xml version = "1.0"?>
<?xml-stylesheet type="text/xsl" href="pcspec.xsl"?>
<computerSale xmlns="x-schema:pcspecschema.xml">
    <computerSpec>
        <computerType>Notebook</computerType>
        <manufacturer>Dill</manufacturer>
        <model>Longitude CS</model>
        <diskCapacity units="GB">5</diskCapacity>
        <ram units="MB">64</ram>
        <cpu units="MHZ">500</cpu>
        <price currencyCode="ECU">1500</price>
    </computerSpec>
    <computerSpec>
        <computerType>Notebook</computerType>
        <manufacturer>Dill</manufacturer>
        <model>Longitude LS</model>
        <diskCapacity units="GB">8</diskCapacity>
        <ram units="MB">128</ram>
        <cpu units="MHZ">650</cpu>
        <price currencyCode="ECU">2500</price>
    </computerSpec>
</computerSale>
```

Figure 11.3: XML document (pcspec.xml)

Inspection of the XML source code shows that the tags do not refer to *presentation*, as did the HTML tags, but to data *content*. With XML users can make up their own tags. This raises the question of what happens if they make up different tags. For example, maybe supplier A uses the tag <ram> and supplier B uses the tag <random access memory>. Therefore, standards are needed to get the best from XML. If computer suppliers – or engineering organisations – adopt a common standard for describing computers then search engines will be able to make meaningful comparisons. Standards are also important if organizations are to automate the interchange of data, such as purchase orders. Fortunately, there are organizations working on industry-specific standards. RosettaNet is developing an XML specification for supply chain management. They have developed 5000 words and have 3500 words specific to the IT supply chain, e.g., 'mouse left button'. This is great for data interchange within industries, but there are also going to have to be standards that cross industries and communities.

Coordination of the production of standards means that bodies are needed to develop and act as custodians. There are many standards being developed in a wide range of industries, including Accounting, Banking, Advertising, Automotive, Financial, Insurance, Computer graphics, and Legal. Repositories of XML data standards (or, more properly, XML *schemas*) are being established by BiZTalk and XML.org. BizTalk is led by Microsoft and has an advisory panel that includes RosettaNet, the US Department of Defense (DoD), and CommerceOne. BiZTalk has around 250 schemas covering 11 industry categories. XML.org is an OASIS (Organization for the Advancement of Structured Information Standards) initiative with sponsors that include IBM, Oracle, Sun, and CommerceOne. XML.Org has links to more than 100 schema-producing organizations listed in 45 categories. The Microsoft initiative differs from XML.org in having a commercial product, the BizTalk Server, which will provide a platform for XML-enabled business data interchange.

11.2.1 XML data definitions

The definition of a set of tags is called an XML schema. These were originally defined as document type definitions (DTD), but these used non-standard XML tags. A schema that is written in XML itself is replacing the DTD. This is a purer and ultimately more flexible approach, since an XML schema is indeed now just another XML document, albeit one that happens to be describing other XML documents. In the example in figure 11.3, the *xmlns* tag tells the browser to check the document against its schema (figure 11.4) – if it does not conform then an error message will appear in the browser. It is not a requirement that all XML documents area checked against a schema, but clearly this makes sense when processing documents such as purchase orders.

The XML schema can be stored anywhere on the web and accessed as needed (this is known as a namespace).

```
<?xml version="1.0"?>
<Schema name="computerSale_schema_ver_1"
    xmlns="urn:schemas-microsoft-com:xml-data"
    xmlns:dt="urn:schemas-microsoft-com:datatypes">

<AttributeType name="units" dt:type="string"/>
<AttributeType name="currencyCode" dt:type="string"/>

<ElementType name="computerType" content="textOnly"/>
<ElementType name="manufacturer" content="textOnly"/>
<ElementType name="model" content="textOnly"/>

<ElementType name="diskCapacity" content="textOnly">
      <attribute type="units"/>
</ElementType>

<ElementType name="ram" content="textOnly">
      <attribute type="units"/>
</ElementType>

<ElementType name="cpu" content="textOnly">
      <attribute type="units"/>
</ElementType>

<ElementType name="price" content="textOnly">
      <attribute type="currencyCode"/>
</ElementType>

<ElementType name="computerSpec" content="eltOnly"
order="many">
      <element type="computerType"/>
      <element type="manufacturer"/>
      <element type="model"/>
      <element type="diskCapacity"/>
      <element type="ram"/>
      <element type="cpu"/>
      <element type="price"/>
</ElementType>

<ElementType name="computerSale" content="eltOnly"
order="many">
      <element type="computerSpec" maxOccurs="*"/>
</ElementType>

</Schema>
```

Figure 11.4: XML schema (pcspecschema.xml)

The XML schema in figure 11.4 shows how the basic XML building block, the element, is defined and used to create higher order elements. At the lowest level are elements such as manufacturer and computerType. These cannot be broken down into further detail but they can be combined to create higher order XML entities, in this case the element computerSpec. The element computerSale can comprise of many (zero, one, or more) instances of the element computerSpec. Notice that some of the elements have attributes defined, such as price, which has an attribute called currencyCode. This is analogous to the idea of entities and attributes that we used in information modeling and database design. Although there are similarities between XML schemas and UML class modeling, note that the XML schema is a hierarchical (tree-type) structure and a single UML data structure can be implemented in many different ways using XML.

11.2.2 Displaying XML in a browser

The XML tags relate solely to the meaning of the data as described by the XML schema. Therefore we need a way of formatting the data for display on different devices, such as an Internet browser. Data can be presented in a browser using the latest versions of Internet Explorer and Netscape. There are two main ways of doing this on the client (browser) side – cascading style sheets (CSS) and the XML Style Language (XSL). CSS version 1 supplemented HTML's existing formatting capabilities and provided a powerful facility for managing the look and feel of a web site. With CSS version 2 the W3C tackled the requirements of a style language more seriously, allowing all the formatting of a document to be described. The XSL transformation engine (XSLT), such as the one supplied with IE5, provides style sheet capabilities and a whole lot more besides. Using XSLT it is possible to transform the data, for example to exclude some data or to sort the data before display in the browser (figure 11.5). Currently, XSL is only supported by IE5, which rather limits its use on public access web sites.

```
<?xml version="1.0"?>
<xsl:stylesheet xmlns:xsl="http://www.w3.org/TR/WD-xsl">

<xsl:template match="/">
   <xsl:apply-templates />
</xsl:template>

<xsl:template match="computerSale">
   <html>
   <head>
      <title>PCs for sale</title>
   </head>
   <body bgcolor="#FFFFFF">
   <h2>Personal Computers for Sale</h2>
   <xsl:apply-templates />
   </body>
   </html>
</xsl:template>
```

```
<xsl:template match="computerSpec">
        <font face="Arial, Helvetica, sans-serif" size="3"
        color="#336699">
        <p>
        <b>PC specification:</b>
        <br><em>PC Type:</em> <xsl:value-of
            select="computerType" /></br>
        <em>Manufacturer:</em> <xsl:value-of
            select="manufacturer" />
        <br><em>Model:</em> <xsl:value-of select="model"
            /></br>
        <em>Disk:</em> <xsl:value-of select="diskCapacity" />
            <xsl:value-of select="diskCapacity/@units" />
        <br><em>RAM:</em> <xsl:value-of select="ram" />
            <xsl:value-of select="ram/@units" /></br>
        <em>CPU:</em> <xsl:value-of select="cpu" />
            <xsl:value-of select="cpu/@units" />
        <br><em>Price:</em> <xsl:value-of select="price" />
            <xsl:value-of select="price/@currencyCode" /></br>
        </p>
        </font>
</xsl:template>
</xsl:stylesheet>
```

Figure 11.5: XSL presentation (pcspec.xsl)

The XML data file (pcspec.xml) contains no information about how the data should be presented in the browser. This is supplied by the style sheet, pcspec.xsl (figure 11.5). Don't worry about the details of the XSL language – the main message is that all the formatting, including sorting if needed, is specified here. The XML implementation produces the same results when viewed in a browser as the HTML in figure 11.1 – superficially, the user will see no difference in the way the data is displayed. For the transformation engine to check whether the XML data in pcspec.xml is valid an XML schema needs to be specified (pcspecschema.xml). This is not a requirement; the XML parser in the IE5 browser will check that the document pcspec.xml is *well-formed* (e.g., matching opening and closing tags are present), but will only check that the document is *valid* if a schema is specified.

11.2.3 Time to ditch HTML?

In the long term it is likely that XML will replace HTML, but it will be an evolutionary change. There is a massive investment in HTML and too many people are comfortable with HTML to throw it out straight away. This means that we are going to have to live in a hybrid world where it won't be safe to build XML-only sites, unless you can control the browser software that people use as might be possible on an Intranet. So for now, this means that server-side processing should be used to detect the browser type and serve up XML or convert the XML to HTML server-side before sending it to the browser.

11.2.4 Business applications of XML

XML is an interesting technology because it allows the content of a web page to be separated out from its presentation, but what are the *business* applications of XML?

Intelligent searching

Consumer e-commerce: e.g., find the cheapest price for a PC anywhere in the world. This would need PC manufacturers to agree a PC markup language that they could all use to describe their products. IBM have launched the first XML search engine to search for XML tags and schemas. A similar approach is also relevant to purchasing decisions, sourcing suppliers, finding acceptable cost/service combinations, etc. Because there is agreement on the data formats it will be possible for intelligent agents to go out and negotiate on our behalves.

Web automation for business to business transactions

Once a standard is agreed for the data format of orders then the processing of orders can be automated, as long as the order documents conform to the order XML schema (this is a use of XML for traditional EDI – electronic document interchange). Different industries and interest groups need to develop their own XML standards to facilitate interchange. For example, the Inland Revenue will have an XML standard for tax returns so they can be filled in online and if they conform to the tax return XML schema then they can be processed automatically by the Inland Revenue's computer systems. Different software suppliers could develop different tax return packages with varying degrees of sophistication but as long as they all produce documents that conform to the Inland Revenue schema then they can all be processed by the Inland Revenue.

Intranet development and knowledge management

Content is separated from style, so we can change the formatting at a stroke (we could achieve this with cascading style sheets – CSS). With XML an organization can go a step further and build standard definitions of its data and begin to manage the organizations' knowledge by structuring it so it can more easily be retrieved and reused. When coupled with a content management system (CMS) the power of the web can begin to be harnessed by organizations.

Delivery to different platforms

Again, separating content and presentation means the same content can be directed toward different display devices. It can also be used to integrate legacy systems, using XML structures to get data out of and into legacy systems that need to be integrated with the Internet (one of the key issues in e-business).

The XML schema specifies the data content, but not the way in which it is displayed. The display can be handled by the client device; for example, the client might be desktop computer with Internet Explorer, but it might be a personal digital assistant or a mobile phone running the wireless application protocol (WAP). As an aside, you will see that web pages for serving up to a mobile telephone via WAP are written in WML – wireless markup language. WML documents use an XML schema to define the tags that constitute valid WML. Unfortunately, today, WML does not separate data and presentation any better than does HTML, but over time this will change.

11.2.5 XML and databases, XML and Java

We discussed earlier the merits of object oriented (OO) DBMS. Many thought that relational DBMS would go away and be replaced by object technology. In practice, RDBMS have survived and gone from strength to strength. OODBMS are used in more specialist applications, such as computer aided design (CAD), while RDBMS have been extended with many of the features of an OO environment.

The situation is not dissimilar with XML. Some applications may warrant an XML document server that can store persistent XML objects. Many applications are likely to store the data in an RDBMS and to convert it to XML on output, and to convert XML to SQL on input. Today you could write this easily enough in a scripting language such as ASP or a heavier duty programming language C++, but tools are being added into products to make this easier for the developer and seamless for the user.

XML is basically a way of defining data structures. In object oriented terms it is less powerful when it comes to defining the behaviour of objects. However, Java is strong at defining and encapsulating behaviour, but less useful for defining and exposing data structures (the key thing about OO is that you don't need to know the data structure to use an object – this is internal and hidden from the client). By combining XML and Java it is possible to have a document object whose behaviour is given by a URL that indicates a Java applet that knows how to display, manipulate, process, interact with the XML document (this is analogous to the namespace where the schema is defined). Unlike the namespace, where there needs to be a definitive master version, there can be lots of Java applets that can add behaviour to an XML schema. For example, the user could use a range of different Java applications to complete their tax return – as long as all the applications conform to the definitive tax return schema. One way of exposing an interface on the web to allow others to make use of existing services is Microsoft's .NET framework.

11.2.6 XML, web services, and .NET

Microsoft's .NET initiative is a framework and vision for the future of Internet computing. One of the most important elements of .NET is web services. Using web services organizations can interface their software applications with those of their trading partners to conduct business-to-business (B2B) e-commerce, or to link the front office and back office applications within their own organization (Enterprise Application Integration – EAI). For web services to work there needs to be a standard way of defining an interface to a web service – in .NET this is accomplished using WSDL (Web Services Description Language). WSDL interfaces are defined with XML. The interface needs a way of invoking operations in the application and a way to return results to the client. In web services this achieved using SOAP (Simple Object Access Protocol). SOAP is also defined in XML. The final part of the picture is a directory to help clients find available web services – UDDI (Universal Discovery, Description and Integration). SOAP is used to read and write the contents of the UDDI database, so once again we see that XML, via SOAP, is a core .NET technology.

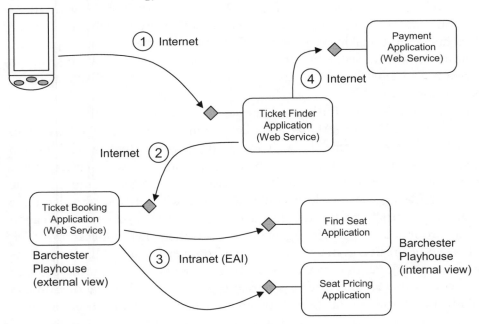

Figure 11.6: Web services for the Theatre Booking Application (adapted from Chappell, 2002, p. 51)

Let us see how web services could be used in the case of a theatre booking system. Rather than implement the business logic layer as a closed and proprietary software interface we could open it by making it into a web service that can be exposed on the Internet for access by client software applications (figure 11.6). Assume that a theatre-goer wants to book a theatre performance using a personal digital assistant (PDA) and a wireless connection to the Internet. The user enters detail of the type of production they want to see and when (step 1). The Ticket Finder application is a web service that can access many theatre booking systems to find the user a suitable production and performance dates. The Ticket Finder application uses the Internet to access a ticket booking application, such as the one operated by the Barchester Playhouse. For this to work, the Barchester Playhouse needs to have implemented its ticket booking system as a web service and make it available via the Internet to the Ticket Finder application (step 2). In step 3 the Ticket Booking application interacts with Seat Availability and Seat Pricing applications to price and reserve the seats. These applications are run internally and are accessed via an Intranet. It is possible that they are pre-Internet legacy systems that have been extended to support a web service interface, thus integrating them as part of a larger, Internet-based ticket booking system. Finally, the Ticket Finder application takes payment using a further web service (step 4).

The web services component of the .NET framework allows organizations to collaborate in providing end user functionality (such as finding performances and making payment). The .NET framework also provides organizations with a platform for enterprise application integration that can integrate pre-Internet legacy systems as part of a larger and publicly available Internet application.

We introduced ColdFusion components as a way of structuring the business logic of the TicketManager application in chapters 9 (technical design) and 10 (software construction). The good news is that a ColdFusion component can be made available to the outside world as a web service simply by changing the parameter ACCESS="public" to ACCESS="remote" in the <CFFunction> tag. The ColdFusion MX server will generate the necessary WISDL automatically on the fly, thus allowing the TicketManager application to be incorporated by partner organizations into their own applications. Web services can be created in many technical environments, but ColdFusion makes it about as simple as one can imagine. In summary, component-based, web service compatible architectures have great promise for B2B collaboration and should be the starting point for web-based information systems development.

11.3 Content management systems

All organizations that have a website (and that is nearly all organizations) must have a content management system, whether it be a manual process enacted by a single web manager or a decentralized system for producing and publishing web content supported by sophisticated technologies. CMS is primarily a process, not a product, and we define it as *'an organizational process, aided by software tools, for the management of heterogeneous content on the web, encompassing a life-cycle that runs from creation to destruction'* (Goodwin & Vidgen, 2002).

As with many new IT trends, web content management systems (CMS) is in part a practical response to a pressing business problem – how to organize and manage large-scale web sites – and in part a technology push on the part of software suppliers. Early to market software suppliers, such as Interwoven (www.interwoven.com) and Vignette (www.vignette.com), are finding many others jumping on the CMS bandwagon. Some of these offerings are extant software products that are being re-positioned (or possibly just re-branded) in the CMS domain. Some of the 'new' CMS products are rooted in document management, while others have developed from customer relationship management, e-commerce, and software configuration management. In the crowded CMS marketplace there is some confusion about what constitutes CMS – many suppliers define it in terms of the product they sell – hence our definition above.

11.3.1 Issues in web content management

Many organizations have created a website and most have established some infrastructural support for their website, such as a web manager or a web services department. There has been an explosion of content on web sites as the potential of the web for internal and external communication is recognized. For a web site to 'live and breathe' it must be fed with new content and out of date content must be removed. Organizations therefore need to encourage the activities of content providers. However, increased activity in content generation has raised a number of issues, all of which can cause problems if not properly managed:

- *Bottlenecks.* The web management function can become a bottleneck for content revision. Content arrives in different forms and has to be edited – usually manually – into a form suitable for publishing on the web. Funnelling content through a web manager resource can lead to delays in publishing on the web
- *Consistency.* Where web editing is devolved to departments there can be inconsistencies in the look and feel of the site and variable quality of layout and content
- *Navigation.* If structure and content are not closely controlled, there is a danger that navigation and search capabilities will suffer. This is of major importance, as without these, it becomes hard for the user to find the required information thus degrading the value of the entire Intranet

- *Data duplication.* In many cases, the content on the web is a copy of data held in a departmental or institutional system; changes to one system are manually replicated in the other systems. Ideally, data will not be stored redundantly in the organization. There will be one source accessed by all business applications, whether internal or external. Where data needs to be copied then replication should be automated and controlled
- *Content audit and control.* Unauthorized content may appear on the website. Material published on the web should be subject to a review and authorization process to ensure that it is acceptable from a marketing and legal viewpoint. Procedures and controls need to be defined to manage the web publishing process as well as user roles, such as creator, editor, and approver
- *Tracking.* To use content effectively it is necessary to know things about the content, such as who created it, when was it created, and when was it last updated. The ability to track and reconstruct the changes that have occurred to content is an important part of content management
- *Business processes.* Content is often tied tightly to business processes. For example, the production of a market intelligence report is a complex business process, involving data collection, data analysis, and the generation of commentaries and forecasts. Not only is the 'final' report published on the web, but also updates and revisions are likely to be needed on a regular basis. The business process and web content management need to be integrated, allowing content to be published internally for inspection and review and only released once it has been approved. Furthermore, the process itself may need to be redesigned to take account of differences between paper and web publishing.

Although many CMS packages are aimed at large organizations with tens or hundreds of thousands of pages, smaller organizations are also running into the problems caused by a lack of control over the content management process.

11.3.2 Genesis of web content management systems

CMS solutions must be capable of dealing with data with different degrees of structure. Some content will have a high degree of structure, such as employee records, and be amenable to being broken down into tables and stored in a traditional relational database system. Other content will be low in structure, such as a video clip of an Internet consultant talking about security issues. In between will be range of content, such as a health and safety manual or an in-house magazine, which will display more or less degrees of structure. A CMS must be capable of managing content in different media and with different degrees of structure, which suggests a combination of traditional data management and document (hypermedia) management technologies.

Many e-commerce products have specialized CMS facilities to address the maintenance of product and customer data. There is also much to learn from software configuration management, which is concerned with aspects of change such as versioning and audit trails. From an enabling perspective, technologies that support semantic interoperability, such as XML (eXtensible Markup Language) and RDF (Resource Description Framework – Dekker et al., 2000) provide a basis for sharing and the automated interchange of content between partners, i.e., humans are not the only users of web sites.

In figure 11.7 we show how the three antecedents of CMS – document management, customer relationship management, and software configuration management – together with enabling technologies and web semantics can be combined to provide a platform for CMS systems.

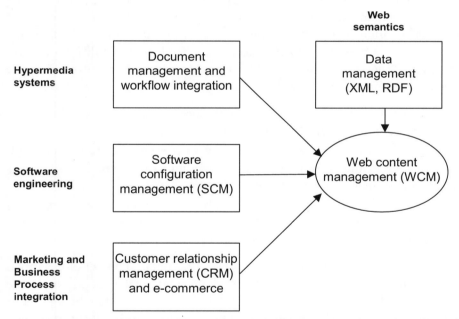

Figure 11.7: Antecedents and enablers of web content management (Goodwin & Vidgen, 2002)

The antecedents also point to the range of disciplines that are encompassed by CMS. Research areas in hypermedia and document management, software engineering, marketing, and business process design are all relevant, underpinned by data management and web semantics. This diversity of interest suggests that although the idea of CMS is intuitively simple to grasp, the different emphases and permeable boundaries will make it a difficult area to tackle both in research and in practice.

11.3.3   A web content management systems framework

The integrated view of web content management developed above provides a basis for developing a framework that brings together a range of content management related issues and requirements (figure 11.8).

Content life-cycle

At the core is the content life-cycle and a logically unified repository. The content life-cycle covers all stages, from creation to destruction of content components. New content will arrive from a number of sources, including electronic documents (e.g., from word-processors, such as MS Word), paper documents, web page templates (e.g., press releases, new product descriptions), web design tools (e.g., MS FrontPage, Macromedia DreamWeaver), and direct edit on the web into the repository. In many cases, the source will require some sort of *review*. This may be a review in terms of acceptable content, or it may be a review to determine the optimum place for the data within the structure of the system. The original data may require *storage* prior to publication and this may need to be continued after publication if it is published in a different form. With regard to *publication*, apart from the obvious requirement of making the content available, this should include:

- *Authentication* – which is concerned with identifying the user through a mechanism such as a user id and password or biometrics
- *Personalization* – which relates to the ability to present different users with different views and different data depending on preferences, access profiles, role, previous accesses, etc.
- *Transformation* – which is concerned with constructing (e.g., combining subcomponents into new documents) and transforming content at the time of delivery.

There is often a requirement to *archive* the data. This could happen automatically after a given date, or it could be a manual process, with the archives stored online or offline. Finally, at some stage, there may be a need to remove (*destroy*) the content permanently. The repository is a collection of data stores that cater for components with more or less structure, including relational and object-oriented databases, document stores, file systems, etc. The CMS must give seamless access to the content components regardless of where and how they are stored.

Organizational integration

Content is generated by and in support of business processes, which indicates a workflow and application perspective. To take advantage of the web effectively it is likely that some of the workflows will need to be redesigned, possibly to incorporate computer mediated communication and collaboration. This suggests that content management may go beyond routine automation and require, be constrained by, or initiate organizational change. As with any information technology, the consequences are likely to be unpredictable and are as much social as they are technical. The CMS core (content life-cycle and content component repository) must therefore be integrated with business processes and workflows and the existing business information systems that support those processes.

CMS process management

Management of the CMS process suggests a range of activities that need to be catered for, including data management, metadata management, and site management.

Data management is essential if content is to be exchanged, reused, shared, and searched intelligently. It is increasingly likely that web content will be marked up using XML and presentation will be defined using the style language XSL. To define and manage the XML data structures a modeling notation is required, such as the Unified Modeling Language (UML). If UML class diagrams are used to model the data structures (possibly represented in RDF – resource description framework), then XML documents can be thought of as physical implementations of an underlying and consistent enterprise class diagram. Connallen (www.rosearchitect.com) has shown how UML diagrams can be mapped into the hierarchical structure of XML documents. These hierarchies need to be shown to be consistent with the class diagram, i.e., that the UML schema can be derived by navigating through the class diagram. The combination of UML/RDF/XML is a promising approach to enterprise-wide data management.

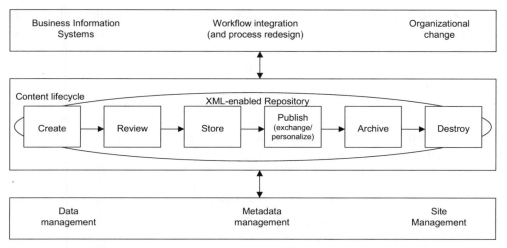

Figure 11.8: Web content management framework (adapted from Goodwin & Vidgen, 2002)

Metadata is the information that needs to be stored about a data item for an agent to use it. For example: expiry date, source, revision history, title, keywords, date created, time to archive, and version number. The metadata might also define how content can be combined to make new/virtual documents; for example, can this section be combined with that one? In what order? Is there a pre-requisite/co-requisite? 'Bursting' documents into subcomponents has great potential for data reuse but is going to be difficult to implement and control. Consequently, content management systems should be expected to have sophisticated metadata capabilities.

Site management is concerned with web site design and structure. Content must be separate from style and be device-independent. It should be possible to change the look and feel of the site by changing a style sheet. It should be possible to add a new device, such as a personal digital assistant (PDA), without affecting the content structure.

The content life-cycle suggests that there will be a number of roles to be considered: content contributor, content publisher, content consumer, web designer, web developer, content manager, design/navigation manager. This list is not necessarily exhaustive and neither does it imply that in all cases, all these roles will require separate individuals. However, the list does indicate the type of roles that will need to be considered in managing the CMS process.

11.3.4 CMS illustration: Intranet development

We will use our model to critically examine an Intranet development programme that has been ongoing for some time. The company concerned is an autonomous division of a major multi-national organization. Early in 2000, senior executives within the division decided to 'reinvent' the Intranet and take it forward in a more proactive manner. Views tended to be short term – 'Let's just get something up and running' was a common comment. However, despite this short termism, a top-level structure was formulated with the agreement of all of the relevant departmental and business process managers. Furthermore, each of the managers agreed to take responsibility for the content of their areas.

The project started well. A prototype site was built and agreed and templates were provided to allow various groups to contribute content in a consistent fashion. However, despite advice to the contrary, further progress was poor and that can be explained through the following factors:

- There was little or no investment
- Executive interest and attention drifted away
- There was no project champion
- There was little or no central control.

Some sections of the Intranet, typically those with proactive owners or resident 'techies' who liked to play with web pages, expanded greatly and at the end of 2000 were up-to-date and perceived to be useful. Other sections of the Intranet had, after 12 months, no content whatsoever.

In terms of content management, the CMS process is manual, localized, and has little overall control. A common site look and feel and consistent navigation is achieved in part through web page templates, although this still requires content providers to be adept at using a web-authoring tool. Groups that happen to have web-authoring skills do quite well in terms of content, but frequently they rely on a web enthusiast whose actual duties are often very different. This can lead to a loss of activity in the areas of work that the content provider should be involved in and an under-recording of the time actually spent in generating and maintaining content. Groups without web-authoring skills have to rely on the very small central 'corporate' resource. This underlines the problems of the 'web manager bottleneck' mentioned above.

The Intranet is providing value in localized areas, but has not matured into a corporate resource and first point of call for help and information.

The CMS framework as a diagnostic tool

In our case study, it is clear that there has been little thought about many of the areas of figure 11.8 in the organization we considered. There has been almost no thought of business processes and work flows other than in the initial choice of top-level divisions of the Intranet. It has been considered almost entirely as just another means of distributing information rather than as a possible tool to streamline and redesign processes.

There have been culture clashes between the decentralized tradition of some departments and the more centralized needs for a corporate Intranet structure. In a recent paper, Rosabeth Moss Kanter (2001) describes one of the ways to fail in moving your company onto the Internet which is equally true in this Intranet case:

> Under the banner of decentralization and business unit autonomy, reward each unit for its own performance, and offer no extra incentives to cooperate in cyberspace. Keep reminding divisions that they are separate businesses because they are different, and that's that.

Only in one or two small areas has there been an alignment between technology, structure and needs.

If we now look at the content life-cycle from figure 11.8 we again find discrepancies. First and foremost, there is no central strategy for, or control of, content. It is created randomly, rarely reviewed and published in an ad hoc manner. No one has thought about archiving or what happens to out of date data. Old items are rarely removed. There is no concept of data or metadata management other than a basic, free-text search engine. Site management is poor due to lack of skills, resources and experience.

Finally, we see little definition (or even understanding) of roles within the company. There are, by definition, a significant number of real or would-be content contributors as there are content consumers. However the roles of content publisher, web designer, content manager and design/navigation manager are combined into a very small part of one person who has little understanding of, and who has had no training in, any of them.

Summary

- XML is a basic building block for the separation of meaning and presentation of data.
- RDF goes beyond XML in allowing semantics to be expressed unambiguously as graphs rather than hierarchically-structured documents.
- Content management systems (CMS) provide an infrastructure to help organizations manage large-scale web sites and address issues such as the web manager bottleneck.
- CMS build on the XML family of technologies.
- CMS is primarily a process, not a product. We define it as 'an organizational process, aided by software tools, for the management of heterogeneous content on the web, encompassing a life-cycle that runs from creation to destruction'.

Exercises

1. For an industry in which you have worked or have experience of, what XML and RDF standards exist for that industry? How might the industry be affected or transformed by the uptake of common data standards?
2. What problems does your organization face in managing the content of its web site today?
3. What are the formal procedures for web publishing? Are these procedures followed (if not, why not)?
4. What benefits would your organization obtain from implementing a CMS? If your organization already has a CMS what implementation issues have had to be faced?

Further reading

Chappell, D., (2002). *Understanding .NET: a Tutorial and Analysis.* Addison Wesley.

Davenport, T. H. and Prusak, L., (1998). *Working Knowledge.* Harvard Business School Press.

Decker, S., Melnik, S., Van Hamelen, F., Fensel, D., Klein, M., Broekstra, J., Erdmann, M. and Horrocks, I., (2000). The Semantic Web: the Roles of XML and RDF. *IEEE Internet Computing,* September–October: 63–74.

Moss Kanter, R., (2001). The Ten Deadly Mistakes of Wanna-Dots. *Harvard Business Review,* 79(1): 91.

Nakano, R., (2002). *Web Content Management: a Collaborative Approach.* Addison Wesley, Boston, MA.

Goodwin, S. and Vidgen, R., (2002). Content, Content, Everywhere … Time to Stop and Think? The Process of Web Content Management. *IEE Computing & Control Engineering Journal.* 13(2): 66–70.

12

Reflections on WISDM

12.1 Introduction

To pull the strands of the WISDM framework together we introduce a real-life web-based information system development case study. The case is concerned with a UK-based small to medium size enterprise (SME) as reported by Vidgen (2002). Following the case we will introduce some theory into the WISDM framework to provide a basis for reflecting on the practice of information system development.

12.2 The Global Drinks case

12.2.1 The client organization in 1998

Founded in 1991, Zenith International Ltd is a business consultancy specializing in the food, drinks and packaging industries worldwide. The main business activities are market analysis, strategic advice, technical consulting projects and conference organization. In spring 1998, the strategic aims of Zenith were to create a global presence, to broaden the product range, and to develop complementary skills (e.g., a synergy of market intelligence reports and consultancy). In September 1998 Zenith launched its first web site. The adoption of the Internet by Zenith is explained well by Mehrtens et al. (2001), whose model comprises three factors: perceived benefits (e.g., sending product information to prospective customers), organizational readiness (e.g., high levels of Internet familiarity by staff and senior management support), and external pressure (mainly from existing customers who want the firm to communicate with them electronically).

Zenith can, therefore, be categorized as a stereotypical SME Internet adopter. Given these factors, it is not surprising that the first stage of the web site implementation was to create a web presence and to provide marketing information about Zenith companies and their services and products. Although customers could not buy digital documents on the web site they could place orders online for subsequent delivery of paper reports. Two of the most successful features of the site were the online conference booking forms and the Chairman's newsletters. In summary, the site was typical of a cyber-brochure, informational site, with elementary order taking facilities.

12.2.2 The Global Drinks e-commerce project 1999–2001

Analysis of competitors showed that the larger market research companies were making reports available online (e.g., Gartner, Datamonitor) and issuing user identification and passwords to customers. The success of the company web site launched in 1998 gave Zenith the confidence to explore e-commerce and the online delivery of market research content. In October 1999 Zenith and the University of Bath established a two-year Teaching Company Scheme (TCS).

The objective of the TCS programme was to build an online Global Drinks Service (GDS). In 1999 the GDS was a paper-based survey of beverage consumption data, together with textual analysis, for all countries with analysis across product groups (e.g., soft drinks) and products (e.g., bottled water, fruit juices). This information is of value to the marketing and planning departments of organizations involved in the drinks industry, including ingredients suppliers, manufacturers, retailers, and packagers. In its paper form a customer was expected to buy the complete survey – all countries, all products, all years – and to renew a subscription on an annual basis if it wanted a new report with updated consumption data. By making this information available online Zenith would be able to supply information in 'byte-sized' chunks on demand.

12.2.3 Outcomes of the intervention

The project plan anticipated version 1.0 of the GDS being complete 12 months into the two-year project with the remaining 12 months being used for monitoring and iterative development. In Internet time 12 months might well seem to be excessive, but the time-scale needed to reflect the training requirements of the Teaching Company Associate (a recent graduate and novice developer) and allow the Associate to gain experience and confidence through working on technically less demanding pieces of work, such as a redesign of the company's main web site. Throughout the project rapid application development and prototyping were used. This approach allowed

Zenith researchers and managers to see a working system quickly and for the developers to continuously check their understanding of the requirements. The internal prototype was evolved into a production system, culminating with the first live version of the GDS being delivered ahead of schedule ten months after project commencement. This first release allowed for end-to-end purchasing: customers could select the data they wanted to purchase, pick a user id and password, pay by credit card using a secure third party, and have immediate access to the data purchased (www.globaldrinks.com).

Once the initial version of the GDS was delivered, new releases followed at roughly two-month intervals. New facilities included: more sophisticated calculations (e.g., country to country comparisons of percentage growth in beverage consumption per capita) and improved graphical presentation, a report store allowing textual commentaries to be purchased in Adobe Acrobat (pdf) file format, a database of more than 1500 links to drinks manufacturer sites, an email news service, daily news available by mobile telephone using WAP (wireless application protocol), and real-time generation of user selected data in the form of an Excel spreadsheet. A revenue stream of GDS sales was created in the first year of the project and the financial targets for revenue generation specified in the project proposal for the two-year period were exceeded. From a TCS and company perspective the project was judged to be a success. In the context of an e-commerce web application, the GDS project was an important input to the shaping of WISDM, particularly with regard to the contents of the methods matrix.

12.3 Web IS Development methods

The methods used in the development of the GDS are presented using the four quadrants of the methods matrix in figure 12.1.

12.3.1 Organizational analysis

SSM is particularly relevant in situations characterized by complexity and pluralism of stakeholder interests. The GDS project was perceived by the client organization to be simple/unitary. In organizational terms the project was perceived to be 'simple' – it was an e-commerce bolt-on to existing operations (i.e., another channel for marketing and sales). Stakeholder interests were unitary, i.e., there was agreement on both the ends – success would be measured chiefly by the ability to generate revenue – and the means. Given this reading of the situation, the explicit introduction of SSM would not have been perceived as meaningful in this context. However, some form of organizational analysis was needed. For an e-commerce project an external orientation is essential, since the aim is to sell products and services to customers. The organizational analysis consisted of building an e-commerce strategy for Zenith and conducting a market survey. The e-commerce survey was concerned with aligning the development project with Zenith's wider business strategy in the context of industry forces. The market survey focused on customers and included a postal and telephone survey to determine attitudes to the Internet, e-commerce (particularly making online payments), and to find out their research information requirements. Organizational analysis and value creation were tackled through formulating an e-business strategy, as described in chapter 4.

12.3.2 Information analysis

UML (Unified Modeling Language) use cases were developed to describe the major functionality of the proposed system, including registration and purchase, research queries, and maintenance. Given that the Global Drinks Service is a data-intensive application that would be implemented around a relational database, it is not surprising that the heaviest use of UML was in the development of class diagrams. Limited use was made of OO principles, such as encapsulation and inheritance, because it was known that the implementation environment had no explicit support for OO mechanisms. Although the analysis was approached from a logical stance, i.e., independent of the implementation platform, the methods used were influenced by the choice of technical platform for implementation. Some use of UML sequence diagrams was made, but again, the target environment meant that these were perceived as having less value due to a knowledge that the implementation would take the form of web pages – an environment notoriously antithetical to OO (Connallen, 2000).

12.3.3 Work design

Sociotechnical design approaches, such as ETHICS, are concerned with achieving a suitable match between job satisfaction and the efficiency objectives of the organization. The GDS project was conceived as a standalone initiative that would target external customers and have minimal impact on working practices within the organization. In practice, this was not entirely the case. The initial load of the GDS data to the database was a typical development activity, i.e., data conversion. However, 9 months later (18 months into the project) it was necessary to load in the next year's data. This was a routine business process that did impact on the internal business processes of the research department, i.e., the GDS project had implications for work that had not been accounted for. If the annual updates had met with user resistance from the research staff who were not involved directly in the GDS then the project may have faltered. Although a full-blown ETHICS investigation into the internal workings of Zenith would have been inappropriate to the GDS project, the experience served as a reminder that even the most independent seeming of projects can have an impact on work practices.

The primary user of the GDS was the external customer. These customers use the GDS to support their own work practices, such as marketing and production planning, and to that extent ETHICS could be applied to understanding how the GDS might contribute to the quality of their work life. However, given the difficulties of gaining access to customers it is more appropriate to treat the customer's organization as a black box and to assess user satisfaction through an instrument such as WebQual, as described in chapter 7. As part of the TCS programme the Zenith main web site was redesigned and WebQual was used to assess the quality of the site before and after the redesign. A similar assessment will be conducted on the GDS web site. Where it is inappropriate or too expensive to do a detailed work-study, as may be the case with external customers, the WebQual questionnaire approach is a suitable instrument for the assessment of user satisfaction.

12.3.4 Technical design

The physical requirements of the implementation were clear: a database was needed together with some technology to link the database to the web. The project team selected Allaire's ColdFusion server together with Microsoft Access (later upgraded to MS SQL Server) database. Graphical presentation of database query results was achieved using Seagate's Crystal Reports and web site design was accomplished using Macromedia DreamWeaver with Fireworks and Flash for graphics and animation. The choice of platform was driven by a mixture of the technology available on a limited budget and the previous experience of the team members. The budget affected the hosting decision insofar as an ISP (Internet service provider) was needed since the option of Zenith hosting its own dedicated server, or even co-hosting with an ISP, were not viable options.

From a logical design perspective, the GDS started as a relatively straightforward application. The database did not have a lot of tables and the program logic was simple. As the project progressed and more functionality and tables were added the application gained in complexity. It became clear that some structure was needed to manage this complexity. The structure came in the form of a three-tier architecture that allowed database, business logic, and presentation layers to be separated out. By building the business logic in ColdFusion using components it is possible to achieve a pseudo-OO implementation. Unfortunately, the scripting approach to web development does not sit well with OO, which meant that the UML diagrams became less relevant as the design moved from the logical to the physical. However, use was made of UML-style interaction diagrams to model the interaction and flow of web pages.

Possibly the greatest challenge was in the design of the web user interface. The University supervisor, a traditional system developer, had little aptitude for this area of development. Fortunately, the TCS Associate proved to have a flair for graphics and web aesthetics. If this had not been the case, the project would have had to be supplemented with the skills of a graphic designer. We also found that the best way to learn about web page design and web navigation and flow was to copy exemplars. For example, the Amazon.com registration and ordering flow proved an excellent template – the Amazon.com site is consistently rated highly for ease of use and many Internet users are familiar with its interface. Taking inspiration from exemplar sites might not be innovative, but it does provide a tried and tested route to follow, as long as proprietary methods, such as Amazon.com's 'one-click ordering' are not infringed.

12.4 Reflections on the case

In this section the differences between web-based IS development and traditional, pre-Internet development are considered, followed by reflections on the role of methodology in IS development. The outcome of this reflection is a revised WISDM framework for IS development in general. In chapter 3 Baskerville & Pries-Heje (2001) outlined ten characteristics of Internet development, which are used here to analyse the GDS case:

Time pressure: The users and senior management expected early and frequent delivery of prototypes.

Vague requirements: The high level aims of the project were clear (deliver research data to customers via the Internet) but the detailed requirements were unknown (e.g., how would the research data be packaged, priced, and presented to the user in graphical format?).

Prototyping: The detailed requirements were explored and developed through successive prototypes. Since a formal requirements dictionary was not kept the prototype became the detailed specification.

Release orientation: The release early and often approach of open source software was followed throughout, for internal prototypes and for the production system. This helped the development of the requirements specification and enabled new features to be delivered to customers on a regular basis in response to comments and feedback.

Parallel development: Analysis and design were conducted in parallel throughout the project, each informing the other.

Fixed architecture: A three-tier architecture was adopted at a later stage of the project to manage the complexity and to avoid being overwhelmed by the software maintenance task.

Coding your way out: Coding your way out was a fact of life. Emergency fixes and last minute requirements led to 'hacks' being made, with the documentation left to catch up later, 'when things are quieter'.

Quality is negotiable: The benchmark for quality is customer perceptions, rather than the internally focussed perspectives of the product and the software development process.

Dependence on good people: Given the timescale and the small project team, dependence on good people was an absolute requirement. An able Associate who is quick to learn was an essential prerequisite to the success of the project. However, it is particularly difficult to predict the learning ability and aptitude of a novice developer and to a rather worrying extent the project is largely dependent on the 'luck of the draw'. With larger projects there might be some resilience to developer variability – with Internet time projects with small numbers of specialized resources (e.g., graphic design, database design) getting the personnel resources wrong has catastrophic implications

Need for new structures of IS development: This may be the case where there is a traditional systems development department in existence, but in the case of the GDS project the team were working in a green field situation and created working structures and routines as the project unfolded.

Although the ten concepts capture the emergent WISDM and our experience on the GDS project well, as we pointed out in chapter 3, it is less clear that the concepts really capture the differences between web-based IS development and traditional IS development. However, there are differences between web-based projects and traditional IS development, but these differences are more to do with concrete content than with abstractions (table 12.1).

As Internet projects become broader in scope requiring greater integration with front office, back office, and legacy IT systems of all sorts, then Internet projects will become yet more difficult to distinguish from traditional IT projects. Traditional IS projects would also benefit from giving more attention to strategy, customers, and design aesthetics and therefore the distinctions in table 12.1 should, over time, become less pronounced and ultimately disappear altogether.

12.5 Methods and methodology in IS development

The elaborated WISDM framework is shown in figure 12.1. Each of the aspects in the methods matrix has been annotated to highlight the different emphases that IS development projects are subject to as the developers move around the matrix. Organizational analysis is stereotyped as *envisioning* and creative thinking, information modeling with *rationalizing* and a 'rage for order', work design with *championing* and representing stakeholder interests, technical design with *engineering* and problem solving, and HCI with *aestheticizing* and a notion of design as style. A successful web-based IS project is likely to need a mix of all five aspects, but the mix will vary from project to project, reflecting the contingent nature of the emergent methodology.

Turning to the role of methodology, at the centre of the framework in figure 2 is the generation of a local and contingent methodology (WISDM), generated through the struggle of the change agents with the situation and the methods. The emergent methodology only becomes visible through engagement and practice. Methodology in this sense is an outcome of action rather than pre-existing, being created and recreated through action and the day-to-day practice of system development.

Dimension	Traditional IS projects	Internet/e-commerce projects
Strategy	The strategic dimension is abstract	The strategic dimension is tangible and visible and relates closely to business goals
	The strategic dimension is addressed indirectly, through broad notions such as strategic alignment. Often the strategic dimension is not addressed at all	Strategy is addressed directly, particularly for e-commerce projects in which a revenue stream is generated
User	The typical user is an employee	The typical user is a customer who makes payment for goods and services
	Users can be trained and consulted directly. System use might be mandatory	Usage is not mandatory and the customer won't attend training sessions
	User needs can be understood through work studies	User needs can be understood through sales and marketing methods
	Job satisfaction is a key aim	Customer satisfaction is a key aim
Design	The development focus is on the internals of the design: the database, the programs and an architecture (e.g., three-tier) A prosaic user interface design providing basic usability is sufficient	The development focus is on the web site as a visual artefact. The development cycle might start with a mock-up of the user interface. Graphic design skills and a feel for web aesthetics are essential

Table 12.1: Stereotypical differences between traditional IS development and Internet projects (Vidgen, 2002)

Although methodology as contingent and locally situated practice might be described as amethodical (Truex et al., 2000), it is not a series of random actions. There are structures that guide and shape the creation of methodology, such as the IS methods and perceptions of the problem situation in figure 2.

These structures are not objectively given, but must be interpreted – drawn upon and made sense of – in a specific situation by the human actors enacting change. Because there are multiple human actors involved in system development there are multiple meanings created as people interpret the IS methods and the problem situation in different ways. The structures that are drawn upon (perceptions of the methods and the situation) are what enable meaningful action to be taken. However, at the same time, taking action is what produces and reproduces those structures as we learn about and adapt to the local situation. Through this continual flux of negotiation and renegotiation a local IS development methodology emerges – it is contingent in the sense that it is a product of the individuals, the situation and the methods that they draw on.

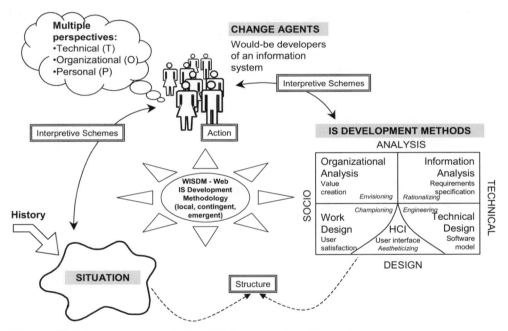

Figure 12.1: The elaborated WISDM framework (Vidgen, 2002)

Summary

The Multiview framework has been used to explain how a web IS development methodology (WISDM) emerged on an e-commerce development project, the Global Drinks Service (GDS), in a UK-based SME. The methods used in the development project reflected the experiences and skills of the developers, the situation, and the type of project. Three key areas where an e-commerce project differs from traditional IS development were identified: a strong and direct link with business strategy, the need to incorporate sales and marketing skills to address the needs of the user as customer, and a bolstering of traditional IS development skills with a graphic design sensibility. Five stereotypical roles in IS development were identified through the methods matrix: envisioning, rationalizing, championing, engineering, and aestheticizing. The project also gave insights into the structures that developers draw on in the production of a local IS development methodology, suggesting that our attention should move from the idea of methodology as fixed structure to one of methodology as doing and practice.

Further reading

Baskerville, R. and Pries-Heje, J., (2001). Racing the e-bomb: How the Internet is Redefining Information Systems Development. In: *Realigning Research and Practice in Information System Development*, (Eds, Russo, L., Fitzgerald, B. and DeGross, J.), IFIP TC8/WG8.2 Working Conference, Boise, Idaho, USA, July 27–29.

Connallen, J., (2000). *Building Web Applications with UML*, Addison-Wesley, Reading, MA.

Mehrtens, J., Cragg, P. and Mills, A., (2001). A Model of Internet Adoption by SMEs. *Information and Management*, 39, 165–176.

Truex, D. P., Baskerville, R. and Travis, J., (2000). Amethodical Systems Development: the deferred meaning of systems development methods. *Accounting, Management and Information Technology*, 10 (1), 53–79.

Vidgen, R., (2002). WISDM: Constructing a Web Information System Development Methodology. *Information Systems Journal*, 12, 247–261.

Walsham, G., (1993). *Interpreting Information Systems in Organizations*, Wiley, Chichester.

Barchester Playhouse
Case Study

A1 Introduction

The (fictional) Barchester Playhouse is the county theatre for Barsetshire and is located in the county town, Barchester. The theatre was built in 1877 and has an interior designed by Frank Matcham, the eminent Victorian theatre designer. Because of the historical importance of the theatre the interior is listed by the Department of Heritage and is subject to restrictions concerning what changes can be made to the fabric of the theatre building. The theatre has seating for 750 people and puts on a range of productions. The theatre is a 'receiving house'; productions are presented at the theatre rather than having its own company of actors. The mission of the theatre is to be 'The theatre for Barsetshire'. The Playhouse pursues its mission through a range of activities:

- Developing a programme that is high quality and accessible – a mix of 'money-spinners' and more demanding work
- Acting as a resource for the people of Barsetshire. For example, there is a 'Reachout' programme for presenting productions at schools. Tours of the theatre are arranged for school parties and local societies
- Maintaining the historic building and developing theatre staff
- Being part of the community of Barchester and the County. For example, social and charity events are held in the theatre rooms and there is an active Theatre Club.

The principal revenue streams for the Playhouse are ticket sales and ancillary services, which include the bar, catering, programme sales, and merchandising (e.g., t-shirts and mugs). The revenue stream is supplemented by funding from the Arts Council, Barchester Borough Council, and Barsetshire Council. There is also some corporate sponsorship by local companies. For an annual subscription fee members of the Theatre Club are entitled to discounts on ticket prices, priority allocation of tickets for popular productions, and attendance at social events organized by the theatre.

A.1.1 The organization of the Playhouse

The organization of the theatre is shown in figure A.1. There is a chief executive who has overall responsibility for running the theatre including administration, marketing, mounting of plays, etc. It is the responsibility of the chief executive to ensure that the theatre is successful as a whole. The chief executive makes the final decision regarding which productions are to be presented at the theatre. She has a long history in the theatre business and has extensive contacts throughout the industry.

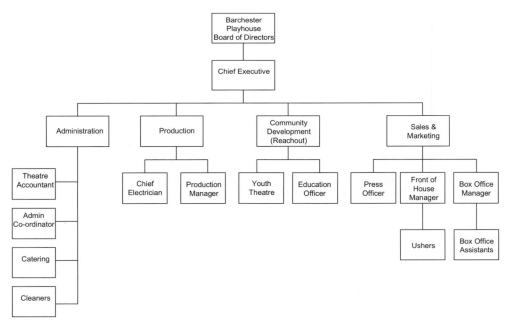

Figure A.1: Barchester Playhouse organization chart

The accountant looks after the quarterly tax returns, is responsible for checking takings at the end of each of run of a performance and advises the administration manager on the financial viability of any new project. The accountant is also responsible for the day-to-day administration of the theatre, including catering and cleaning services. The marketing manager oversees the work of the box office manager. The box office manager runs the box office and is responsible for two full-time and three regular part-time staff.

A.2 Current box office operations

All ticket sales are made via the box office, either in person at the physical box office in the foyer or by telephone to the box office telephone sales office. If a third party, such as the Tourist Information office in Barchester, is asked to book tickets on behalf of a visitor then the Tourist Information officer rings the box office. When a booking is made customer details are recorded in case any last-minute changes to performance details occur, such as a performance being cancelled, and to gather data for marketing purposes.

The box office staff are responsible for: selling tickets for cash, cheques or credit (made in person or by telephone), making reservations, answering queries about seat availability, producing reports of takings by show, by category and by day, and providing theatre management and show promoters with daily reports on sales and reservations. A study estimated that the box office staff is executing something like 20 different processes regularly and that they perform about 30 different processes altogether. Currently, many of these processes rely for their speed and accuracy upon staff keeping a substantial volume of information in their memories. For example, the current system has no facility for storing details of customers waiting for cancellations and box office assistants currently keep hand-written notes of waiting lists and returns.

A.2.1 Current IT systems

The current box office system was installed in 1987 and was developed on a bespoke basis by a small software house that has since ceased to trade. The software was built using a database product and fourth generation language that are no longer marketed or supported. The box office application was developed before Windows become widely available and runs under the MS-DOS operating system with a character-based, green screen interface. The application is installed on four networked personal computers available at the time, but now very much out of date. Three of the computers are in an office where telephone orders are dealt with and the fourth computer is in the box office in the theatre foyer. The four ticketing computers are networked to each other, but in a dedicated fashion using an old and non-standard networking protocol developed specifically for this application by the software house.

The Playhouse has a website, but it is hosted on a low-level business plan and is a basic cyber-brochure providing information about the theatre and the current programme of events. There are no facilities for booking tickets. In the administrative offices of the Playhouse there are numerous PCs. These are a mix of old Pentium IIs with a few newer Pentium IIIs and IVs. The PCs are used for word-processing, accounting, and standalone MS Access databases.

Processes and data supported by the current box office system

The main areas of processing are:

- Maintenance of standing data – production details, performance details, theatre details
- Enquiries about performances
- Taking orders for tickets
- Ticket production
- Management reporting.

The data held on the computer system is used to support the processing of ticket sales, the allocation of seats to customers, and the printing of tickets. The system is also used to answer enquiries made by the general public and to provide reports for the theatre management. The computer system contains details of each of the physical seats in the theatre and specific details of the use of each seat at a specific performance.

Issues with the current box office system

Details of the members of the Theatre Club are not held on the box office system. A manual list is maintained on a word-processor in the marketing manager's office and new versions printed off periodically once a number of changes to the membership have been recorded. Mail shots are mail-merged using word-processing software.

Periodically, data is stripped from the box office system and transferred to a standalone marketing database implemented in Microsoft Access. This database is used to generate mail shots to publicise forthcoming productions. The data is unreliable – many of the addresses are suspected to be out of date and there are duplicate names that result in multiple postings to the same person. Furthermore, there is no easy way of matching who has bought tickets against the mailing lists in the marketing database, which makes it difficult to build up a profile of customers.

A.3 Motivation for change

Box office receipts have risen steadily, as has the average number of nights a week the theatre is in use. During the 17 week period to 28 February 2002 box office takings averaged £47,500 a week. During the 2002 pantomime season, when as many as three shows were taking place during the day, transaction volumes were at an historic high and the box office became a bottleneck, possibly selling fewer seats than it might have done. In September 2001 the theatre was being booked for an average of 5 nights each week. As a result, pressure to investigate the possibility of upgrading the current box office computer system developed. The theatre manager has commissioned a local software house, Nimbus, to conduct a feasibility study into upgrading or replacing the current computer system. The brief given to Nimbus is that the feasibility study must take account of opportunities provided by the Internet.

A.3.1 Perceptions of the theatre

The Barchester Playhouse has recently received the results of market research into the local community's requirements of the theatre. The results show that the theatre is perceived to be primarily a middle-class domain that does not appear to welcome the unwaged and economically disadvantaged. The feeling was that the members of the Theatre Club initiative serves to consolidate the theatre as a centre for a wine-drinking, four-wheel drive-owning, golfers who seem more interested in restoring the Playhouse's historic interior than in staging contemporary plays. Disabled people in the community feel that the Playhouse's management have done little to improve access facilities, although this is not easy given the theatre's architectural importance and planning constraints. Their impression is that although theatre staff are polite they tend to treat them as a special case, which makes some of the disabled theatre-goers feel uncomfortable. The Playhouse already receives a small subsidy from the Arts Council and is hoping to get further funding from the local council, which is keen that the theatre be made accessible to a wider range of members of the local community. This is part of the council's policy of bringing life back to the business and retail areas of Barchester at nighttime.

A.4 Requirements of the theatre booking system

The new theatre booking system should be designed to assist the operation of the box office of the Barchester Playhouse. The focus of the investigation is restricted to the allocation and issuing of tickets for theatre performances to customers and the maintenance of related data, such as seating plans, productions, pricing, and performance schedules. The booking system will need to be integrated with other areas of operation of the theatre, such as accounting.

Theatre layout

The Barchester Playhouse has the following requirements of a new box office management system. The new system should hold details of the theatre layout, an illustration of which is shown in figure A.2. The theatre comprises three parts – Balcony, Circle, and Stalls.

Theatre productions and performances

The theatre puts on productions, such as 'The Importance of Being Earnest' by Oscar Wilde and 'Julius Caesar' by William Shakespeare. Each production will have many (i.e., one or more) performances taking place on a specific date and at a particular time (some productions will have matinees as well as evening performances). A schedule of performances is established for each production.

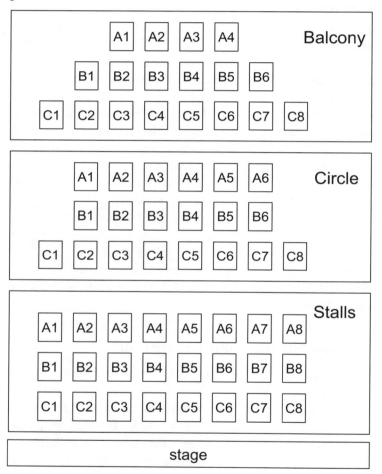

Figure A.2: Theatre layout

Ticket prices

The ticket price is determined by a combination of the production and the part of the theatre. For example, tickets for a children's production, such as 'The Wind in the Willows', might cost £3.50 in the stalls and £4.50 in the circle, while a production of 'Hamlet' could cost £8.50 for the stalls and £10.50 for the circle.

Ticket sales

A ticket sale is made up of one or more seats at a performance (figure A.3). For example, a theatre-goer could buy two tickets to see 'Hamlet' on 13 April 2001 and two tickets to see 'Julius Caesar' on 16 May 2001. The total cost of the tickets in a transaction is calculated (£25 in figure A.3) and stored with the details of the transaction. The transaction ID is generated automatically by the computer system and the date is filled automatically with today's date. The individual price per seat should be retrieved from the standard ticket prices for the production and shown automatically when a performance and seat are entered. The ticket price per seat can be changed; for example, the box office manager can decide to sell off spare seats cheaply just before the performance begins. This means that the actual price achieved for each seat at a performance can differ from the standard ticket price and therefore the price achieved must be recorded against the seat at performance. The payment method (e.g., cash, credit card, cheque) should be recorded at the time of the sale.

Theatre:		Barchester Playhouse
TransactionID:		A83742
Date:		03-Apr-2002
Payment method:		credit card

Date of Performance	Time of Performance	Title of production	Part of theatre	Seat no.	Seat price
13/04/02	19.30	Hamlet	Stalls	C3	5.00
13/04/02	19.30	Hamlet	Stalls	C4	5.00
16/05/02	15.00	Julius Caesar	Circle	B2	7.50
16/05/02	15.00	Julius Caesar	Circle	B3	7.50
				£ Total	25.00

Figure A.3: Ticket sale transaction report

A.4.1 Roles and attitudes of those involved in the analysis

Theatre accountant: Interested in costs/benefits, worried about the possible affect of a computer system on his position within the theatre. Rather defensive and often unwilling to give information about his job.

Theatre box office manager: Has detailed knowledge of how the box office operates (or thinks she has). Is anxious to improve the situation in the Box Office and will seek to find a compromise when any conflict occurs.

Box office clerk (full-time): Has worked for a long time in the box office and is very comfortable with the current system. Has built up a practical knowledge of box office activity over many years and seen just about every exceptional situation that can arise, although would find it very difficult to articulate this knowledge. Part-time box office clerks are used at busy periods, but there is a high turnover of part-time box office staff. The box office in the foyer is open from 10 am to 1 pm and 2 pm to 5 pm Monday to Friday.

Marketing manager: Is keen to find new channels for ticket sales and promotion of the Playhouse. Wants to get a better understanding of who visits the Playhouse and to build stronger relationships with theatre-goers. Is currently studying part-time for an MBA at the University of Barchester.

Chief executive: Has an interest in the future strategic development of the theatre but is naturally an 'includer'. Above all she wants everyone to be happy with any decision made and wants a broad range of consultation. Her attitude to IT is 'agnostic' – she concedes that IT may be strategically important but has to be convinced over and over.

Representative from the Arts Council: Concerned about the role of the theatre in the local community. Will take a broader view of the theatre and is likely to question why the local council and the Arts Council should provide subsidies to the Barchester Playhouse.

Project manager of Nimbus: Sees his role in testing the group's output and will be critical of any and all ideas proposed.

Software designer from Nimbus: Wants his own ideas accepted by the rest of the group. Either becomes withdrawn or gets annoyed if he doesn't get his own way. Has a strong technical rationality and tends to see the situation as a problem that can be solved through the application of information technology (so long as people don't get in the way).

B

Research Student Admissions Case Study

B1 The current process

The Business School at the University of Barchester offers MPhil and PhD degrees by research. With full-time study the MPhil typically takes one year (two years part-time) and the PhD three years (five years part-time) to complete. The School handles applications to study for research degrees in the following way. Initial enquiries can be taken by the Director of Postgraduate Research (DPR), by the School's research office administrators, by the receptionist in the School office, or centrally at the Graduate Admissions Office. Inquiries are received by post and by email. A research office administrator then sends the enquirer a postgraduate prospectus for the University together with an application form and a few pages of additional information about the Business School, including details of the School's research centres (this information is also available on the School's Web site). The prospectus is a glossy colour production; the additional information is in the form of photocopies of word-processed documents. The DPR will often talk to the enquirers about their application, for example to help them decide whether a research degree is for them, to discuss funding opportunities, and whether the Barchester Business School is appropriate for their proposed area of study.

Once the enquirer has completed an application form and returned it to the University, then he/she becomes an official applicant. An acknowledgement letter is sent out by the research office administrator within 7 days to confirm receipt of the application.

All research applications must include a brief research proposal, which is used to identify potential supervisors and to assess the quality of the proposal. In a few cases, if the DPR does not feel that the proposal is suitable, or the applicant not appropriately qualified, then a polite and carefully worded letter of rejection will be sent (usually 4 weeks after the application was received). More normally, a decision on rejection is made after the application has been reviewed by potential academic supervisors.

Applicants must be funded to carry out their studies. Some are self-funded, some are seeking scholarships and grants, and others hope to do teaching for the Business School in return for payment of fees and all or part of their living costs. This means that strong applicants without funds can be rejected if a funding source cannot be identified. The University as a whole operates an Overseas Research Student (ORS) grant, but funding is tight and highly competitive and only the very best qualified students have a chance of gaining an award. Non-EU (European Union) students are not eligible for UK and EU research council studentships.

If the applicant is considered suitable then the search for a suitable supervisory team begins. A 'green form' is completed for all applicants. The green form acts as a control sheet on which the date the application is received is recorded; it is also used to log the progress of the application through the application process. On the basis of the DPR's knowledge of the research interests of academic members of staff, the DPR will try to match the application to potential supervisors. Probationary lecturers and lecturers without PhDs may only supervise students jointly with a suitably qualified member of staff. Given that there are around 80 academic members of staff, the DPR has difficulty in remembering the research interests and eligibility of all the members of staff, particularly for new and newly qualified personnel (the Business School is experiencing a period of growth and new staff join on a regular basis). Typically, the DPR will highlight two or three potential supervisors and put their names on the green form. The form, together with the application and the proposal, is then forwarded to the first name on the list. The recipient makes comments on the form and then passes the file to the next person on the list. It is not unknown for applications to sit on academics' desks for weeks and even months at a time, particularly during out of term time. Although applications do not get lost, they can be mislaid and there is considerable effort expended in the research office tracking down applications that are due to be returned by potential supervisors. The research office administrator currently logs and tracks the progress of applications using an Excel spreadsheet.

Once all the members of academic staff identified by the DPR on the green form have seen the application it will be returned to the DPR and a decision will be made. If a suitably qualified and willing supervisor, or supervisory team, can be identified then the DPR will request the University to issue a formal offer to the applicant.

Around 500 applications are received each year, of which about 60 become accepted offers. Of the 60 offers accepted, 5 or so will have come from 'done deals' where the applicant is already known to the supervisor and there is little doubt about the outcome. Supervisors can be wary of taking students on who they have not met before, as the supervisor/PhD student relationship lasts for at least three years and is a significant commitment on both sides that needs to work on a professional and on a personal level. For UK-based applicants it may be possible to invite the applicant for interview; for overseas students this is often not possible and it can be difficult to make a decision on the basis of a relatively brief research proposal and a telephone call. However, the School is keen to increase the number of high quality PhD students (i.e., those that complete successfully within the allotted time period) since this is a key factor in building the School's research profile and is also taken into account in the University's funding grant. It is possible that some students are lost due to the time taken to process applications: currently anywhere between one month and, in extreme cases, six months, depending on how often the paperwork gets held up.

Internet Resources

C.1 WISDM

WISDM
(www.wisdm.net)

The TicketManager theatre booking application is accessible from here, together with a download of the ColdFusion source code, DreamWeaver templates, and Access database. Developments of the WISDM framework and research papers and general resources on IS development will be added to the site as they become available.

C.2 Development tools

Tools required for the TicketManager application

Microsoft Access
(www.microsoft.com/office/access/default.asp)

The TicketManager application is built on a Microsoft Access 2000 Database, which can be bought as a standalone product or as part of the Microsoft Office Professional suite. Because Access is a client database rather than an industrial strength server application it is not recommended that Access be used for production databases on the Internet. Access can cope with a small number of concurrent users, but for a robust solution a server database such as

Microsoft's SQL Server or Oracle is recommended. Access can be used to good effect as a client for SQL Server for applications that are run in-house.

Macromedia DreamWeaver MX
(www.macromedia.com/software/dreamweaver/)

The DreamWeaver MX web authoring tool ships with a single user version of ColdFusion MX server for development use. Fully functional trial versions (time limited) of the DreamWeaver MX products can be downloaded from the Macromedia site. DreamWeaver MX gives you everything you need to develop active web sites locally. To deploy the web site live an Internet server and ColdFusion MX will be required (or a ColdFusion enabled ISP).

Macromedia ColdFusion MX
(www.macromedia.com/software/coldfusion/)

The Allaire ColdFusion Server was acquired by Macromedia in 2001. Fully functional trial versions (time limited) of the ColdFusion MX server product can be downloaded from the Macromedia site.

Optional tools for the TicketManager application

Rational Rose
(www.rational.com)

The Rational Rose UML toolset is an industrial strength family of products covering modeling and software development. Trial versions can be downloaded for evaluation.

Microsoft Visio
(www.microsoft.com/office/visio/default.asp)

Visio is a comprehensive graphical modeling package with support for process modeling, UML notations, and database design. It is an excellent aid for making rich pictures and for preparing UML diagrams, although lacking the software engineering power of the Rational products.

Computer Associates ERWin
(www3.ca.com/Solutions/Product.asp?ID=260)

ERWin is a powerful database modeling and design tool. It will support the development of large-scale and complex applications, but is straightforward to use and integrates tightly with database products such as Microsoft SQL Server.

Macromedia Fireworks
(www.macromedia.com/software/fireworks/)

Fireworks is an image editing and graphic design package aimed specifically at web designers. Fireworks can be used to automate mundane tasks such as the generation of rollover images. It is tightly integrated with DreamWeaver and can also be purchased as part of the Studio MX package, which includes Flash and Freehand as well as DreamWeaver and Fireworks.

C.3 Web design

ProjectSeven
(www.projectseven.com)

Project Seven supply professionally designed web site templates developed in DreamWeaver and Fireworks. The templates can be modified by the user and provide an excellent starting point building a sophisticated web site.

Jakob Nielsen
(www.useit.com)

Jakob Nielsen's site has many articles and resources on user interface design and web usability.

WebQual
(www.webqual.co.uk)

The home site for the WebQual instrument. Research papers can be downloaded in pdf format.

C.4 Other useful sites

Open Source
(www.opensource.org)

A good place to start an exploration of the open source community. The site contains definitions of open source and useful frequently asked questions (FAQs).

ColdFusion hosting

Advances.com, media3.net, and virtualscape.com are US-based organizations that provide hosting services for ColdFusion. In the UK see firstserv.co.uk and in Europe see www.hotchilli.com/subpages/hosting/coldfusion.htm.

ColdFusion Developer Journal
(www.coldfusionjournal.com)

Although subscriptions are not cheap outside of the US, the ColdFusion developer journal is a great source of tips on using ColdFusion and for keeping uptodate with the latest developments in the ColdFusion product set.

Gelon.net
(www.gelon.net)

Gelon provide a free wap emulator that runs in a PC browser. This is a useful and cheap way to build and test m-commerce applications.

Index